Kojiki-den, Book 1

Motoori Norinaga, age 61, self-portrait.

Kojiki-den
Book 1

Motoori Norinaga

Introduced, Translated, and Annotated by
Ann Wehmeyer

With a Preface by
Naoki Sakai

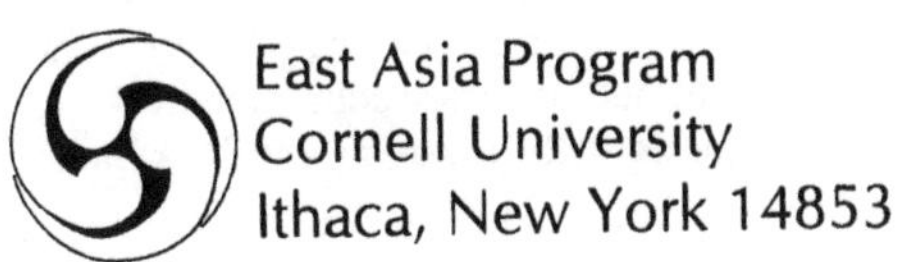
East Asia Program
Cornell University
Ithaca, New York 14853

The Cornell East Asia Series is published by the Cornell University East Asia Program and is not affiliated with Cornell University Press. We are a small, non-profit press, publishing reasonably-priced books on a wide variety of scholarly topics relating to East Asia as a service to the academic community and the general public. We accept standing orders which may be cancelled at any time and which provide for automatic billing and shipping of each title in the series upon publication.

If after review by internal and external readers a manuscript is accepted for publication, it is published on the basis of camera-ready copy provided by the volume author. Each author is thus responsible for any necessary copy-editing and for manuscript formatting. Submission inquiries should be addressed to Editorial Board, East Asia Program, Cornell University, Ithaca, New York 14853-7601.

Cover motif of ancient bells and illustrations on pages ii and xx are reprinted courtesy of Motoori Norinaga Ki'nenkan, Matsusaka.
Cover design: Karen K. Smith.

Number 87 in the Cornell East Asia Series.

ISSN 1050-2955
ISBN 1-885445-87-3 pb
ISBN 1-885445-57-1 hc

Contents

Preface

In the *specifically national and nationalist context* of Japanese history, hardly any book, treatise, or unified body of script surpasses in historical significance Motoori Norinaga's *Kojiki-den* which consists of forty four volumes of the revised and phoneticized text of the *Kojiki*, detailed and extensive commentaries and interpretations on the original text. Of course, there were many classical works produced in the Japanese archipelago before Motoori's time. One might easily mention some exceptionally important texts that were produced in Japan long before the *Kojiki-den*, such as the *Nihonshoki* or *Chronicle of Japan*, Kûkai's *Jûjûshinron*, the *Tale of Genji*, the *Kokinshû*, the *Tales of the Heike* and Zeami's No playscripts. Some of these texts had been repeatedly commented upon, recited, referred to as evidence of certain truths or had sometimes served as kernels of institutionalized knowledge and beliefs. Yet it is important to note that the *Kojiki-den* is one of the earliest works which claimed its worth only in the restricted context of Japanese national history. And this claim itself is rather astonishing. In general education as it was taught in *Terakoya* tutoring schools in the seventeenth and eighteenth centuries, for example, the canonical texts that were regarded as classics were primarily the Four Books and Five Classics of Confucian traditions, and there hardly existed an acknowledged need to distinguish Japanese texts from Chinese ones and to teach Japanese children Japanese classics. Just as we do not insist upon finding the features of national character in the texts of the Koran and the Bible or in the textbooks of mathematics and biology today, so most people in East Asia did not seek the conspicuous traits of national history in the classics. Obviously social formations were not organized on the basis of a desire for national identity so that people lived free from the tenets of the nation-state, and accordingly the classics they worshipped stood indifferent to national identification. Therefore, we cannot help noticing something extremely novel and eccentric in Motoori's insistence upon a distinction between the Chinese orientation of the *Nihonshoki* and the Japaneseness inherent in the *Kojiki*. While the *Nihonshoki* and the *Kojiki* both were historiographical attempts in the eighth century to construct the histories of the Yamato dynasties and the Imperial lineage, Motoori Norinaga reconstructed the entire *Kojiki* on the assumption that Japanese *national or ethnic* language existed when it was originally written, and he thereby turned the *Kojiki* into a self-consciously Japanese text. Thus from the outset, Motoori's *Kojiki-den* insists on reading the text of the *Kojiki* on the explicitly declared premise that it is written in the *Japanese* language. How should we assess the significance of Motoori's insistence on Japanese language? Were many previous writings such as the *Manyô-shû* or *Ten Thousand Leaves,* the *Kokinshû* and the *Pillow Books* of Seishônagon not also written in Japanese? Is it a truism that statements in the *Tale of Genji,* for instance, were mainly written in *Kana* characters as opposed to its many contemporary documents that were composed in *Mana* or literary Chinese? Such a demand for the recognition of the Japanese as an ethnic/national linguistic identity could be given rise to only when a massive transformation of discursive formation was under way.

What was at issue in Motoori's project of writing an extensively annotated revision of an ancient mytho-historiography taking some thirty five years was an on-going epistemic change in the ways in which people apprehended what were meant by speaking, hearing, writing and reading. Perhaps it is more accurate to say that this change involved plural eruptions of the new *regimes* of narrating, reciting, listening, writing and reading and that it occurred not homogeneously throughout the imagined whole of that contemporary Japan but dispersedly and sporadically in eighteenth century social formations in the central regions of the Japanese islands. Moreover, the change was essentially discursive, so, to use Michel Foucault's terminology, it cannot be identified at the level of what historical texts as 'documents' testify to but rather at the level of the texts' historical 'monumentality'; neither can it be recognized as what the authors wanted to say in and through the texts nor as individuals' or collective opinions. I would not attribute the eruptive emergence of these new regimes to any single genius or personality, scholarly group, school, or a Zeitgeist. Yet, undeniably, around that time some people began to see various forms of representation and textuality differently and to engage textual production in manners that had hitherto been unknown.

What we now can find in Motoori's work as well as in treatises by some Confucian scholars of the so-called *Kogaku* affiliation such as Ogyû Sorai was not merely an introduction of one more interpretation of the ancient text, but also the creation of a new set of regimes (reading, writing, reciting, narrating, and so forth) whereby the classic text was re-created. Therefore, it is impossible to understand Motoori's work simply in terms of his discovery of ancient Japanese language, Japanese phonetics, syntax, and grammar, and so on, that is, in those terms which are believed to have existed before Motoori's and Kogaku scholars' interventions. It seems that what Motoori achieved by 'reading' the *Kojiki* was to establish the conditions of possibility for the knowledge of Japanese language to emerge. As a result of these changes, the possibility of talking about Japanese ethnic or national language emerged. In other words, Motoori and others invented Japanese language as an object of systematic knowledge in the 18th century. In this respect, compared with the *Kojiki-den*, the previous canonical works clearly lacked the sense of national affiliation, and, even though some of them were in so-called Japanese inscription systems, these works did not claim to belong to the lineage of particularly *Japanese* literature. There are a few other well-known texts of the eighteenth century which can be seen as testimony to these epistemic changes or discontinuities, but they could not highlight the new enunciative possibility which was given rise to along with these changes as dramatically as the *Kojiki-den*. This is to say, the writing of the *Kojiki-den* inaugurated the 'modern' prescription of the national imaginary. We cannot not recognize the aura of modernity in the *Kojiki-den* precisely because, generally speaking and even beyond the context of Japan's history, the imaginary affiliation with nation and national culture and tradition is specifically modern.

How did the *Kojiki-den* re-articulate or newly invent the senses of reading, writing, reciting and narrating? In this respect, the problem of *Kana*, *Mana*, and phoneticism and ideography is crucial. However, a precaution must be taken in order to deliberately avoid the culturalist scheme in which the unities of Japanese culture and Japanese language are supposed to be existent trans-historically throughout Japanese history.

It is important to keep in mind that today's readers, regardless of whether they are resident in North America, Japan or European Community countries, inhabit the social and discursive formations that are markedly modern. To the extent that they take the modern regimes of reading, writing, reciting, narrating, and so forth for granted, they tend to assume the regularities sustained by these regimes to be universally valid, and become incapable of imagining the possibilities of other regimes. It is imperative to historicize our own regimes as well as those of the *Kojiki-den* in order not to fall into the pitfall of culturalism. For the culturalist assumption that Japanese language and culture have continued to exist since antiquity is not so much a thesis affirmed by historical evidences as one that is required to supplement their inability to imagine the possibilities of other discursive formations.

Of course, the term 'modern' is overdetermined, and there are so many different ways to define modernity. What I mean by 'modern' in this instance is a particular manner in which the regimes of reading, writing, reciting, narrating, and so forth are arranged in social formations characteristic of the nation-states, and I think that, as far as those regimes are concerned, there seems to be a certain commensurability among many 'modernized' societies in the world despite different historical developments and geopolitical conditions. The sense of this commensurability was aptly expressed by Benedict Anderson's well-known phrases 'modules of the nation-state' and 'print culture' both of which strongly suggest the transferability of modernity and its essential uprootedness (although I do not agree with Anderson's summary representation of the modernity of the modern regimes of reading, writing, reciting, narrating and so on by print culture) and which implicitly deny the evolutionary and linear model of modernization.

Here I want to stress the transferability or transplantability of modernity mainly for two reasons. First, the modern regimes of reading, writing, reciting, narrating, and so forth can be practiced even if regimes in other behavioral spheres remain non-modern. In our case of eighteenth century epistemic changes, there is no doubt that the polity, i. e., the Tokugawa shogunate-domainal system, was antithetical to the idea of the nation-state, but these modern regimes could inhabit, so to say, or co-exist with rather 'feudal' politico-social formations. (My claim of the modern regimes' transferability derives, however, much less from the observation of their particular traits than from my refusal to regard a society as an organic whole.) Although I have no intention of claiming that the epistemic regimes which were emerging in the eighteenth century would continually grow into the post-Meiji ones, it is possible to see a certain commensurability between those regimes which underwrote the *Kojiki-den* and the ones which sustained the production of knowledge in the late nineteenth and early twentieth centuries in disciplines such as national history and national literature. Secondly, the transferability and uprootedness of modernity simultaneously creates two contrasting but mutually supplementary conditions, one that allows for comparing many areas in the world in the relationship of *equi-valence*, and another contrasting one which calls for an obsessive emphasis on the historical authenticity and irreplaceability of a particular area and its inhabitant population. Just as in the scheme of trade balance, two contrasting areas are presented as differing but being on the commensurate *e-valuation*, on the one hand. Yet each area is supposed to be recognized as unique and exceptional so that it constitutes itself as an organic unity, on the other. It goes without saying that the insistence on the irreplaceable historical uniqueness of Chinese antiquity by Ogyû Sorai and of Japanese antiquity by Kamo Mabuchi, an insistence which Motoori emphatically repeats in favor of Japanese uniqueness against Chinese empty generality in the *Kojiki-den* and his other writings, unambiguously testifies to the necessity of these two conditions according to which the distinctive unity of the Japanese linguistic and cultural sphere could be figured out within an international configuration. In this sense, Motoori's obsessive emphasis on the particularly Japanese nature of the *Kojiki* and his evaluation of the superiority of Japanese traditions over other ethnic or national ones may be viewed as indicating the prototypical international consciousness, somewhat on a parallel with the development of internationalism and nationalism in eighteenth and early nineteenth century European anthropology on national characters and racial taxonomy without which the idea of the national sovereignty would have been inconceivable.

Here, let me note that the transferability of modernity is an issue that had nothing to do with the factual transfer or importation of cultural and social artifacts and institutions from one area to another. There has always been a transfer of that nature between areas in East Asia from antiquity. Instead I would like to suggest that, as the distinction of the domestic and the foreign increasingly played an important role in organizing the representations of various social relations, certain cultural and social institutions began to be evaluated in terms of this distinction. The best example can be found in the case of *kana*.

From the late nineteenth century when the national compulsory education was established by Japanese government, the writing system has been standardized. Today school children in Japan are taught 46 basic *hiragana* characters and 46 *katakana* characters. *Hiragana* and *katakana* characters form two parallel alphabetical systems, and each *hiragana* character has a corresponding *katakana* character and they are understood to express 46 basic phonetic units. Since the end of the Second World War the Japanese Ministry of Education has adopted the policy of making the *hiragana* the main system of phonetic characters and the *katakana* a supplementary one so that *katakana* are now used mainly to transcribe foreign names and pronunciations, and occasionally for onomatopoeia. By the time they graduate from the secondary schools usually at the age of fifteen, Japanese children are expected to have learned from two to three thousand *kanji* (*hanzi* in Mandarin Chinese or the characters of the Han) characters which are supposed to function as ideographic symbols in addition to *hiragana* and *katakana*. And the overwhelming majority of verbal publications such as daily newspapers, weekly and monthly magazines, academic monographs, novels, poetry, government ordinances, business correspondences, official licenses, insurance policies, and textbooks are written in a mixture of these *hiragana, katakana*, and *kanji* characters.

So often the co-presence of two heterogeneous inscriptional principles in Japanese writing has been pointed to as a sign of the 'peculiarity' of Japanese language and, by extension, Japanese culture in general. It is widely believed that, whereas *kanji* characters are multivocal with respect to their phonetic expressivity but are univocal in their ideation, *kana* characters are univocal with respect to their phonetic expressivity and non-vocal in their ideation. Etymologically, *kana* in *hiragana* and *katakana* derives from the opposition between *kana* and *mana*, ad hoc characters as opposed to true characters. And it is believed that, since *mana* have been identified unambiguously with Chinese ideographic characters of *kanji, kana* must imply something inherently Japanese and phonetic. But, to what extent does this characterization of *kanji* and *kana* in terms of nationality hold up?

Since there were no standardizing governmental regulations about the uses of characters until the Meiji period, there used to be many more than the 46 *hiragana* and 46 *katakana* characters which the Japanese use today. In a sense, one was allowed to almost arbitrarily invent *kana* characters out of *kanji* characters through simplification and abbreviation although unofficial standardization could be recognized particularly in *katakana*. Here, let us ponder over the fact that *kana* meant an ad hoc or makeshift character. It was a sort of shorthand whereby to outline a proper *kanji* character without drawing all the necessary brush strokes that constitute its graphic unity. We must recall that, except for very simple ones, one typical *kanji* character involves from five to thirty strokes when it is written in the so-called 'square style.' Written in the fluid and more individualized 'grass style,' the graphic complexity of a *kanji* character can be reduced. Furthermore, by abbreviating more strokes one could create a graphic *ad hoc* symbol which refers to the original *kanji*. The simplified character thus obtained is usually called *hiragana*. *Katakana* is also obtained from the *kanji* character through a similar but somewhat different procedure.[1] And it seems that *kana* is a sign indicating a *kanji* character, a graphic sign that refers to another graphic sign. The way in which the *kanji* character can be simplified varies from one person to another, and, accordingly, *kana,* particularly *hiragana,* very much retains the signatory quality of calligraphy. Yet it should be invariably true that, unless one is familiar with a wide variety of handwriting traits, the handwritten text of *kana* is in due course extremely difficult to read. In order to decipher those ad hoc characters, one would have had to know which *kanji* characters they originated from. Precisely because kana is a doubly articulated sign, the decipherment of it required some reference to the knowledge of the primary signs, i. e., of *mana* until the sense of *kana*'s double articulation was totally erased by the general shift from wood block printing to movable printing in the Meiji period.

Even a cursory survey like this about the opposition between *mana* and *kana* demonstrates that, unless certain conditions are imposed upon the systematic uses of *kanji* and *kana* characters, the *mana* and *kana* opposition cannot be equated to either the binary of the ideographic and the phonetic, or of Chinese and Japanese. What is overlooked in the binary evaluation of *kana* is that all the groups of characters, *kanji, hiragana*, *katakana,* and even *manyôgana*, could serve differently according to the way a desire for meaning is invested in those graphic signs, that is, according to a specific ideology to which the sign is submitted. In other words, neither hieroglyphy, phoneticism, nor ideography is characteristically inherent in the graphic constitution of the character. As the use of *manyôgana* best exemplifies, the *kanji* character can be used phonetically. At the same time, however, no graphic sign is purely phonetic or ideographic; it is always not only multiply but also overly determined. In this sense it is probably misleading to treat any graphic sign as pertaining to a system unless we are conscious that to do so is to determine it unitarily and to repress other copresent possibilities. This is to say that a hiragana character, for example, can be an ideographic *kanji* character drawn in grass style, a phonetic symbol indicating a specific phonetic unit and so forth, *at the same time.*

What the *Kojiki-den* declares unambiguously is the inauguration of a completely different way of relating the agent/subject of writing and reading to those graphic signs, and I have collectively called these newly emerging regimes whereby to relate oneself imaginarily to inscription 'phonocentrism.' By re-transcribing the original text of the *Kojiki* in which neither *hiragana* nor *katakana* characters were used at all into a new text of the *Kojiki* which is mainly in *hiragana* characters, Motoori Norinaga—or the discursive change at large, to be more precise—destroyed the previous regimes of reading, writing, reciting, narrating and so forth which allowed for the overdeterminacy of graphic signs, and replaced them with ones in which different inscriptional ideologies—ideologies in each of which a particular imaginary relationship to inscription is invested—such as ideography, hieroglyphy, phoneticism and so on were discriminated against one another.

In the previous regimes, characters were permitted to shift their ideological register fairly freely and could float, so to say, from the status of phonetic signifier to that of ideographic signifier, to that of illustrative symbol. Perhaps the best example of this ideological overdeterminacy can be found in calligraphy in which each character is not immediately determined with respect to its ideological register. Is a calligraphic piece of Tang poetry, for instance, a text to read, to look at, or to recite? To determine a calligraphic text solely as a text to recite is, in fact, tantamount to denying it its essential quality as calligraphy. Nevertheless, what Motoori attempted to do in his *Kojiki-den* was to determine the text of the *Kojiki* unitarily as a text to recite, and to prove that it should be possible to exclude other relationships to this text. Of course, to exclude other inscriptional relationships to this text and to determine this text unitarily as a text to recite was, for Motoori, to recover the original recitational voice and gesture of ancient Japan. It is as a consequence of this 'phonocentric' transformation that the co-presence of two heterogeneous inscriptional principles in Japanese writing began to be perceived as a marker of the 'peculiarity' of Japanese language and, by extension, Japanese culture in general. In other words, Motoori and others could detect the heterogeneous constitution of graphic signs as an abnormality of their contemporary social and cultural formations, thanks to the installment of phonocentrism, and they began to allocate these inscriptional ideologies according to geopolitical mapping, phoneticism for Japan and ideography for China. Consequently it was made possible to construe the abnormality of their contemporary formations as a trait of contamination by alien influence in terms of the relationality of geographical areas. Even today this type of assessment of Japanese uniqueness still dominates culturalist literature on Japan, no matter whether it is produced by American Japan experts, European journalists or Japanese writers of the Nihonjin-ron discourse.

Here, it is important to note that phonocentrism I refer to here is not so much an insistence on the superiority of alphabetical phonetic writing over non-phonetic writing as a belief that these different ideologies can be distinguished from one another, and that I closely follow Jacques Derrida in his discussion of phonocentrism.

The phonocentric reorganization of the regimes also created the possibility of discovering the spoken language of the native *illiterate* people which could not be recorded in ideographic *kanji* characters, but which on rare occasions manifested itself in spite of ideographic oppression. Thus, through phonocentrism, a group of writers in the eighteenth century could project into antiquity an archetypal unity of Chinese or Japanese language of which they could only find remnant fragments in their contemporary world. So Ogyû Sorai, Kamo Mabuchi, Hattori Nankaku, and Motoori Norinaga among others posited the archetypal unity of Chinese or Japanese language in the past and thereby rendered it possible to talk about the loss or fragmentation of the social whole in eighteenth century social formations on the Japanese islands. In this sense, the unity of Japanese language and the Japanese ethnos were invented out of the phonocentric reorganization of discourse as two absences: Japanese language and Japanese ethnos were thus stillborn in this discourse in the eighteenth century.

Such an invention of the unity of Japanese language and the Japanese ethnos cannot be equated to the institutionalized unity of the Japanese language and the Japanese nation in the post-Meiji periods. For one thing, the sort of discourse which I think emerged in the eighteenth century never occupied a hegemonic position in social formations, then. For another, we must always caution ourselves against a culturalist temptation to equate a discursive formation to something like national culture or tradition. The point about consciously using the term 'discourse', though there are indeed other motifs and effects than this, is to prevent in advance a confusionism between national culture or tradition from a coherent arrangement of various regimes and pragmatic conditions for the possibilities of the emergence of certain sorts of statements. This is why I must characterize the emergence of the unity of Japanese language and Japanese ethnos as that of that of stillbirths. Today it is believed that both of them are taken to be self-evident by the majority of people who are concerned with Japan in one way or another. In this respect, neither the unity of the Japanese language nor the Japanese ethnos is dead. This means that, at certain points, they were resurrected. We simply cannot flatten the pre-resurrection and the post-resurrection stages onto a smooth continuity in the name of Japanese history.

In the domain of the current production of knowledge on Japan, however, it is urgent to remind ourselves that, as the term

Kokugaku means 'the study of the country (Japan),' Japanese studies, not only in Japan, such as *Kokubungaku* (Japanese Literature) and *Kokushi* (Japanese History), but also in the United States, Europe and other regions, have continued to produce new knowledge on Japan in the mode set by the whole idea of *Kokugaku*. Of course, at modern universities, disciplines and regiments whereby knowledge on Japan is being produced have been modified massively since the 18th century and they radically differ from the *Kokugaku* and *Kogaku* formats. But, there are traits of cultural and national essentialism which many of the so-called Japanologists in Japan, the United States and elsewhere unwittingly inherit from the *Kokugaku*.

Our complicity with the *Kokugaku* will continue unless we are ready to call into question how such a complicity between some of the regimes mobilized in the *Kojiki-den* and our own scholarship is inevitable. It goes without saying that this is not exclusively a problem of Japanese peculiarity but also of modernity in general.

Naoki Sakai

February 1996

Notes

[1] The third category of *kana*, *manyôgana*, is concerned with a particular use of the *kanji* character. Since it does not involve the process of graphic abbreviation or simplification, it does not differ from the *kanji* character graphically. It is a category of *kana*, whose categorical identity is based upon the particular way in which desire is invested in these signs.

Translator's Acknowledgements

I would like to express my thanks to a number of people for lending me their expertise in working on this project. I discussed many matters of interpretation with Yasushi Toda, and benefitted greatly from his insight. Cynthia Chennault and Lening Liu willingly clarified issues pertaining to Chinese thought and Chinese language. S. Yumiko Hulvey read the entire manuscript, and made many suggestions which contributed to refinement of style. Nancy Bedinger generously proof-read the work. I am indebted to Jo Tyler for her careful reading and editing of the manuscript in the final stages.

I am also grateful for two grants from the Center for East Asian Studies at the University of Chicago, and a grant from the Division of Sponsored Research at the University of Florida in support of this work. I owe my inspiration for this project to H. D. Harootunian, who suggested I take a look at this text.

Note on the format of the text

This translation is based on the edition of *Kojiki-den* found in Ôno Susumu, ed. *Kojiki-den*, in *Motoori Norinaga zenshû*, Vols. 9-12 (Chikuma shobô, 1968-1974). At the time when Motoori wrote his *Kojiki-den*, it was the convention to write notes in half-size characters in single-spaced columns immediately following the item concerning which the note was written. In Ôno Susumu's edition of the *Kojiki-den*, these notes have been enclosed in bold brackets, with the characters in a slightly smaller-sized print. I have indicated these notes by keeping them as is in the text, and enclosing them in angular brackets (< . . . >). In many cases, these notes are quite long. I have put glosses and the like in parentheses, and material I have added to the text such as dates in square brackets ([. . .]).

As discussed in the biographical introduction, the *kô-otsu* vocalic distinction was something which Motoori discovered and presented in this text simply as a matter of a differentiation in the use of *man'yôgana* to represent certain syllables. I have represented the distinction in examples from the *Kojiki* and the Man'yôshû with the convention of a diacritic for the *otsu*-type (*ï, ë, ö*), and plain vowel for the *kô*-type (*i, e, o*), based on the Aoki et al. edition of the *Kojiki*, Jôdaigo jiten henshû i'inkai, eds., *Jidai betsu kokugo daijiten: Jôdai-hen*, and Ôno Susumu et al. eds., *Iwanami kogo jiten*.

The format of Chapter 9, "Naobi no mitama" (The Spirit of Rectification), differs from the rest of the text. Here, Motoori has arranged the text in a series of precept-like headings, with explanation of each indented beneath. I have retained this format, with the explanations indented from the left.

All endnotes, which are given at the end of each chapter, are my own. Unless otherwise indicated, all translations of quotations are my own.

The following abbreviations have been used in the notes:

MNZ	*Motoori Norinaga zenshû*. Ôno Susumu and Ôkubo Tadashi, comps. Chikuma shobô. 1968-1975, 20 Vols.
NKBT	*Nihon koten bungaku taikei*. Takagi Ichinosuke et al., eds. Iwanami shoten 1957-68, 102 Vols.
NST	*Nihon shisô taikei*. Ienaga Saburô, et al., comps. Iwanami shoten. 1970—, 67 Vols.

Kojiki-den, second manuscript copy, 1798, 44 volumes and open book face.

Biographical Introduction

The discipline of *kokugaku* (nativism) began as the philological study of ancient Japanese texts with the goal of discovering the ancient mentality and spirituality of the Japanese prior to their contact with continental epistemes. The Buddhist priest Keichû (1640-1701) is considered to be the forerunner of the nativist movement. The objectivity of his commentaries on literature, and his investigation of the use of kana syllabary, were an inspiration for Motoori. The second major figure in nativism was the scholar Kada no Azumamaro (1669-1736), whose family formed a long line of Shinto priests. Employed by first the imperial court and later the Tokugawa shogunate, he lectured and published on the major texts of antiquity. He also petitioned the shogunate, unsuccessfully, to establish a school for nativism in Kyoto. Kamo no Mabuchi (1697-1769), the third major figure of nativism, also the son of a Shinto priest, was a member of Kada no Azumamaro's school. His major work of commentary, the *Man'yôkô* (1760-68), was a study of each of the poems of the *Man'yôshû*. He also wrote ideological works on language in general in which he argued in favor of the superiority of the Japanese language, and linguistic analyses of such phenomena as verbal conjugation.

Motoori Norinaga (1730-1801) considered himself a student of Kamo no Mabuchi. He was a prolific scholar who made significant contributions to a number of different fields. In his study of literature, he developed the concept of *mono no aware,* the idea that the true value of literature lies in its ability to convey human sensitivity and emotion, and not in the transmission of didactic moralization. His linguistic analyses of the orthography, sound system, and grammar of Japanese constitute a major part of the native grammatical tradition. He also wrote works having to do with his notions of Shintoism and the nature of government. With the work of Hirata Atsutane (1776-1843), who viewed himself as the successor to the school of Motoori, the nativist movement began to focus more exclusively on the elucidation of the true nature of Shinto, and the role it should play in the everyday lives of the people.

Book 1 of Motoori Norinaga's forty-four book great commentary on the *Kojiki* (712), the *Kojiki-den*, commonly referred to as the "Sôron" (Introduction) plus "Naobi no mitama" (The Spirit of Rectification) which closes it, stands on its own as a text for several reasons. The first is the argument Motoori presents in favor of the historical and linguistic value of the *Kojiki*, as opposed to other histories of Japan, in particular, the *Nihonshoki* (720). The second has to do with the philological principles Motoori sets forth for the reading of the *Kojiki*; among them, the identification and systematization of nearly all of the Chinese graphs used as *man'yô-gana,* and the establishment of readings for various postpositions, verbal suffixes, and conjunctions. "Naobi no mitama" advocates the Japanese "Way of the Gods" as superior to the "Ways" of other countries, in particular those of China, and provides a spiritual statement further bolstering the superiority of the *Kojiki,* less tainted with the rhetoric and ideology of China than the other histories which followed it. Book 2 of the *Kojiki-den* contains a *kun* reading and interpretation of the preface to the *Kojiki*, plus a genealogy. The remainder of the Books assign a *kun* reading and provide a commentary on the main body of the entire text of the *Kojiki*.

Motoori is thought to have begun his study of the *Kojiki* in 1764, at the age of 34, the year after his first and only meeting with Kamo no Mabuchi. He finished the commentary in 1798, at the age of 68, having worked on it virtually every year in this three-decade span.[1] Roughly half of the *Kojiki-den* was published in his lifetime: Books 1-5 (1790), Books 6-11 (1792), and Books 12-17 (1797). The remainder, Books 18-44, appeared posthumously in 1822.[2] "Naobi no mitama" appeared separately, first of all, in 1771, and the fourth draft of this text was eventually published as the final section in Book 1 of the *Kojiki-den*.[3] A handwritten manuscript titled *Kojiki zakkô,*[4] consisting of thirteen chapters in two books, is thought to be one of the first drafts for Books 1 and 2 of *Kojiki-den*, including Chapter 13 of this work, titled "Michi chô ron," which is regarded as a draft of "Naobi no mitama."[5] The date of this work, however, is unknown.

Motoori was born Ozu Tominosuke, the first son of parents Ozu Sadatoshi (1695-1740) and Murata Okatsu (1705-1768), who ran a prosperous cotton wholesaler's business in the town of Matsusaka, in the former province of Ise, now Mie prefecture.[6] Sadatoshi's step-son from a previous marriage, Sadaharu (1711-

1851), was heir to the family. Sadatoshi died when Motoori was ten years old, and thereafter Okatsu raised their four children on her own. Motoori is said to have felt a deep affection for his mother throughout his life. She provided a rich education for him in the form of the Chinese classics, Japanese classical poetry, archery, and the tea ceremony. In 1748, Motoori was adopted by a family of paper manufacturers in the nearby town of Yamada, close to the Ise shrines, but the adoption was revoked after two years.

Upon the death of Sadaharu in 1851, Motoori was made heir, and his mother encouraged him to go to Kyoto for study to pursue a career in medicine. An essay written late in his life indicates that Motoori had a dislike for merchant life;[7] no doubt his mother sensed this and sought a vocation for him more suited to his temperament. In 1852, Motoori went to Kyoto, where he enrolled in the school of Hori Keizan (1689-1757), and at that time adopted the surname of Motoori, the surname of remote samurai ancestors of some two centuries past. Hori Keizan, a Confucian scholar well-versed in neo-Confucianism, the dominant ideology of the day, also corresponded with Ogyû Sorai (1666-1728), who advocated a return to the study of the original, primary texts of Confucianism, and devised his own philological methodology, termed *kobunjigaku* (古文辞学, study of ancient texts and words), by which to do so. Hori Keizan did not limit himself to study of Confucianism; he was also interested in Japanese classical literature, and familiar with the philological works of the early nativist Keichû.

Motoori appears to have written down Ogyû's theories and studied them, as is evidenced by notebooks in Motoori's hand recently discovered titled "Sorai-shû."[8] For Ogyû, the Six Classics represented the true Way of the Sages.[9] Ogyû argued that the meaning of words changes over time, and in order to understand the original intent of the words in the Six Classics, it was essential to have an understanding of the meanings of the ancient words used in the texts. In his view, the "words" represented the actual "facts" of the Way of the Sages. The same notion that facts or events (*kotogara*) may be revealed through language (*kotoba*) is stated explicitly in the first chapter of Book 1 of the *Kojiki-den*, and is reflected throughout the work.[10] Both Ogyû and the nativists termed their fields of study "*kogaku*" (the study of antiquity), and perhaps out of the need to distance himself from the Confucianists, Motoori denied any connection with their approach.

In addition to the Chinese classics, Motoori read many works of classical Japanese literature, giving close attention in particular to the *Tale of Genji* and the *Kokinshû*. He was particularly impressed by the thoroughness of Keichû's commentary on the *Hyakunin isshu* (*Hyakunin isshu kaikanshô*), and Ôno Susumu suggests that the fact that Motoori wrote out a copy of Keichû's *Kokinshû yozaishô* indicates the deep level of Motoori's respect for his scholarship.[11] Motoori also became a student of several prominent waka masters, writing poetry himself and participating in poetic gatherings. He wrote his first major work, *Ashiwake obune*, a treatise on the nature of waka, near the end of his six years of study in Kyoto.

Motoori did his medical training under Hori Genkô (1686-1754), and then the pediatrician Takekawa Kôjun (1725-1780). In 1757 he returned to Matsusaka and set up a medical practice. Shortly after his return, he read Kamo no Mabuchi's recently published treatise on poetic epithets, *Kanji kô* (1757), in which Kamo no Mabuchi advocated study of the *Kojiki* rather than the *Nihonshoki*.[12] It was this text which apparently drew Motoori's attention to the *Kojiki*.

Prior to Motoori's *Kojiki-den*, both Keichû and Kamo no Mabuchi had written commentaries on the *Kojiki,* but only on the songs contained therein. It was not until Motoori that the entire text of the *Kojiki* was given consideration as a unitary repository of the oral tradition of Japan. The *Kojiki* itself had not been circulated widely, and its compilation was not even mentioned in the *Shoku Nihongi*.[13] There are very few extant manuscripts of the *Kojiki*, the oldest being the Shinpukuji-bon manuscript, copied by the priest Ken'yû in 1371-1372. In contrast, there are many extant manuscripts of the *Nihonshoki*, dating from the Nara period or slightly later. The *Kojiki* had simply been eclipsed by the *Nihonshoki*, although both were associated as members of the trilogy of the "Shinto sanbusho" (Three Texts of Shinto), which also included the *Kujiki*. These three histories wrote of the divine age and recorded the important events and lineage of the earliest reigns in Japan, and as such were esteemed as the major repositories of the teachings of Shinto.[14]

A major commentary on the *Nihonshoki*, the *Shaku Nihongi,* appeared in the Kamakura period. This was a collection of "private records," or annotated readings and notes, compiled in the latter half of the thirteenth century by Urabe Kanekata. It was distinguished by discussions of various aspects of the text, such as its origins, correct versus corrupt text, interpretation and explanation of text and songs, in addition to simply presenting notes on the words of the text itself.[15] The medieval commentaries which followed tended to focus exclusively on the chapters in the *Nihonshoki* that dealt with the "Age of the Gods." These works incorporated concepts and symbols from Buddhism and Chinese philosophy to reinforce the right of the imperial line to rule Japan in perpetuity,[16] an approach antithetical to that later taken by Motoori, who sought to erase any trace of foreign ideology in his reading of the *Kojiki.* It was not until the *Nihonshoki tsûsho* (1762) of Tanikawa Kotosuga that a commentary which concerned the entire work appeared.

The publication of the entire *Kojiki* in a woodblock print edition, known as the Kan'ei *Kojiki*, from an Urabe line manuscript in Kyoto in 1644, marked a turning point in the notice given to the *Kojiki*. Heretofore, outside religious circles, its value had been seen as simply a supplementary text useful for understanding the *Man'yôshû* and the *Nihonshoki*. As mentioned above, Keichû wrote a commentary on the songs of the *Kojiki* and the *Nihonshoki*, titled *Kôganshô* (1691). Keichû had referred constantly to the songs in these two texts when he wrote his great commentary on the *Man' yôshû,* the *Man'yô daishô ki* (ca. 1683-1690). This was the inspiration for him to begin his analysis of the songs in the histories. The songs had received previous philological attention in a special section in the major premodern commentary on the *Nihonshoki,* the *Shaku Nihongi*, mentioned above, but Keichû believed that much remained to be clarified.[17]

Later, Kada no Azumamaro gave a series of lectures on the *Kojiki*, compiled as *Kojiki sakki* (ca. 1729). In his estimation, however, the *Kojiki* was far inferior to the *Nihonshoki* in its value as a repository of religious teaching. Kada objected to the mixing of the "Age of the Gods" with the age of human beings in the *Kojiki*, as opposed to the clean separation of the two in the *Nihonshoki*, in which divine affairs are dealt with in the first two books, and titled "Age of the Gods, Book 1," and "Age of the Gods, Book 2." In addition, he deemed the *Kojiki* inferior in comparison to the *Nihonshoki* because he believed the *Kojiki* to merely be Ô no Yasumaro's revision of the *Kujiki*.[18]

Kamo no Mabuchi (1697-1769), on the other hand, valued the *Kojiki* more highly than the *Nihonshoki,* a view which Inoue Minoru asserts is hardly to be seen in anyone prior to Kamo.[19] In an appendix to the preface to his *Engi shiki norito kai* (1746), Kamo states that the value of the *Nihonshoki* is second to that of the *Kojiki*, since the *Nihonshoki* has selected from various texts and recorded the matters of antiquity in classical Chinese, and this textual representation therefore differs from the actual matters of antiquity. The *Kojiki,* in contrast, is a direct recording of the nation's history, and is a text in which respect has been paid to the archaic language. There is no other text which can compare to it for seeing the manner of antiquity and understanding the language of antiquity.[20] Kamo no Mabuchi wrote one minor work on the *Nihonshoki, Nihongi waka ryaku-chû* (1765), and a number of minor works on the *Kojiki*: *Kojiki tôsho* (1757), *Kojiki waka ryaku-chû kakiire* (1757), and *Kana Kojiki* (1768).

As mentioned above, it was apparently Kamo no Mabuchi's treatise on poetic epithets, *Kanji kô* (1757), in which he also advocates study of the *Kojiki,* rather than the *Nihonshoki*, which drew Motoori's interest to the *Kojiki*. Motoori sought a meeting with Kamo no Mabuchi, and their first and only meeting took place in 1763 at the Shinjôya, an inn in Matsusaka, where Kamo no Mabuchi spent the night after touring the Ise Shrines. Motoori was 34 years old at the time, while Kamo no Mabuchi was 67. Their encounter is known as the "evening in Matsusaka," and is recalled well after the event in Motoori's *Tamakatsuma* (1794).[21] At the end of 1763, Motoori enrolled in the school of Kamo no Mabuchi, and they carried on correspondence until Kamo no Mabuchi's death in 1769. Motoori's questions to Kamo no Mabuchi in this correspondence indicate the methodology he used in establishing a reading for the *Kojiki*.[22] In 1767 and 1768, he went over the *Man'yôshû* twice, and was asking Kamo no Mabuchi questions about that text. In 1769, he was asking Kamo no Mabuchi questions about the *senmyô* (imperial proclamations) in the *Shoku Nihongi*, hoping to gain an understanding of the way postpositions were used. Motoori also completed a preliminary study of the *senmyô* in this text in that same year which was titled *Shokugi senmyô monmoku*.[23]

Several of his draft manuscripts and publications from this time indicate that he was establishing a firm basis upon which to determine the readings for the *Kojiki*. In 1771, he completed *Teniwoha himo-kagami*, a chart indicating the relations between the various postpositions, including the rules of *kakari-musubi* agreement.[24] The chart applied not only to the language of archaic song, but also to a vast body of poetry from the Heian period as well, and the work indicates that Motoori had attained a firm grasp of the grammar of the language of antiquity. Also in 1771, the first drafts of *Mojigoe no kanazukai* (1776) and the first chapter of *Kanji san'on kô* (1785) were completed.[25] These works have to do with the pronunciation of Chinese characters, an understanding of which was essential for establishing the reading for the sections of the *Kojiki* written in *man'yôgana*.

Book 1 of the *Kojiki-den* addresses the difficulties in establishing a reading for the *Kojiki*. Chapter 1, "The Texts of Antiquity: Clarification," argues that the *Kojiki* is superior to the *Nihonshoki* because the language of the *Kojiki* represents the true Japanese language of antiquity. Therefore, Motoori maintains that in the *Kojiki*, meaning (*kokoro*), event (*koto*), and word (*kotoba*), are all in accord with one another, unlike the state of affairs in the *Nihonshoki*, in which events have been recorded in the alien language of classical Chinese. Chapter 2, "Discussion of the *Nihonshoki*," presents specific examples from the *Kojiki* and the *Nihonshoki* which illustrate the heavy borrowing of Chinese philosophical concepts and rhetoric to be found in the *Nihonshoki*. Chapters 3, "Discussion of the *Kujiki*, 4, "On the Title of the *Kojiki*," and 5, "Manuscripts and Commentaries," are brief and more narrow in focus.

Motoori outlines the methodology he used in assigning a Japanese reading to the *Kojiki* in Chapters 6 through 8. Chapter 6, "On the Style of Writing," discusses the types of orthography and language that are found in the *Kojiki*. Chapter 7, "On Kana," is a list of all of the *man'yôgana* used in the *Kojiki*, with examples illustrating their usage.[26] Perhaps the most significant linguistic discovery made by Motoori is to be seen in this chapter. Motoori was the first to realize that certain syllables showed a definite pattern in the *man'yôgana* used to represent them. The distinction occurs in the vowels *i*, *e*, and *o*, when they appear in the syllables *ki*, *Fi*, *mi*, *ke*, *Fe*, *me*, *ko*, *so*, *to*, *no*, *mo*, *yo*, and *ro*. Motoori noticed the distinction in almost all of these syllables. Motoori's pupil, Ishizuka Tatsumaro (1764-1823), found that the same distinctions obtained in the *Man'yôshû* and the *Nihonshoki* as well. Neither Motoori or Ishizuka realized, however, that the distinctions in orthography must have reflected a distinction in the sounds of Old Japanese. It was not until the twentieth century, with the work of Hashimoto Shinkichi (1882-1945), that the hypothesis of a distinction in sound was put forth. The hypothesis proposed that there were two sets of vowels, a *kô*-type and an *otsu*-type, for each of the vowels *i*, *e*, and *o*, when they appear in the above-mentioned syllables. The hypothesis quickly became standard theory, but controversy as to exactly what the nature of the sound distinction might have been continues to this day.

In Chapter 8, "On the Method of Reading," Motoori discusses the general principles he used in assigning readings, and also presents a list of postpositions, verbal suffixes, and conjunctions, with a discussion of examples and suggested readings. Ôno notes that his conclusions, based on very limited materials, differ very little from those of scholars of today, who have an abundance of material with which to work.[27] He also states that Motoori's edition of the text of the *Kojiki* remains largely unrevised even today.[28] The most recent edition of the *Kojiki,* however, that of the first volume of the *Nihon shisô taikei*, edited by Aoki Kazuo, Ishimoda Shô, Kobayashi Yoshinori, and Saeki Arikiyo, does differ in significant ways from the readings assigned by Motoori. Kobayashi, who has done extensive research on *kunten* materials from the early Heian period, was responsible for the editing of the text. His approach, which he has termed to be "diametrically opposed" to that of Motoori, was to focus on the Chinese characters, with the hypothesis that there was a fixed usage and reading for each character used as a logograph (*hyôi kanji*).[29] Motoori, on the other hand, viewed Chinese characters with contempt, and argues in chapter 8 that they are "makeshift items simply attached to the text." Motoori's approach to assigning readings was to some extent intuitive, simply assigning a word or item from Old Japanese that was suitable for the context. According to Kobayashi, the main trends seen in those who have emended the readings proposed by Motoori have to do with Motoori's changing the readings of the same character in different contexts, and not following the word order indicated.[30] I have noted in the endnotes when Aoki et al.'s reading of the text differs from that of Motoori in the examples he presents.

The notion that historical "fact" may be revealed through the archaic "word" was a major factor motivating the philological pursuits of the nativists. In Koyasu Nobukuni's view, the nativists had to provide some justification for referring to Japan as a sanctified land, but they lacked the means, other than to say that "our Way is superior to all others," or to state the same in the negative terms "our Way is not like those of foreign countries." [31] Nativists needed to find a means of conceptualizing the Way and giving expression to it; however, this must not simply be a matter of conjecture, but must be based on the facts of "remnants of the Age of the Gods."[32] The *Kojiki,* and also the *Nihonshoki*, describe the events from the "Age of the Gods," and therefore, clarification of the words in these texts had the power to reveal the events from those times. Koyasu states that the *Kojiki-den* may thus be seen as a work which attempts to construct the identity of the Way based on facts from the remnants of antiquity.

Koyasu also links a difference in the grounds for belief in the superiority of the Japanese language on the part of nativists to the difference in the type of text chosen for study. He outlines two schools of thought on the grounds for the superiority of the

Japanese language: one, represented by Motoori, simply posits the tautology that since Japan is the august, imperial country, its language and sounds are pure and superior to all others.[33] Motoori's desire was to establish the true facts of antiquity, and therein discover the true nature of the "Age of the Gods" and of the august, imperial country. The *Kojiki,* being an official record of the events of antiquity, was therefore the ideal text for Motoori to study.[34] The other school of thought, initiated by Kamo no Mabuchi and continued by Hirata Atsutane, held that the Japanese language was superior because it had a divine aspect to it, allowing human beings to communicate naturally with all things.[35]

Atsutane proclaimed that *norito* (ritual prayers) contained a more reliable presentation of the events of antiquity than did the records of the "Age of the Gods" in the *Kojiki*, and, consequently, focused his study on the *norito* rather than the *Kojiki*.[36] Koyasu points to Atsutane's belief that *norito* had been transmitted orally from antiquity, beginning with the two Musubi deities,[37] and to his observation that *norito* had been used as words offered to the gods in the sacred rituals of antiquity as the reasons for his belief that they represented a more accurate version of the "Age of the Gods" than did the official histories.[38]

Ôno Susumu points out that while the belief that "word" (*koto*) may be read as "fact" (*koto*) was a powerful philological tool for Motoori, motivating him to read as widely and as accurately as possible in order to interpret the facts correctly, the same belief, seen from the vantage point of today, can be said to be flawed.[39] The example Ôno uses to illustrate this point is Motoori's failure to reflect on why there should be differing versions of a legend, or what the background could have been which would have given rise to differing versions of a legend. As Motoori was fixated to the idea that words in the *Kojiki* represent actual events, when the *Nihonshoki* presents different textual versions of the same legend, Motoori rejects them as foreign materials added as adornment, or simply fails to give them serious consideration. In Ôno's view, if Motoori had been able to give some consideration to what might have given rise to differing legends, he might have been able to add a new direction or dimension to materials on the "Age of the Gods."

In addition, Ôno points out that for Motoori, the meaning of *koto* (事 event, fact) was that of the *koto* in *kotogara* (matter) and *dekigoto* (happening); i.e. something which originates naturally, proceeds according to nature, and ends up with a certain result. Motoori believed that the events discussed in the *Kojiki* were things which came about naturally.[40] Subsequent scholars of antiquity, such as Tsuda Sôkichi, however, viewed the same *koto* in a different light: that of *suru koto* (doing) and *shigoto* (work), rather than *nariyuku koto* (the development of events). Tsuda argued that human activity has some purpose, and that texts are also written with some purpose. When Tsuda investigated the purpose behind the production of the *Kojiki*, he came to the conclusion that "the sections on the Age of the Gods and descriptions of historical emperors beginning with Emperor Jinmu in both the *Kojiki* and *Nihonshoki*, while based to some extent on materials such as folklore, or reflecting actual historical events, were overall materials compiled after the sixth century with the political purpose of proving the legitimacy of the imperial line to rule over Japan."[41] Thus, in Ôno's view, depending upon one's perspective of the nature of *koto*, one may arrive at a completely different interpretation of the context or even the individual words of a text.

Motoori and the other nativists wrote in a style of language called *gikobun* (imitating ancient texts) which took as its model the poetry and prose of Late Old Japanese, as represented in the literature of the Heian period. The use of some lexical items and grammatical forms from Old Japanese can be seen as well. Much of the time, Motoori gives Chinese loanwords a *kun* gloss, as in the example 漢籍の学問, which is glossed as *kara-bumi no manabi* (study of the Chinese classics), silencing the conventional Sino-Japanese reading of *kanseki no gakumon*. This has the effect of reinforcing his message that Chinese characters are nothing more than makeshift items, attached to an original Japanese text as ornamentation.

It is of course in Books 3 through 44 of the *Kojiki-den*, in which Motoori provides commentary and interpretation of the main text of the *Kojiki*, that his ideas on Shintoism and the culture of archaic Japan are to be found. Book 1, however, as mentioned above, stands in its own right as a kind of manifesto of the nativist project, and may also be used, as it were, as a primer for reading the texts of antiquity, written in a variety of styles and orthography.

Motoori gave lectures on the various classical texts, traveling widely to do so, especially in his later years. He also taught students who enrolled in his school termed the Suzunoya, named after the room added as a partial second floor to his home in 1782. It was in this four and one-half mat room that Motoori wrote the majority of his work. A record kept by Motoori of those enrolled in his school lists 489 names, representing 44 provinces ranging from the Tôhoku area to Kyûshû.[42] One can sense something of the teacher's and the lecturer's voice in the written words of

Motoori, including the *Kojiki-den*. Motoori died in the fall of 1801 after a brief illness, having just completed a successful lecture series in Kyoto in the summer of that year.

Notes

[1] The chronology of writing according to Yoshikawa Kôjirô, Satake Akihiro, and Hino Tatsuo (*Motoori Norinaga*, Nihon shisô taikei 40 <Iwanami shoten, 1978>, p. 626-630), is as follows:

1764 Begins *Kojiki-den*
1767 *Kojiki-den*: Books 3-4
1771 *Kojiki-den*: Naobi no mitama
1772 *Kojiki-den*: Book 7
1773 *Kojiki-den*: Book 8
1774 *Kojiki-den*: Books 9-11
1775 *Kojiki-den*: Book 12
1776 *Kojiki-den*: Book 13
1777 *Kojiki-den:* Book 14
1778 *Kojiki-den*: Books 15-17
1782 *Kojiki-den*: Book 18
1783 *Kojiki-den*: Book 19
1784 *Kojiki-den*: Book 20
1785 *Kojiki-den*: Book 21
1788 *Kojiki-den*: Books 22-24
1789 *Kojiki-den*: Books 25-26
1790 *Kojiki-den*: Books 27-28
1791 *Kojiki-den*: Books 29-30
1792 *Kojiki-den*: Books 31-33
1793 *Kojiki-den*: Books 34-35
1795 *Kojiki-den*: Books 36-37
1796 *Kojiki-den*: Books 38-40
1797 *Kojiki-den*: Books 41-43
1798 *Kojiki-den*: Book 44

[2] Ibid.
[3] Nishimura Sey, "The Way of the Gods: Motoori Norinaga's *Naobi no mitama*," *Monumenta Nipponica* 46:1 (Spring 1991), 21-41; the various draft versions are discussed on p. 22-24.
[4] The text is found in Ôkubo Tadashi, ed. *Motoori Norinaga zenshû*, Vol. 14 (Chikuma shobô, 1972), 1-115.
[5] The thirteen chapters of the *Kojiki zakkô*, with the exception of one chapter which is an index to the personal names, place names, kabane and

uji to be found in the *Kojiki*, correspond more or less to the content of the nine chapters of Book 1 of the *Kojiki-den*. Koyasu Nobukuni (*Motoori Norinaga* <Iwanami shoten, 1992>, 32-33) regards it as a draft of Books 1 and 2 of the *Kojiki-den*, while Ôno Susumu ("Kaidai," in Ôno Susumu, ed., *Kojiki-den*; Motoori Norinaga zenshu, Vol. 9 <Chikuma shobô, 1968>, 15) regards it as a draft of Book 1.

[6] My description of the life of Motoori is based on information in the following works: Matsumoto Shigeru, *Motoori Norinaga*, 1730-1801 (Cambridge: Harvard University Press, 1970); Motoyama Yukihiko, *Motoori Norinaga* (Shimizu shoin, 1978); Muraoka Tsunetsugu, *Motoori Norinaga* (Iwanami shoten, 1928), and Peter Nosco, *Remembering Paradise: Nativism and Nostalgia in Eighteenth Century Japan* (Cambridge: Harvard Council on East Asian Studies, Harvard University Press, 1990).

[7] Katô Shûichi provides the following quotes from Motoori's "Ie no mukashi monogatari" (1798): merchants are "an ignoble people;" Motoori's becoming a doctor was "getting away from the ranks of the business people" (*A History of Japanese Literature*, Vol. 2: *The Years of Isolation* <London: The Macmillan Press Ltd. and Paul Norbury Publications Ltd., 1983>, 182).

[8] Ôno, "Kaidai," 11.

[9] Maruyama Masao, *Studies in the Intellectual History of Tokugawa Japan*, trans. by Mikiso Hane (Tokyo: University of Tokyo Press, 1974), 76.

[10] Ôno, "Kaidai," 11.

[11] Ibid., 10.

[12] Nosco, *Remembering Paradise*, 166.

[13] Ôno, "Kaidai," 8.

[14] Miyake Kiyoshi, *Kada no Azumamaro no koten-gaku*, Vol. 1 (Urawa-shi: Miyake Kiyoshi, 1980), 122.

[15] Sakamoto Tarô, *The Six National Histories of Japan,* trans. by John S. Brownlee (Vancouver: University of British Columbia Press, 1991), 81-82.

[16] Kate Wildman Nakai, *Shogunal Politics: Arai Hakuseki and the Premises of Tokugawa Rule* (Cambridge, MA: Council on East Asian Studies, Harvard University/Harvard University Press, 1988), 328. As a case in point, Nakai discusses Ichijô Kanera's (1402-1481) commmentary on the *Nihonshoki*, *Nihonshoki sanso*: "Ichijô . . . equated Takamagahara with the Buddhist *tenshu*, the highest of the six realms of existence; Amenominakanushi no mikoto, one of the earliest deities to appear at the time of the formation of heaven and earth, with Daibonten (Mahabrahma); and the eight islands of Japan (Ôyashima) with the eight trigrams of the *Book of Changes*."

[17] Hisamatsu Sen'ichi, *Keichû* (Yoshikawa kôbunkan, 1963), 127; Tsukishima Hiroshi, "*Kôganshô* ni tsuite," in *Keichû zenshû*, Vol. 7, ed. by

Hisamatsu Sen'ichi (Iwanami shoten, 1974), 623-651. The text of the *Kôganshô* may also be found in Vol. 7 of *Keichû zenshû*, 457-592.

[18] Miyake, *Kada no Azumamaro no koten-gaku*, 124-125.

[19] Inoue Minoru, *Kamo no Mabuchi no gakumon* (Yagi shoten, 1944), 306.

[20] As quoted in Inoue, Ibid.

[21] *Tamakatsuma*; *Motoori Norinaga zenshû*, Vol. 1, ed. by Ôno Susumu (Chikuma shobô, 1968), 86. It is a question as to whether Motoori is recounting the actual words spoken by Kamo no Mabuchi, or whether he is distilling the essential inspiration and guidance he received at their meeting. According to Motoori's account of their conversation, when Motoori professed his desire to write a commentary on the *Kojiki*, Kamo no Mabuchi stated that he, too, had had the intention of doing so, but that his first priority had been to rid himself of the Chinese mind and inquire into the pure heart of antiquity. In order to do so, he believed, one must gain a good grasp of the language of antiquity, and in his view, the *Man'yôshû* was the best text for such a purpose. Accordingly, he had spent the greater part of his efforts on clarifying that text. Now, he feared that his remaining years were few, and doubted that he would have time to comment on the *Kojiki*. He then encouraged Motoori, who could expect many more years to come, to pursue the project of commenting on the *Kojiki*. Peter Nosco, in his discussion of this event, states that Motoori's version of their encounter cannot be considered a "verbatim account," because the concept of "Chinese heart" (*karagokoro*) was created by Motoori, and does not appear in the writings of Kamo no Mabuchi (*Remembering Paradise*, 175). Motoori's account of the event is also discussed in Shigeru Matsumoto, *Motoori Norinaga*, 1730-1801, 69 ff., and Koyasu Nobukuni, *Motoori Norinaga* (Iwanami shoten, 1992), 14 ff., among others.

[22] Information on Motoori's correspondence with Kamo no Mabuchi, and his publications during this time is based on Ôno, "Kaidai," 14.

[23] This text is found in Ôno Susumu, ed., *Motoori Norinaga zenshû*, Vol. 7, 1-13. Motoori's major study of the *senmyô*, *Shokugi miyomiyo no mikotonori no tokigoto bumi*, was completed in 1800 (*Motoori Norinaga zenshû*, Vol. 7, 185-482).

[24] This text is found in Ôno Susumu, ed., *Motoori Norinaga zenshû*, Vol. 5 (Chikuma shobô, 1970), 1-4.

[25] These texts are found in *Motoori Norinaga zenshû*, Vol. 5, 319-374, and 375-433, respectively.

[26] According to Ôno Susumu, Motoori has neglected to mention very few of the *man'yôgana* which were used, and has made virtually no mistakes in his determination of voiceless and voiced sounds ("Kaidai," 22).

[27] Ibid., 23.

[28] Ibid., 22.

[29] Kobayashi Yoshinori, "The *Kun* Readings of the *Kojiki*," *Acta Asiatica* 46 (1984), 83. Kobayashi first compiled an index of the 45,127 characters appearing in the *Kojiki*, and determined that there were a total of 1,482 different characters used. His working hypothesis in determining the *kun* readings for these was that "there was a uniform consciousness in the use of characters in the main text; an intent can be seen to keep the number of logographs small and to choose characters that are relatively simple; as a matter of principle each character has just one or two *kun* readings; there was a standard-use set of characters in antiquity which was used as the basis, and the text reflects this" ("*Kojiki* kundoku ni tsuite," in Aoki et al., *Kojiki*, Nihon shiso taikei, Vol. 1 <Iwanami shoten, 1982>, 656).

[30] Ibid., 689.

[31] Koyasu, *Motoori Norinaga*, 53.

[32] Ibid.

[33] Ibid., 61.

[34] Ibid., 66.

[35] Ibid., 64.

[36] Ibid., 69.

[37] The "Musubi" deities are Taka-mi-musubi-no-kami and Kami-musubi-no-kami; *musubi* means "divine generative force." The two deities are among the five deities who are the first to come into existence in the creation myth (Donald L. Philippi, trans., *Kojiki* <Tokyo: University of Tokyo Press, 1968>, 47).

[38] Koyasu, *Motoori Norinaga*, 68.

[39] Ôno, "Kaidai," 26-27.

[40] Ibid., 28.

[41] As quoted in Ôno, Ibid.

[42] The record, titled "Jugyô monjin seimei roku," is housed in the Motoori Norinaga Ki'nenkan in Matsusaka, Mie Prefecture. A brief discussion of it may be found in Motoori Norinaga Ki'nenkan, eds., *Meihin zuroku* (Matsusaka: Motoori Norinaga Ki'nenkan, 1991), 78.

1

The Texts of Antiquity: Clarification

From which period did the writings which chronicled the ancient events of previous generations begin? If one thinks of the following passage in the section on Emperor Richû [r. 400-405] in the *Shoki* <the *Nihonshoki*, although in the commentary I will refer to it as the *Shoki*>: "4th year, Autumn, 8th month, 8th day. Local Recorders were appointed for the first time in the various provinces, [who noted down statements, and communicated the writings of the four quarters],"[1)] one can surmise that there were probably literate persons at some date prior to this quite early on in the court who recorded things. As these literate persons must have been recording the events of the day, we cannot know whether they also concerned themselves with the previous ages. Yet, in recording the events of the day, they must also have had occasion to record some of the events which had been transmitted from antiquity. One can conclude, therefore, that the recording of the events of antiquity began at this time.

At the time of the compilation of the *Nihonshoki*, it seems that there existed many ancient texts <one should know this just from the fact that there are many items taken as quotations in the

chapters titled "The Age of the Gods">. In the entry in the *Nihonshoki* for the twenty-eighth year [620] of the reign of Empress Suiko [r. 592-628], it states that Prince Shôtoku [574-622], in concert with Soga no Umako [6th C.], "drew up a history of the Emperors, a history of the country, and the original record of the Omi, the Muraji, the Tomo no Miyakko, the Kuni no Miyakko, the 180 Be, and the free subjects."[2] This is the first time that we see a reference to the recording of historical events in the literature. There is also the passage in the chapter on Emperor Tenmu [r. 672-686], where it states that in the tenth year [681] of his reign, the Emperor gave orders to the Imperial Prince Kawashima and others, twelve in all, to "compile a chronicle of the Emperors, and to record the events of great antiquity." [3] These two works, however, have not been transmitted to later generations. In the preface to the *Kojiki*, it states that in the august reign of Empress Genmei [r. 707-715] at the imperial court in Nara, on the eighteenth day of the ninth month of the fourth year of Wadô [711], Ô nö Yasumarö was commanded to compile the *Kojiki*, and on the twenty-eighth day of the first month of the fifth year of Wadô [712], the work was brought to completion.[4] <There is no mention of this in the *Shoku Nihongi*.[5] >This means that of the ancient texts transmitted to the present, the *Kojiki* is the oldest. Since it is recorded in the *Shoku Nihongi* that the *Nihonshoki* was completed in the fourth year of Yôrô [720] in the reign of Empress Genshô [r. 715-724] at the same imperial court,[6] then this means that the *Nihonshoki* appeared eight years later than the *Kojiki*.

This chronicle [*Kojiki*] does not adorn itself with embellishments (文, *aya*)[7] of graphs (字, *mozi*), and it is stated in the preface that efforts were made to use only the ancient language (古語,

hurukoto),[8] and not to lose the true conditions of ancient times. Despite this fact, however, as I will say again and again, since the appearance of the *Nihonshoki*, the people of this world have in general revered and valued it only, and there are many who do not know even the name of the *Kojiki*. The reasons for this occurred somehow in the flourishing of the study of Chinese writings, wherein people venerated and preferred the ways of that country in all fields. People received pleasure only from works which resembled the format of the national histories of China (漢国, *karakuni*), and when they looked at the purity of the *Kojiki*, they would pronounce that it did not have the proper format of a national history and therefore did not take it up. Certain persons have found my saying this to be strange, and have asked me whether it was not the case that the reason why people compiled the *Nihonshoki* in addition to the *Kojiki*, despite the fact that it had not been long since the *Kojiki* had appeared, was because there were errors in the *Kojiki*. I have answered them that this is not likely to have been the reason. The reason why people compiled the *Nihonshoki* despite the existence of the *Kojiki* was that this compilation of the *Nihonshoki* occurred when there was a flourishing of the desire to study Chinese writings (*karabumi-manabi*) on the part of government officials and others. When they compared this completely unembellished, unadorned text [*Kojiki*] with the Chinese national histories, it was not impressive, resounded only faintly, and was deemed to be insufficient. They thereupon reflected widely upon various things, set up a yearly chronicle, embellished it with Chinese-style words, and created Chinese-style rhetoric (*karabumi-aya*). In so doing, they created a national history which resembled those of China. This was their purpose in compiling the *Nihonshoki.*

To elaborate further, as I stated above, the Imperial Prince Kawashima and others were commanded to compile an imperial history (帝紀) and other matters. Subsequent to that, it is stated in the *Shoku Nihongi* that in the year 714 (Wadô 7), Ki no Kiyohito and Miyake no Fujimaro were commanded by imperial edict to compile a national history (国史).[9] Of these two compilations, the selection by Prince Kawashima and others was begun, like the *Kojiki*, in the reign of Emperor Tenmu [r. 672-686], but it is difficult to know whether the commencement of the compilation of the *Kojiki* precedes or follows the compilation of Prince Kawashima. If the compilation of Prince Kawashima predates the *Kojiki*, then, according to the statement in the preface to the *Kojiki*: "I hear that the *Sumeröki nö Fitugi* (*The Imperial Sun-Lineage*) and the *Saki-tu-yö nö kötöba* (*Fundamental Matters*) possessed by the various houses completely differ from the truth and that many falsehoods have been added to them,"[10] the text compiled by Prince Kawashima would also have been among those which deviated from the true state of affairs and would probably have contained added falsehoods. If this text is later, then what is represented in the *Kojiki* would be something that was rendered sufficiently by the later collection. When we consider, however, that it states in the preface to the *Kojiki* that "time passed, and the imperial reign changed, so this project was not carried out,"[11] then it seems that the *Kojiki* and the compilation of Prince Kawashima were essentially something different. The main point in which they would most likely have differed from one another is that the compilation by Prince Kawashima had added ornamentation and modeled itself on the national histories of China, while the *Kojiki* strives to convey the true state of affairs of ancient times. This aim of the *Kojiki* is apparent in the preface.

Upon commencement of the Nara Period [710-794], this imperial plan was continued, and Ô nö Yasumarö was commanded to write down the ancient matters that Fiyeda nö Are would bring to mind and recite. The history which was later compiled in 714 (Wadô 7) no doubt had embellishments. Then, in 717 (Yôrô 1), Prince Toneri [677-735] was commanded to compile the *Nihonshoki*.[12] The reason why this compilation continued uninterrupted despite there being two ornamental histories was because these histories were insufficient, and did not go along with the great aims. It thus seems that these histories were abandoned and were not transmitted. No doubt not even the names of the texts remained behind. The *Nihonshoki*, however, was superior to those previous histories, and as it was good, it was established as the correct history, and there were no subsequent revisions. The reason why the *Kojiki* seems not to have been abandoned even after the *Nihonshoki* appeared was because, unlike the two texts mentioned above, it did not have much ornamentation, but was rather a text which recorded the true nature (*makoto*) of ancient times. The reason for compiling the *Nihonshoki* was not because there were errors in the *Kojiki*. The two texts differed fundamentally in tone (*omomuki*). If there were errors in the *Kojiki*, they would only have had to correct them. If one considers that the *Kojiki*, too, like the two aforementioned texts, would probably have died out, one must remember that it is only the *Kojiki* which has been transmitted up until the present day.

Other persons say that the matter of whether or not a text is transmitted to a later age is a matter of coincidence, and that it is probably not the case that a text is transmitted because it is good, or, conversely, that a text is not transmitted because it is not good. These persons doubt [the *Kojiki*] by saying that probably in China and in this country, too, many very fine books of ancient times have died out, and many that were not so fine have been widely transmitted. I answer that although that is possibly the case, it is not true of the *Kojiki*. These two histories are recorded in the *Nihon-shoki* and *Shoku Nihongi*, and since they were official histories, even if they were to die out naturally, they would nonetheless have stayed on for some time in the public eye, and people would have known of them. Perhaps only their names could have been expected to survive in later generations, yet not even their names remain, and early on in the Nara period [710-794] there were none who knew of them. In the notes in the *Man'yôshû* clarifying matters of ancient times, one does not encounter any quotations from these works. The *Kojiki* has recorded events just as they were without ornamentation, and since it is a very different type of work than the national histories of China, if there were many errors in it, it should have died out quickly in an age which was so fond of Chinese writings. There would have been no one to pick it up and read it, not to mention transmitting it to later ages. When one considers the fact that it has continued to be transmitted for a thousand years, would it not seem that it had been used by officials, and that ordinary people had read it as well? It is also quoted from in the *Man'yôshû*.[13] <Although, as I have discussed above, we do not know all that we should in these matters, I have more or less covered what is possible to know with regard to a consideration of

the preface to the *Kojiki* and the fragments of the compilations of these two histories.>

People then argue that the task of compilation commanded of Prince Kawashima and the others appears in the *Nihonshoki*, and the compilation of 714 (Wadô 7) and of the *Nihonshoki* appear in the *Shoku Nihongi*, but there is no mention of the compilation of the *Kojiki*. In light of this, it would seem that the *Kojiki* is not a serious, official undertaking like these other histories, but rather an unofficial, trifling undertaking. Furthermore, of the many items treated as individual sections in such chapters as "The Age of the Gods" in the *Nihonshoki*, there are sections which would appear to have been taken from the *Kojiki*. The *Kojiki* thus appears to have been one of many such records existing at the time. Since the *Nihonshoki* and other records are all compilations which have gathered together this and that and are equipped so that there are no insufficiencies, they are not of the same type as the *Kojiki*. Some will ask how the *Kojiki* can be revered and adopted in an equal fashion with these records. To this I answer that the *Kojiki* is one of several works which were selectively chosen from for compilation of the *Nihonshoki*, and that therefore, the *Nihonshoki* is furnished with the *Kojiki*. This is one argument. Since the *Nihonshoki* is indeed a work in which things are widely recorded even down to the year, month, and day in detail, so that nothing is lacking, it of course goes without saying that there are many things which the *Kojiki* does not cover.

Although that is the case, if one is to speak of the superior features of the *Kojiki*, one would first of all note that in ancient times, books did not exist, and the things which people must have conveyed via the mouths of people were not necessarily like the decorative language (文) of the *Nihonshoki*; rather, they were probably like the words (詞) of the *Kojiki*.[14] The *Nihonshoki* strives to resemble the Chinese, and ornaments its figures of speech (文章, *aya*),[15] while the *Kojiki* pays no attention to the Chinese and merely aims at not losing the words (語言, *kotoba*) of ancient times. <I shall speak about the reason for this when I discuss the preface to the *Kojiki* in the next book.>[16]

Meaning (意, *kokoro*), event (事, *koto*), and word (言, *kotoba*) are all things which are consistent with one another. In the world of the ancients, there were the meanings, events, and words of the ancients, and so, too, in the later ages, there exist the meanings, events, and words of the later ages. China, too, has its own meanings, events, and words. The *Nihonshoki* uses the meaning of the later ages to record the events of the ancient age, and because it uses the language of China to record the meaning of our imperial country, there are many things which are not in correspondence with one another. The *Kojiki* contains not a bit of posturing, and since it has recorded things just as they have been transmitted from ancient times, in the *Kojiki* meaning, event, and word are in accord with one another, and what is represented there is the true nature of the ancient age. This is precisely because they have concentrated on using only the language (語言, *kotoba*) of ancient times. Since meanings and events are transmitted by words in written texts, it is the language in which things are recorded which is of primary importance. Furthermore, since the *Nihonshoki* aimed for the style of Chinese works, there are many places where the style of the ancient language of our imperial country is lost. The *Kojiki*, however, uses the ancient language just as it was, and the style of the language of the ancient period is a very beautiful thing.

Suppose one were to take one portion of the *Nihonshoki* which is not of great official importance. One would nonetheless be expected to respect it and use it. The *Kojiki* came into existence as the result of great interest on the part of Emperor Tenmu [r. 672-686], and was recorded in the Nara period [710-794] by imperial command [Empress Genmei, 711], and is, therefore, not an insignificant, unofficial text. When one considers these various factors, it is indeed the *Kojiki* which deserves all the greater value and esteem. Despite this fact, however, in those days only Chinese studies were carried out in a flourishing fashion, and even the laws below heaven were all of the Chinese type. In such an age, even when it came to official works, people fervently revered those that were of the Chinese type and gave them prominent display, while the works which related the truth of previous generations were relegated to obscurity, as if they were unofficial works. This must be the reason why the compilation of the *Kojiki* is not mentioned in the *Shoku Nihongi*.

Subsequently, this neglect increased, and there were few who took up the *Kojiki* and read it. It is quite lamentable that the scholars of subsequent generations claimed that it was not a true national history and gave it little regard. Since there were no other ancient national histories transmitted in Japan, what people would adopt as a model for their style would be something of China. In the matter of works which were felt to be equipped with the proper style, people were pleased only with works which resembled those of China. What would be the harm if one did not feel predisposed to behave in the Chinese way and created a work which did not resemble the Chinese? The practice in this world of taking China as the primary model in all things to determine what is good and what is bad is very foolish indeed.

Through the persuasive efforts of my teacher Professor Okabe (Kamo no Mabuchi Agata Nushi) to promote the study of ancient things while in residence at the Eastern Capital [Edo Shogunate], people have come forth who have become aware of the stain of the spirit of Chinese writings, which has permeated the depths of people's hearts for more than a thousand years, and people in the world are beginning to understand the respectability of the *Kojiki*. This is all due to the meritorious efforts of Kamo no Mabuchi. Such efforts in the path of learning have not existed since the Age of the Gods. I, Norinaga, have begun to understand this spirit through his benevolence, and as the years and months pass have come to realize more and more the stain of the spirit of Chinese writings, and can well see the truth of the pure beauty of antiquity. I have determined, therefore, that in the *Kojiki*, we have the best work (史典, *humi*) among the ancient works, and that the *Nihonshoki* should be placed secondary in importance after the *Kojiki*. Those who aim to study the imperial country should not for a moment be of mistaken thought with regard to this spirit (意).

Notes

1) W. G. Aston, trans., *Nihongi: Chronicles of Japan from the Earliest Times to A.D. 697* (Rutland, VT: Tuttle, 1972; First edition by Japan Society, 1896), Vol. 1:307. *Nihonshoki,* Vol. 1, NKBT 67:427. The *Nihonshoki* is organized in "books" (巻 *kan*), which number thirty altogether. The first two books cover events from the "Age of the Gods," and the rest record the events in the reigns of forty-two successive emperors and empresses, beginning with the legendary first emperor, Emperor Jinmu (r. 600-585

B.C.). Some books cover a single reign, while others cover more than one regnal period; in each case, the change in reign is indicated by a subtitle consisting of the new emperor's name. Motoori refers to the portion of the text dealing with each of these regnal periods as a "book" (巻 *maki*), which I translate throughout as "chapter."

[2] Aston, *Nihongi*, Vol. 2:148. *Nihonshoki*, Vol. 2, NKBT 68:203. The "History of the Emperors" (*Sumera-mikötö nö Fumi*, or *Tennô-ki)*, and the "Original Records" (*Mötö nö Fumi*, or *Hongi*) were destroyed by fire in the overthrow of the Soga family in 645. The "History of the Country" (*Kuni nö Fumi*, or *Kokki*) was seized from the flames by Fune no Fubito Wesaka (Aston, *Nihongi*, Vol. 2:193; *Nihonshoki*, Vol. 2, NKBT 68:265), who presented it to future Emperor Tenji (668-671). There is no later mention of the book (Donald L. Philippi, trans., *Kojiki* <Tokyo: Tokyo University Press, 1968>, 5).

[3] Motoori gives the quotation in abbreviated form. The original passage contains the names of the others so commanded (*Nihonshoki*, Vol. 2, NKBT 68:445, 447; Aston, *Nihongi*, Vol. 2:350). The twelve were ordered to examine conflicting views with the aim of establishing historical fact and to record the results in the two documents mentioned: one an "Imperial Chronicle" (帝紀, *Sumeragi nö miFumi* <Motoori's reading>, or *Sumera- mikötö nö Fumi* <Sakamoto Tarô et al.'s reading>), the other an anthology of myth, legend, and song, the "Events of Great Antiquity" (上古諸事, *Kamu tu yö nö mörömörö nö kötö* <Motoori's reading>, or *InisiFe nö mörömörö nö kötö* <Sakamoto Tarô et al.'s reading>) (*Nihonshoki*, Vol. 2, NKBT 68:593, supplementary note 17).

The first document is thought to be the same document that is referred to, variously, as the *Sumeröki nö Fitugi* (帝皇日継 *The Imperial Sun-Lineage*), the *Teiki* (or *Sumeröki nö Fitugi*) (帝紀 *Imperial Chronicles*), and the *Senki* (or *Saki tu Fitugi*) (先紀 *Chronicles of the Past*) in the *Kojiki* (*Kojiki*, NST 1:15, Kojima Noriyuki, "Kaisetsu," *Nihonshoki*, Vol. 1, NKBT 67:7; Vol. 2, NKBT 68:593, supplementary note 17). It is presumed to have been a genealogy of the succession of emperors. The second document is considered to be the same document as the text which is referred to, variously, as the *Saki tu yö nö Furukötö* (or *Sendai kuji*) (先代旧辞 *Ancient Matters of Former Ages*), the *Honji* (or *Saki tu yö nö kötöba*) (本辞 *Fundamental Matters*), and the *Kuji* (or *Furukötö*) (旧辞 *Ancient Matters*) (Ibid.). These texts appear in the quotation preceding note 10 in the text. See also Philippi, *Kojiki*, 8-15; 41-43, for a discussion of these documents. Aoki Kazuo et al. provide a detailed discussion of what these works might have contained and outline the history of their development (*Kojiki*, NST 1:310-311, supplementary notes 14, 15). Sakamoto Tarô also outlines their probable content, and states that both were composed of materials that had been transmitted orally and first put down in writing "around the sixth century" (John S. Brownlee, trans., *The Six National Histories of Japan* <Vancouver: UBC Press; Tokyo: University of Tokyo Press, 1991>, 44).

4) *Kojiki*, NST 1:14, 16.

5) The *Shoku Nihongi* (*The Nihongi Continued),* the second of the "Six National Histories" compiled by the imperial decree of Emperor Kônin (r. 770-781), was completed in 797. It is a chronological history covering the period from the accession of Emperor Monmu (r. 697-707) through the year Enryaku 10 (791) of Emperor Kanmu (r. 781-806).

6) "720. Fifth Month: Prince Toneri, upon imperial command, completed the *Nihongi.* Thirty chapters and a genealogy were presented to the Emperor." Hayashi Rokurou, ed., *Shoku Nihongi* (Gendai shichôsha, 1985), Vol. 1:168.

7) Cynthia Chennault (personal communication) has suggested to me that Motoori's focus on the language of antiquity, and his view of Chinese logographic symbols as pure embellishment superimposed upon that language, implies that he dismisses the Chinese view of the graph as a reflection of the sacred patterns of heaven, interpreted through man. Motoori glosses the graph 文 with the reading of *aya* "pattern" or "rhetorical ornamentation." The traditional interpretation of the original meaning of the Chinese graph 文 (*wen*) has to do with pattern or design: "Wen [consists of] intersecting strokes, representing a criss-cross pattern" (Hsu Shen's *Explanations of Simple and Compound Characters* <*Shuo-wen chieh-tzu*, ca. A.D. 100>, in James J. Y.

Liu, *Chinese Theories of Literature* <Chicago: University of Chicago Press, 1975>, 7), and the term is used to refer to various naturally occurring patterns such as the patterns on cowrie shells and tiger skins, as well as the ornamental patterns created by humans in woven silk and painted designs (Liu, 7). Liu points out that early on, however, *wen* was used in "figurative and abstract" senses as well. He cites the "Commentary on the Decision" under the twenty-second hexagram, *Pi* ('Grace') in the *Yijing* (*Book of Changes*): "Contemplate the configurations [*wen*] of heaven to observe the changes of seasons; contemplate the configurations of man to accomplish the [cultural] transformation of the world," and notes that the passage "draws an analogy between the 'configurations of heaven' (*t'ien-wen*) and the 'configurations of man'" (*jen-wen*) (Liu, 18). It was through contemplation of these configurations of heaven and earth that the trigrams of the *Yijing* were developed, and subsequently, from these trigrams, the logographic writing system: "In ancient times, when Pao-hsi ruled over the world, he lifted his head and contemplated the signs in heaven; he bent down and contemplated the orders on earth. He contemplated the patterns [*wen*] on birds and beasts, and the suitabilities of the earth. He drew [ideas] from his own person, and from objects afar. Thereupon he first invented the Eight Trigrams." ("Appended Words," the *Yijing*, in Liu, 18).

Motoori concentrates on "pattern" as "rhetorical embellishment," and ignores any notion that graphs may be representative of "pattern" in a deeper sense. In a passage in chapter 8: "On the Method of Reading" (p. 145), he describes Chinese graphs as makeshift items attached to Japanese texts, representing no type of underlying deep reality.

8) Specifically, Ô nö Yasumarö indicates his intention to preserve the language of the texts memorized by Fiyeda nö Are (?670-?690). In the preface to the *Kojiki*, he outlines the problems inherent in the use of Chinese graphs to write the Japanese language:

> In antiquity, both word (言 *koto*) and meaning (意 *kokoro*) were unsophisticated, and it is difficult to form sentences which discuss these events with the use of Chinese graphs. When I use Chinese graphs for

their meanings alone, the words do not correspond to the intended meaning. Yet, when I relate the events through the use of Chinese graphs for their sound values only, the account becomes too lengthy. For this reason, I have related some passages with some graphs used for their meaning and others for their sound, and other passages with the graphs used only for their meaning. When the meaning of a passage is not readily apparent, I have added explanatory notes, but when the intended meaning is easily understood, I have added nothing. (*Kojiki*, NST 1:16.)

By writing "古語" (ancient language) and glossing it as "*hurukoto*" (ancient words/events), Motoori is able to convey the double sense of 'ancient language and ancient events'. The deliberate use of non-conventional glossing also has the function of reinforcing Motoori's argument that Chinese graphs are nothing more than pure ornamentation superimposed on the true Japanese text. Motoori also uses the terms 古言, 上ツ代の言, and 古への語言 to refer to the language of antiquity. Edo nativists used the term 古言 to refer to the language of ancient Japan; the materials they studied are from the period of Japanese which Japanese linguists now refer to as 'Old Japanese' (上代語 *jodaigo*) (Hayashi Ôki, "Kogo," in Kokugogakkai, eds., *Kokugogaku daijiten* <Tôkyôdô, 1980>, 423). Those persons writing from the perspective of Western linguistics define 'Old Japanese' as the language of the Nara period (710-794), while those writing from the perspective of *kokugogaku* define it as the language of the time prior to and including the Nara period ("Nara-chô jidai oyobi sore izen no kotoba") (Yoshida Kanehiko, *Jôdai jodôshi no shiteki kenkyû* <Meiji shoin, 1973>, 3).

[9)] Hayashi Rokurou, ed., *Shoku Nihongi* (Gendai shichôsha, 1985), Vol. 1:114. See Sakamoto Tarô for a history of the usage of the term 国史 (*kokushi*, 'national history') (*The Six National Histories of Japan*, 3-6).

[10)] *Kojiki*, NST 1:14.

[11)] *Kojiki*, NST 1:14. This was the project whereby Emperor Tenmu (r. 672-686) would correct the genealogical record and the anecdotal material to pass on to future generations. Apparently, the project did not progress beyond the first step, which was to have Fiyeda nö Are commit the documents to memory.

There is no established theory regarding the connection, if any, between the two projects ordered by Emperor Tenmu. It is generally agreed that both Prince Kawashima and his group, on the one hand, and Fieda nö Are, on the other, were directed to work with the same source documents, one, an imperial genealogy, and two, an anecdotal anthology. Kojima Noriyuki presents two possible scenarios for the relation between the two projects ("Kaisetsu," in *Nihonshoki*, Vol. 1, NKBT 67:6-9). The first scenario is that of Hirata Toshiharu, whose theory is that the project of 681 entrusted to Prince Kawashima and his group was designed to correct the corrupt system of *uji* (lineage) and *kabane* (rank) titles. Their efforts to this end were not successful, however, due to the complications of self-interest. Emperor Tenmu then turned to Fiyeda nö Are, and the result of this later project was the new eight-rank *kabane* system, established in 684. The *Kojiki* resulted from the recording of what Fiyeda nö Are memorized. The *Nihonshoki*, on the other hand, had no connection to either of these projects, and was initiated in 714 in the national history commanded at that time. This is the history mentioned in the quotation preceding note 9 in the text. The second scenario is that of Kojima. In his view, the format and purpose of each project was essentially different. Prince Kawashima and his group received their command in the Great Hall of State (Daigokuden), a public setting. The project was to be an official government undertaking, and this is why as many as twelve persons were entrusted with the task. The project commanded of Fiyeda nö Are, however, was one commanded privately by Emperor Tenmu to Fiyeda nö Are individually, and was a modest project to be undertaken only for the Emperor himself.

Kojima argues that Fiyeda nö Are's efforts came first, and that Emperor Tenmu's intention was to rid the documents of falsehood and establish truth. The task proved to be too much for the efforts of one individual, however, so the Emperor then turned to Prince Kawashima and his group and initiated a large-scale project. This large-scale project was not completed in his reign, but was continued in successive generations, and finally reached completion in the form of the *Nihonshoki* in 720.

The *Kojiki* appeared during the reign of Empress Genmei (r. 707-715), who was married to Prince Kusakabe, son of Emperor Tenmu. Kojima suggests that she may have had an interest in seeing to the completion of the work that Emperor Tenmu left unfinished at his death. She therefore had Ô nö Yasumarö record what Fiyeda nö Are recited, and this became the *Kojiki*, which appeared in 712. See also Philippi, *Kojiki*, 7, for discussion of the motive of Empress Genmei.

Sakamoto Tarô also discusses the connection between the *Kojiki* and the *Nihonshoki*, and his view corresponds to the scenario outlined by Kojima and presented above (*The Six National Histories of Japan*, 33-36).

12) According to Sakamoto Tarô (*The Six National Histories of Japan*, 35-36), it is not known exactly when Prince Toneri received the command. As the third and only surviving son of Emperor Tenmu at that time, he would have been the logical choice to assume responsibility for the project, given the Kojima scenario outlined in note 11 above. Sakamoto believes Prince Toneri's role in the compilation to have been that of a supervisory figurehead (Ibid., 37).

13) According to Ôno Susumu ("Kaidai," *Kojiki-den*, MNZ 9:8), there are two references to the *Kojiki* in the *Man'yôshû*.

14) The term 詞 (*kotoba*, Chinese *ci*) refers, in Chinese, to written or spoken language, and can be used to indicate a word or a phrase, while the term 文 (Chinese *wen*) refers only to the written word (Cynthia Chennault, personal communication).

15) Motoori's use of the term "文章" (Chinese *wen-zhang*, glossed here as "*aya*" 'figure of speech') to represent mere rhetorical flourish here again indicates rejection of the Chinese view of the patterning of words as a representation of the deeper underlying patterns of heaven and earth. James J. Y. Liu, (*Chinese Theories of Literature*, 100), discusses the meaning of the second morpheme *zhang* in the compound *wen-zhang*, and notes that in the *Book of Poetry* "the word chang [*zhang*] occurs altogether eleven times . . . , four times meaning 'patterns' with reference to patterned material, once

referring to 'patterns' formed by stars in the sky, three times meaning 'outward adornments' (once with reference to speech), once meaning model,' once 'statutes,' and once 'splendid' or 'shining.'" Liu interprets the meaning of the compound wen-zhang as "pattern-pattern" or as "verbal pattern,". . . in either case implying formal pattern and beauty."

It is clear that for theorists of Chinese literature, such as Liu Hsieh (d. ca. 523), the pattern and beauty possible in linguistic expression was akin to the natural ornaments nature/heaven allows life forms to adorn themselves with. The patterns in linguistic expression were for those theorists, therefore, not mere rhetorical flourish, but rather were imbued with, in Liu's terms, a "metaphysical aestheticism" (Liu, 21). The following quote from Liu Hsieh's *The Literary Mind: Elaborations* (*Wen-hsin tiao-lung*, ca. 502) is an illustration of this notion (from Liu, 102):

> The writings of the sages and enlightened men are known collectively as "literary patterns" [*wen-chang*]: what are they if not ornamentations! Now, water, which is by nature mobile, forms ripples; trees, which are solid in substance, give forth blossoms: these are examples of outward beauty [*wen*] attaching itself to inner substance [*chih*]. If the tiger and the leopard had no beautiful patterns [*wen*], their hide would be no different from a dog's or a sheep's; the rhinocerous has hide, but this relies on vermillion varnish for color [when made into armor]: these are all examples of inner substance awaiting outward beauty.

16) Motoori compares the preface to the *Kojiki*, which is written entirely in classical Chinese and contains ample reference to the Chinese theories of *qian* (the heavenly principle) and *kun* (the earthly principle), and *yin* (the female force) and *yang* (the male force), with the main body of the *Kojiki*, which contains no reference to any of the theories of the Chinese. He then argues that the fact that these Chinese terms are found in the preface is an indication that such concepts were not a part of the native transmissions from antiquity. The preface, in his view, serves to illustrate the difference between

the Japanese truth (*makoto*), i.e. the main body of the text, and the Chinese ornamentation (*kazari*), i.e. the preface (*Kojiki-den*, MNZ 9:66).

Motoori also argues that the fact that Fiyeda nö Are was commanded to learn the texts and commit them to memory, so that they could be recited aloud apart from any text, is an indication that Emperor Tenmu placed high value on the language, and not merely the content, of the texts (*Kojiki-den*, MNZ 9:72,73).

2
Discussion of the *Nihonshoki*

Now, to say that I will explain the *Kojiki*, why do I discuss the *Nihonshoki*? Since antiquity, people have for the most part valued and taken up the *Nihonshoki* only, and scholars through the ages have devoted their energies to this text. Although there are so many commentaries on the books on the "Age of the Gods" to the point of being irksome, response to the *Kojiki* has been half-hearted and people have not found it to be a text which merited devotion of their energy. To ask why this should be so, it is simply because people of the world have been attracted to nothing but the spirit of Chinese writing, and have completely forgotten the spirit of antiquity of our great country. Therefore, the clearing away of the confusion caused by the Chinese spirit, and establishment of justification for reverence of the *Kojiki* should constitute a sign-post for the study of native things (*mi-kuni no manabi*). Since people do not realize that the *Nihonshoki* is full of embellishments and do not fully understand the circumstances of its compilation, it is difficult to dispel the deep illness of the Chinese spirit. Accordingly, if this illness is not dispelled, it is difficult to express the good points of the *Kojiki*. Unless people realize the good points of the *Kojiki*, they will not be able to understand the true path to the study of antiquity.

Our discussion should begin with the fact that the very title itself of the *Nihonshoki* is unacceptable. In the naming of this text, we have followed the names of Chinese histories, such as the *Han shu* (*History of the Former Han Dynasty*)[1] and *Jin shu* (*History of the Jin Dynasty*)[2] and added the name of our country. In China, since the name of the country changes from generation to generation, if the name of the age is not included in the title, it will be difficult to understand. In our imperial country, however, the imperial throne has continued along with the universe throughout the ages, and since there is no change in the throne, there is no need to divide it into ages and speak of things in that way. To put the name of our country on such a work is an act which is a type of comparison, but to just what is it that this title corresponds? It seems to be nothing more than a contrast to China (*kankoku*), and is a title created in deference to China. <In later histories, people followed this custom in creating titles, and it is all the more unsettling that the name of this country was attached even to the records of the *Montoku jitsuroku* .>[3] Indeed, why was it that later generations praised this type of title as a noble thing? To my mind, it is quite unsatisfactory, and seems to be a title which is quite peripheral as well. Some persons have suggested that the title of *Nihonshoki* was given with the intent of showing it to China, but such was by no means the case. <If it were the case that the title was given with major consideration to the fact that it would be shown to the people of other countries, it would be all the more misguided.>

As for the style of what is written in the *Nihonshoki*, by virtue of the fact that efforts were made to have it conform completely to the Chinese [histories], it is full of nothing but ornamentation of both meaning (*imi*) and form (*kotoba*), and there are many parts which differ from the speech and essential facts of ancient times. First of all, at the beginning of the first book on "The Age of the Gods," where it states: "In ancient times when heaven and earth had not yet separated, and the female and the male were not differentiated, all was round like the egg of a chicken . . . subsequently, the gods were born in the midst of heaven and earth,"[4] this is all individual fabrication on the part of the compilers, who gathered bits and pieces from the works of Chinese writings and wrote them down. By no means are such things to be found in the legends transmitted from ancient times. The words which follow: "Therefore, it is said that in the beginning of heaven and earth, the land of the nation was drifting about just like a fish floating in the water,"[5] are in fact part of the legends transmitted from ancient times. Because the text states "Therefore, it is said," we can know that the preceding section is something which has been added later and is ornamentation. If this were not the case, then what, indeed, would be the meaning of the two characters 故曰? The tone of the first account is undeniably cunning, and is without a doubt in the Chinese spirit. It is definitely not in the spirit of the ancient age of our imperial country. A person who wishes to reflect upon ancient times and understand them should be able to discern this on his own. How can it be, then, that given that the state of affairs in the beginning of heaven and earth must truly have been as they are described in the legends transmitted from ancient times, people nonetheless borrowed the annoyingly intricate and cunning legend of a foreign country and placed it at the very beginning of the text? <One old manuscript has 一曰 'one version' for 故曰

'therefore, it is said,' so if this edition contains the correct version,[6] then the latter expression is a mistake, and there should be no reason to use it. This is because 'therefore' is an indication that the legend of another country has been given primary focus, while the native legends transmitted from ancient times have been put to the side.>

The legends of Chinese writings, including the accounts of the beginnings of heaven and earth, are all things which an ordinary individual created in his own mind through conjecture that established an arbitrary logic for things. Our legends transmitted from ancient times, however, are not of this sort; they are not words which someone suggested, but exactly those very words which have been transmitted from very ancient times. In a comparison of the two, it is the Chinese writings which sound quite logical, and lead one to assume that, indeed, things must have been as described. The Japanese legends transmitted from ancient times sound insignificant and simple. It is for this reason that all have been attracted solely to Chinese writings, and there is no one, from Prince Toneri[7] through successive generations of scholars up until the present time, who has not been quite captivated by them.

The reason why everyone has been so attracted to Chinese writings is because the clever people of ancient times, in thinking deeply about all kinds of things and seeking a reason for them, created the legends in such a way that all would assume that, indeed, things must have been so. With clever brushes, they skillfully wrote these things down. Human knowledge, however, has limitations, and as the true underlying principle does not lie in something that can be measured and known, how can we know that such things as the beginning of heaven and earth should have been due to some purported principle of logic? Such guesswork is grossly in error much of the time even for things that are proximate. To think that with the application of principles of logic, there is nothing that cannot be known with regard to both the beginning and the end of heaven and earth, simply results in the inability to realize that there are limitations to human knowledge, and that the true principle is difficult to fathom. To accept things in the belief that everything corresponds to an underlying principle is simply a mistake.

Whether, in truth, things do or do not correspond to an underlying principle is not something which ordinary people should be able to know. Since those who created the principle are ordinary people, and those who believe in it possess ordinary minds, how could they possibly pass judgment with regard to its suitability? Even the sages in China who are spoken of so grandly are of limited intelligence, and there are many places beyond the reach of their wisdom. How, then, can the explanations of those who are inferior to them in intelligence be sufficient to compel our belief? Nonetheless, generations of scholars have been deceived by these explanations of conjecture without realizing it. They even go so far as to judge the places adorned with Chinese words to be the essence of the Way, which is quite astonishing. As for the initial passage in the *Nihonshoki*, it is best to pass over it as something akin to a preface, added as ornamentation.

Subsequently, the following two passages appear: "The principle of heaven alone created these two deities. Thus, they produced males consisting purely of the male force,"[8)] and "The principles of heaven and earth combined together and thus produced male and female deities."[9)] These are also fabricated words added to the text at the whim of the compilers. The evidence for this is that the concept of the principles of heaven and earth (乾坤, *qian* and *kun*) did not exist in our imperial country.[10] Since it did not exist in the ancient language, it is clear that it must derive from some source other than the legends transmitted from ancient times. If such passages were from the transmissions of antiquity, they would have the words *amëtuti nö miti* (天地之道, 'the Way of heaven and earth'). If it were a matter of a mere difference in graphs, where they had written 乾坤 ('heaven and earth') for 天地 *amëtuti* ('heaven and earth'), this would still be acceptable, but their writing about these deities as if they came into existence by means of the principles of heaven and earth completely contradicts the truth of the matter. These deities[11] came into existence solely through the august deities Taka-mi-musubi-nö-kamï and Kamï-musubi-nö-kamï, but here it will be impossible for one to discern this principle of origin.[12] To write cleverly of the events as 'a transformation of heaven and earth' (乾坤の化) is a mistake of Chinese learning (漢意, *karagokoro*).

Furthermore, they write Izanagi-nö-mikötö as 'male deity' (陽神), and Izanami-nö-mikötö as 'female deity' (陰神).[13] In like fashion, the passage "the female Deity was the first to utter an exclamation of pleasure, and the law of male and female was therefore broken,"[14] is a mistake of Chinese learning. The principles of yin (陰) and yang (陽) do not exist in Japan.[15] In our imperial country, in the age when there did not yet exist a writing system, there were no such words. In the transmissions from ancient times, only the expressions *wogamï* 'male deity', *megamï* 'female deity,' and *mewo nö kötöwari*, 'the principle of the female force and the male force', should have been used. To rewrite these in Chinese terms not only results in a difference in graphs, but also constitutes a hindrance to study. Thus, persons who are not quite so clever will conclude, when looking at this text, that the deities called Izanagi-nö-mikötö and Izanami-nö-mikötö were simply given makeshift names, and that in reality we can explain them in terms of the "creation of yin and yang" (陰陽造化). Or, they will assume that we can explain them in terms of the principle of divination in Chinese writings, or the principles of "yin and yang and the five agents," [16)] which would result in events from the Age of the Gods being described with provisional fabrications. This is because the legends transmitted from the past are completely cloaked in the Chinese spirit, and it is difficult to establish the true Way. No doubt in the beginning, the compilers did not realize that this would be the outcome, and wrote using such expressions as mere ornamentation, thinking that it was a good thing to give words a Chinese cast. The result, however, was that in later ages such expressions became a vehicle for the invitation of all sorts of heterodoxies, and formed the root of all difficulties for a detection of the true Way.

From very ancient times, these principles of yin and yang have penetrated the depths of people's minds, with everyone accepting them as natural principles of heaven and earth. Indeed, people have no doubt been of the opinion that there was no instance of any thing or event deviating from these principles, but their minds have, nonetheless, been deceived by the explanations of Chinese writings.

When we wash away the spirit of Chinese writing and carefully consider things, 天地 is simply *amëtuti* ('heaven and earth'), 男女 is simply *mewo* ('female and male'), and 水火 is simply *himidu* ('fire and water'). Each of these has its own characteristics, but they are all works of the deities, and the principle underlying all of this is quite mysterious and miraculous, and not within the realm of human comprehension. Nonetheless, it is the habit of Chinese people to force themselves with their own individual minds to consider thousands of principles, and to explain everything by creating the terms yin and yang. They then proceed to expound on this matter as if all things in heaven and earth are none other than these principles. <One would assume that since yin and yang are merely terms created by the Chinese, and originally formed a private theory unique to China, it would not be an issue in other countries. If one looks at the Buddhist sutras of India, things like the origin of the world and the human body are explained in terms of the four elements of earth, water, fire, and wind. There is no mention of such theories as yin and yang and the five agents. Although the characters themselves can be seen on occasion, one would assume that they are only superficial changes to the text to make it Chinese. There is no discussion of them as theoretical principles. India is a country which debates the underlying principles of things in an even more complicated fashion than does China, but we should acknowledge the fact that the concepts of yin and yang are a private theory of China.>

The concepts of yin and yang are something which a wise person created after careful consideration, and because in six or seven cases out of ten, they appear to account for things, generations of people have accepted them without a doubt. When it comes to the question of what sort of theory it is that will account for yin and yang, however, it cannot be determined. There is also the concept of *taiji wu ji* ('The Supreme Ultimate is Ultimateless'),[17] but here again, when it comes to the question of what sort of theory will account for it, it is difficult to determine the underlying principle.

In truth, both yin and yang and *taiji wu ji* are worthless terms of no value, small principles in the realm of the limits of the narrow reach of human intelligence, to which various names have been given.

In the first place, Ama-terasu-oFo-mi-kamï is the deity of the sun, and a female goddess, while Tuku-yömi is the deity of the moon, and a male god. This is proof that the concepts of yin and yang do not fit the true principles, and people should realize that it is contrary to the transmissions of ancient times.[18] To cling in confusion to these principles of yin and yang, and to go so far as to distort the transmissions from ancient times in the attempt to force them to conform to this principle, is not acceptable. Writing the names of deities such as 美都波能賣神 (Mitu-Fa-nö-me-nö-kamï) as 罔象女,[19] and 綿津見 (Wata-tu-mi) as 少童,[20] is also done in deference to the Chinese model and is an unpleasant style of writing.

Similarly, in the section on Emperor Jinmu [r. 660-585 B.C.], the imperial decree which reads: "At this time the world was given over to widespread desolation. It was an age of darkness and disorder. In this gloom, therefore, he fostered justice, and so governed this western border. Our Imperial ancestors and Imperial parent, like gods, like sages, accumulated happiness and amassed glory" is not in the style of antiquity, in either content or language.[21] It is a passage fabricated by the compilers and added as ornamentation. The same can be said with regard to the following passage from the section on Emperor Sujin [r. 97-30 B.C.]: "The Emperor issued a decree, saying: When our Imperial ancestors gloriously assumed the Supreme Rank, was it for the benefit of themselves alone?"[22] The reason why most of the imperial decrees of many generations are like this seems to be because these decrees were things added as ornamentation to the chapters dealing with antiquity. This is why there are many passages which are quite difficult to read in the archaic language.

In the *Shoku Nihongi*, imperial decrees in the ancient language <those which are called *senmyô*> and imperial decrees in Chinese are recorded separately. When one considers the fact that even as late as the Nara period, Chinese-style expressions are hardly to be seen in the words of the imperial decrees issued in that time, then one can easily imagine just how much more archaic the words of the imperial decrees must have been in the periods of antiquity. The words of the imperial decrees in the *Nihonshoki* are not archaic in the slightest, and are extremely Chinese in letter and spirit.

Passages which for the most part have clever Chinese-style words such as the following, representing the words of the emperor in the section on Emperor Jinmu [r. 660-585 B.C.], "It is the part of a good general when victorious to avoid arrogance,"[23] all sound like ornamentation. Language is something which has its own style in each age and corresponds to the human actions and feelings of the time. The reason why there are so many instances in the *Nihonshoki* where the language does not correspond either to the conditions of antiquity or to the human actions and feelings of antiquity is because there is too much ornamentation of classical Chinese.

The following passage, also from the section on Emperor Jinmu, is likewise not in accordance with the conditions of antiquity: "I am the descendant of the Sun-Goddess, and if I proceed against the sun to attack the enemy, I shall act contrary to the way of Heaven."[24] <The *Kojiki* states merely that "As the child of the

sun-deity, it would be inauspicious for me to fight facing the sun.">[25] There is also the section "owing to to my reliance on the Majesty of Imperial Heaven, the wicked bands have met death . . ." <up to "will this not be well?" It is entirely Chinese in spirit>.[26]

Furthermore, the character 天 'Heaven' in expressions such as "to commit a sin against Heaven," represents the notion of 天 'Heaven' in the Chinese sense, and does not correspond to antiquity. <The same can be said of expressions such as 天命 'Heaven's mandate,' 天心 'the will of Heaven,' 天意 'the will of Heaven,' and 天祿 'the emolument of Heaven.'> The 天 'Heaven' in these passages is something which lies in the upper reaches of the sky (*sora*), and is nothing more than the country in which the deities of heaven reside; it is not something which possesses a mind or spirit. Therefore, there is no "way of Heaven," and nothing which is to be called the "authority of Heaven." There is no cause for the "commission of sin." To speak of Heaven as if it had a spirit, and to regard human fortune and misfortune, indeed, everything in the world, as the result of the acts of Heaven, is something which is Chinese, and is mistaken. <Nonetheless, the expression *amëtuti nö kökörö* ('spirit of heaven and earth') is to be seen in the imperial proclamations in the *Shoku Nihongi*, and expressions such as *amëtuti nö nasi nö manima ni* ('according to the will of heaven and earth') are written in the poems of the *Man'yôshû*. Such expressions are evidence that Chinese influence was already being reflected by the time of the Nara period [710-794], and that things which were contrary to the spirit of antiquity were included in the works of the time. The reason why people speak of a myriad of things as 天 'Heaven' in foreign countries is because they have no correct transmission of legend from the Age of the Gods, and they are unable

to realize that everything in this world is an act of the gods. Expressions such as 天帝 'Emperor of Heaven' or 天之主宰 'Councilor of Heaven' seem to indicate a deity, but these are not words spoken with the knowledge that a deity truly exists. They are merely makeshift terms, and as they are actually spoken with the principle of Heaven in mind, they differ from the expression 天神 'heavenly deities.' To read the expression 皇天 as *amë nö kamï* ('heavenly deities') in the Japanese reading does not correspond to the ancient meaning of 皇天 (Chinese *huang tian* 'bright sky'). Since this is done, however, with the knowledge that the proper graphs for the expression *amë nö kamï* are 天神, this reading is fine. Nonetheless, it is a mistake to interpret the meaning of 皇天 as 天神 based on this reading. When looking at the *Nihonshoki* it is necessary at all times to keep this distinction in mind. Otherwise, one will be overwhelmed by the Chinese meaning.>

The preoccupation of the compilers with the ornamentation of classical Chinese resulted in this type of discrepancy. People of later ages, misguided by the Chinese meaning, were not aware of this type of distinction. When they looked at these passages, they regarded the reading of *ama tu kamï* ('heavenly deities') as a makeshift reading, with the real meaning being *ten* ('heaven'), with the result that this expression, in particular, has become an obstacle to study. <*Ama tu kamï* are deities which have a living body like human beings. The expression is not a makeshift term spoken with hollow principles of logic like the Chinese meaning of 'Heaven.' The 天 in 天神 refers only to the country the deities dwell in, and 神 is not synonomous with 天.>

In the section on Emperor Suizei [r. 581-549 B.C.], the passage "This Emperor was of distinguished manners and appearance. As a child he possessed the vigor of manhood; when he grew to manhood, his form was gigantic. He excelled in warlike accomplishments, and his will was resolute in the extreme,"[27] is not a transmission from antiquity which has been rewritten in Chinese characters, but rather seems to be a fabricated account of events in antiquity which has been added as ornamentation by the compilers. The same can be said with respect to the following passage from the section on Emperor Sujin [r. 97-30 B.C.]: "The Emperor . . . was of a quick intelligence, and in his boyhood was fond of manly devices. When he grew up to manhood, he was of wide culture and circumspect in his behavior."[28]

In the section on Emperor Ôjin [r. 270-310], the passage describing Awaji-shima is simply too ornate and is quite clearly Chinese: "There is a confusion of peaks and cliffs; hills and valleys succeed to one another. Fragrant herbs grow luxuriantly; it is washed by the long billows."[29] The same can be said with respect to the following passage in praise of a horse from the section on Emperor Yûryaku [r. 456-479]: "[a red courser, which] dashed along like the flight of a dragon, with splendid high springing action, darting off like a wild goose. His strange form was of lofty mould; his remarkable action was of extreme distinction."[30]

The following passage, from the section on Emperor Jinmu [r. 660-585 B.C.], has completely distorted the truth due to its ornamentation, and has become an obstacle to study: "Ukeshi the Younger prepared a great feast of beef and sake, with which he entertained the Imperial Army."[31] The same can be said with respect to this passage from the section on Emperor Sujin [r. 97-30 B.C.]: "Would it not be well to commit the matter to the Sacred Tortoise and thereby ascertain the cause of the calamity?"[32] In our imperial country, even in antiquity people did not eat beef, nor did they use tortoise shells for divination. <Although the intention of the compilers in writing "beef and sake" and "sacred tortoise" was merely to ornament the text with classical Chinese, persons reading this text take these items to be fact, and such passages thus become a hindrance to study. Eating beef and using tortoises for divination are the customs of a foreign country.>

In the section on Emperor Keikô [r. 71-130 B.C.], when Yamatö-takeru-nö-mikötö is about to set off for the eastern country, there is the passage: "The Emperor took a battle-axe, and giving it to Yamato-dake no Mikoto, said . . ."[33] In ancient times, a spear or double-edged sword would have been bestowed, but certainly not a "battle-axe". This is why the *Kojiki* states that a very long spear of *FiFiragï* wood was bestowed, which is the true version.[34] The compilers, in the attempt to force the text into the Chinese style, wrote down "battle-axe". Adornment of the words is perhaps permissable, but to write in such a manner that one changes the very things themselves is going too far. There are other examples of this type which a person looking at the text should pay attention to.

In the section where Emperor Keitai [r. 507-531] is still in Mikuni of Echizen, when Omi and Muraji consult with one another and go there to urge him to assume the imperial throne, and they are refused, it states: "Then the Emperor Wohodo, facing the west, declined three times, and facing the south, declined twice."[35] In that age, such an action would not have occurred. This passage is something lifted directly from Chinese writing. What could possibly have been the purpose of giving the text so much Chinese flavor that even the actions of people are fabricated embellishments?

Other parts of the text also differ from the style of antiquity. The following passage from the section on Emperor Suizei [r. 581-549 B.C.] is one such example: "First year, Spring, 1st month, 8th day . . . He honored the Empress by granting her the title of Kwoodaigoo (皇大后) or Grand Empress."[36] <Later reigns are also recorded in this fashion, based on this example>. In antiquity, the title 大后 (*oFogisaki*) referred to the emperor's principal wife, and the emperor's mother 大御母 (*oFomihaha*) was called *oFomioya* (大御祖). <I will discuss this in detail in the section on the palace of KasiFara in Book 2 of the *Kojiki.*[37] In antiquity, 皇后 was to be read *oFogisaki*, and 皇大后 was to be read *oFomioya*; to read 皇大后 'empress dowager' as *oFogisaki* 'empress' does not fit.> To refer to the empress in a conspicuous way once the reign of her child has commenced as 皇大后 (*oFomioya*) is not a custom of antiquity. The title of the emperor's mother was originally 大御親 *oFomioya*. <In antiquity, there were words but no writing system, so it is unlikely the title 皇大后 existed.> Changing titles conspicuously in this fashion is originally Chinese. Furthermore, recording things down to the year, month, and day is also Chinese. I have discussed elsewhere the matter of giving months and days to the events of antiquity.[38]

There are many things in the *Nihonshoki* which merit discussion, but here I have quoted and discussed only passages ornamented in the spirit of Chinese writing which are likely to become an obstacle to the study of antiquity. It should be understood that other examples of a similar type are much like these. All theories in the Chinese spirit appear to be profoundly logical, and easily penetrate the human mind. As they are things which can easily cause confusion, those reading the *Nihonshoki* must not forget this for an instant.

It is very difficult to devise a reading for the *Nihonshoki*, and the reason for this is as I have discussed above: there are many passages which have added ornamentation in the style of Chinese writing. If one is to read the text literally, then one should read it just as one would read Chinese, including the pronunciation of the characters. Yet, when one considers the fact that there are also occasional notes which indicate Japanese readings, then it would seem that it is not the case, after all, that one must read the text in a strictly Chinese fashion. If one tries to read it entirely in ancient Japanese, there are many places that will be problematic. Furthermore, if one tries to force a reading by taking the meaning of the characters, the result is that while the words themselves will be the words of our imperial country, the meanings and the connections between the words will, for the most part, be Chinese. Therefore, if one is to read the text in ancient Japanese which is true to form and meaning, the only choice is not to stick too literally to the style and to the characters, but rather to assign a reading based on the language of the *Kojiki* and the *Man'yôshû* after one has thought carefully about the general sense of the passage as a whole. In doing so, there will no doubt be places which should be read by discarding ten characters here and twenty characters there. As the people of today have their own individual and collective idiosyncracies, however, it is difficult for them to interpret and understand the words and meanings of antiquity completely and without error. This is why the *Nihonshoki* is difficult to read correctly in every detail.

The readings which are written down on extant manuscripts of the *Nihonshoki* are for the most part based on ancient Japanese <and many of the readings which appear in the *Kojiki* are based on those readings in the *Nihonshoki*>, and there are many ancient words to be found in this text. The problem is that in places which are embellished with classical Chinese, the readings are based on the characters just as they appear in the text, with the result that the meaning is not that of antiquity, and the connections between words are entirely Chinese. One should take these factors into consideration when viewing these manuscripts.

Notes

[1] *Han shu* (漢書, *History of the Former Han Dynasty*) is the Standard History which records the first half of the Han Dynasty (206 B.C.-A.D. 25), and was compiled by Ban Biao (A.D. 3-54), his son Ban Gu (A.D. 32-92), and daughter Ban Zhao (A.D. 1st century).

The titles of the Standard Histories took the form of dynasty name plus the morpheme *shu* (書, Monograph) beginning with the *Han shu*. The term *shu* in the titles derives from the new Monograph section which was added to the Basic Annals (本紀 *ben ji*) style of official dynastic history writing by Si-ma Tan (d. 110 B.C.) and his son Si-ma Qian (145?-90? B.C.), in the *Shiji* (*Records of the Historian*). The Monograph section dealt with historical changes in rituals, astronomy, fiscal administration, natural omens, etc. Si-ma Tan and Si-ma Qian also added a Collected Biographies section, a practice which later historians continued (Endymion Wilkinson, *The History of Imperial China: A Research Guide* <Cambridge: Harvard University Press, 1973>, 72-73).

Sakamoto Tarô discusses the various theories regarding the naming of the *Nihonshoki* (*The Six National Histories of Japan*, translated by John S. Brownlee, <Vancouver: UBC Press, 1991>, 30-33). The theory which he supports holds that the compilers chose the title of *Nihonshoki* based on the Standard Histories style of China, and gave the work the title of *Nihon sho* (日本書, *History of Japan*). As their work did not include a Monograph or a Biography section, however, they added the term "Chronicle" (紀 *ki*) in a smaller graph at the end of the title to indicate that this was only the Annals section of the *Nihon sho.* As the manuscript was copied, the size of the graphs was ignored, and the whole thing was written simply as a single title, *Nihonshoki.* See Sakamoto for further discussion on this matter, and on the issue of the alternate title of *Nihongi* (日本紀).

2) *Jin shu* (晋書, *History of the Jin Dynasty*) is the Standard History of the Jin Dynasty, and covers the years 265-419. It was compiled by Fang Xuan-ling (578-648), et al.

3) The full title is *Nihon Montoku Tennô jitsuroku* (*Veritable Records of Emperor Montoku of Japan*). Completed in 859, it is the fifth of the Six National Histories, and covers the reign of Emperor Montoku (850-858).

4) "古天地未レ剖、陰陽不レ分、渾沌如二鶏子一, . . . 然後、神聖生二其中一焉。" (*Nihonshoki*, Vol. 1, NKBT 67:77, lines 1-3). The compilers selected one of the Chinese creation myths which resembled that of Japan from a text such as the *Huai-nan tzu*, a collection of essays on various schools of thought written or compiled by scholars at the court of Liu An (d. 122 B.C.), Prince of Huai-nan, or the *Yiwen leiju*, a general encyclopedia compiled by Ou-yang Xun (557-641), and adopted it as the model for this passage (*Nihonshoki*, Vol. 1, NKBT 67:76, headnote 2).

The Chinese classics were used as source materials for the *Nihonshoki* in two ways. One was as a source of historical material; the other was as a source of suitable rhetorical embellishment. Sakamoto Tarô states that there is just one instance of the former: in the record of Empress Regent Jingû (r. 201-269), events in her reign were taken from the *Wei zhi* (*History of the Kingdom of Wei*) and the Jin-dynasty *Diary of Activity and Repose*, which refer to a woman ruler of Wa, who could have been the Empress Regent Jingû. Regarding the latter type of use, Sakamoto states that the compilers turned to the Chinese texts for rhetorical embellishment when the original source material was primarily in Japanese (*The Six National Histories of*

49-51). See also Kojima Noriyuki, "Kaisetsu," in *Nihonshoki*, Vol. 1, NKBT 67:17-23, for a discussion of the Chinese classics used as source material.

5) "故曰、開闢之初、洲壤浮漂、譬猶三 游魚之浮二 水上一 也。" (*Nihonshoki*, Vol. 1, NKBT 67:77, line 3).

6) None of the extant manuscript editions of the *Nihonshoki* contains the phrase 一日 for 故日 (Ôno Susumu, ed. *Kojiki-den*, MNZ 9:517, supplementary note "page 8, line 14").

7) Appointed compiler of the *Nihonshoki*. See chapter 1, note 12.

8) "乾道獨化。所以、成二此純男一。" (*Nihonshoki*, Vol. 1, NKBT 67:77, line 5.)

9) "乾坤之道、相參而化。所以、成二此男女一。"(*Nihonshoki*, Vol. 1, NKBT 67:79, line 15).

10) *Qian* (heaven) and *kun* (earth) are the first two trigrams in the *Yijing*: "The way of *ch'ien* [*qian*] constitutes the male, while the way of *k'un* [*kun*] constitutes the female. *Ch'ien* knows the great beginning, and *k'un* acts to bring things to completion. *Ch'ien* knows through the easy, and *k'un* accomplishes through the simple" (*Book of Changes*, "Appended Remarks," pt. 1, ch. 1, in Wing-tsit Chan, trans. and comp., *A Source Book in Chinese Philosophy* <Princeton: Princeton University Press, 1963>, 248). The Appendices of the *Yijing* equate *qian* and *kun* with the forces of *yang* and *yin*, respectively, and these united forces of heaven and earth, male and female, give rise to all worldly phenomena: "*Ch'ien* is a *yang* thing; *k'un* is a *yin* thing. The *yin* and *yang* unite their forces, and the hard and the soft gain embodiment, thus giving manifestation to the phenomena of Heaven and Earth" (*I Ching*, Appendix III, in Fung Yu-lan, *A History of Chinese Philosophy*, Vol. 1: *The Period of the Philosophers*, trans. Derk Bodde <Princeton: Princeton University Press, 1952>, 385).

11) The first deities to appear in the creation myth, and referred to collectively as the "seven generations of the Age of the Gods" (*Kojiki*, NST 1:20, lines 2-3; *Nihonshoki*, Vol. 1, NKBT 67:79, line 16).

[12] On the basis of the names of these two deities, and due to the fact that they come at the very beginning of all creation, Motoori believed that all things, beginning with heaven and earth, came into existence through their divine creative force. (*Kojiki-den*, MNZ 9:129). Motoori explains that the *taka* and *mi* of Taka-mi-musubi-nö-kamï are honorifics, as is the first *kamï* of Kamï-musubi-nö-kamï. *Musu* means 'to come into existence and thrive,' while *Fi* is 'spirit' or 'force', and the compound *musubi* means 'miraculous, divine spirit which creates all things'. His interpretation has been widely accepted (*Kojiki*, NST 1:316, supplementary note 3).

The two deities are introduced in the opening lines of the *Kojiki*: "At the time of the beginning of heaven and earth, there came ing [*sic*] into existence in Takama-nö-para a deity named Amë-nö-mi-naka-nusi-nö-kamï; next, Taka-mi-musubi-nö-kamï; next, Kamï-musubi-nö-kamï. These three deities all came into existence as single deities, and their forms were not visible" (Philippi, *Kojiki*, 47; *Kojiki*, NST 1:18, lines 1-3). In the *Nihonshoki*, however, they are not introduced in the main narrative; rather, they are listed in the fourth version given of the account of creation (*Nihonshoki*, Vol. 1, NKBT 67:79, line 4), and Motoori criticizes the *Nihonshoki* with respect to this (*Kojiki-den*, MNZ 9:130).

The three deities introduced in the opening lines of the *Kojiki* are the same deities that are mentioned in the first section of the preface to the *Kojiki*: "However, when heaven and earth were first divided, the three deities became the first of all creation" (*Kojiki*, NST 1:10, line 2; Philippi, *Kojiki*, 37).

[13] Izanagi and his spouse Izanami, the final deities to be born in the seven generations of the Age of the Gods, are commanded to solidify the land below the Plain of High Heaven (Takama-nö-Fara), and thereafter bear many islands and other deities. Their names are assumed to share the same initial root, and end with suffixes indicating gender. Philippi analyzes the names as *iza-*, from *izanapu* 'to invite', plus *-nagi* 'male suffix' and *-nami* 'female suffix' (*Kojiki*, 482). Ôno Susumu, Satake Akihiro, and Maeda Kingorô, on the other hand, assume *izana-* 'to invite', due to the fact that the marriage resulted from direct

invitation, and *-ki* (the same *-ki-* as in *okina* 'man') denoting 'male', and *-mi* (the same *-mi-* as in *omina* 'woman') denoting 'female' (*Iwanami kogo jiten* <Iwanami shoten, 1974>, 91).

14) Aston, *Nihongi*, Vol. 1:20. " 陰神先發二喜言一。既違二陰陽之理一。" (*Nihonshoki*, Vol. 1, NKBT 67:89, line 10).

15) The yin or passive force is associated with the female, while the yang or active force is associated with the male: "The *yang* and *yin* are conceived of as two mutually complementary principles or forces, of which the *yang* represents masculinity, light, warmth, dryness, hardness, activity, etc., while the *yin* represents femininity, darkness, cold, moisture, softness, passivity, etc. All natural phenomena result from the ceaseless interplay of these two forces" (Derk Bodde, "Translator's Note," in Fung Yu-lan, *A History of Chinese Philosophy*, Vol.1: 7).

16) The "five agents" (五行, *wu xing*) are metaphysical forces which produce one another in the fixed order of wood-fire-earth-metal-water. In another cycle, they are related in another order in which they overcome one another: fire-water-earth-wood-metal. Each agent is associated with a particular season, dynastic rule, color, direction, etc. such that the rise and fall of all heavenly and earthly phenomena can be explained by their activity (Wm. Theodore de Bary, Wing-tsit Chan, and Burton Watson, comps., *Sources of Chinese Tradition*, Vol. 1 <New York: Columbia University Press, 1960>, 198-204).

The concepts of yin and yang and the five agents originated independently, but were later combined into a single metaphysical cosmology by Zou Yan (305-240? B.C.) (Wing-tsit Chan, *A Source Book in Chinese Philosophy*, 244).

17) Zhou Dun-yi (1017-1973) redefined Confucian cosmology by taking a concept mentioned once in the third Appendix to the *Yijing*, that of the Supreme Ultimate (太極, *tai ji*), and placing it as the ultimate source of all phenomena. To illustrate the cosmology, he drew a diagram titled "Diagram of the Supreme Ultimate," and explained its working in a commentary to the diagram: "The Ultimateless (*wu chi* 無極)! And yet also the Supreme Ultimate (*t'ai chi*)!" (Fung Yu-lan, *A History of Chinese Philosophy,* Vol. 2: *The Period of Classical Learning*, trans. Derk Bodde <Princeton: Princeton

University Press, 1953>, 435). Wm. Theodore de Bary et al. hypothesize that Zhou Dun-yi's characterization of the Supreme Ultimate as also the Ultimateless was the result of the incorporation of the Taoist and Buddhist ideas of nonbeing and Emptiness. The notion of "Non-ultimate" refers to the fact that the original source of all phenomena is "pure and undifferentiated" (*Sources of Chinese Tradition*, Vol. 1, 457).

18) According to the principles of yin and yang, the moon should be a female goddess, and the sun, a male god.

19) Mitu-Fa-nö-me-nö-kamï is a water goddess born in the urine of Izanami. Her name is written in *man'yôgana* in the *Kojiki* (NST 1:28, line 12), but with the Chinese term 罔象 (*wang xiang*) in the *Nihonshoki* (Vol. 1, NKBT 67:89, line 14; 91, line 5). The 罔象 (*wang xiang*) is defined as a "water spirit" in the section on flooding in the *Huai-nan tzu*, while *Zhuangzi*, in the section on mastering life, mentions it as being the ghost which is particular to water (*Nihonshoki*, Vol. 1, NKBT 67:89, headnote 23).

20) Wata-tu-mi (*wata* 'sea' + *tu* 'connective particle' + *mi* 'spirit') is not the name of a single deity, but rather an element found in the names of deities of the sea (Philippi, *Kojiki*, 630). The first deity of the sea is born by Izanagi and Izanami after they have given birth to various islands. In the *Kojiki*, this is a single deity, introduced as "god of the sea, named OFo-wata-tu-mi-nö-kamï" (大綿津見神) (*Kojiki*, NST 1:26, lines 5-6). In the rendition in the *Nihonshoki*, they give birth to "gods of the sea, who are called Wata-tu-mi-nö-mikötö (少童命)" (*Nihonshoki*, Vol. 1, NKBT 67:91, line 10). The next gods of the sea are born when Izanagi bathes in the river to purify himself of the pollution incurred in the land of Yömï, and are named Sökö-tu-wata-tu-mi-nö-kamï, Naka-tu-wata-tu-mi-nö-kamï, and UFa-tu-wata-tu-mi-nö-kamï (*Kojiki*, NST 1:40, lines 1-3; *Nihonshoki*, Vol. 1, NKBT 67:95, line 13). In the *Kojiki*, these names are written, as above, in a combination of *kun*-phonograms (綿 *wata* 'floss', presumably homophonous with an archaic word for 'sea'; 津 *tu* 'harbor', for connective particle *tu*; 見 *mi* 'to see', for *mi* 'spirit'), and *kun* (神 *kamï* 'god'). In the *Nihonshoki*, they are written with Chinese graphs used for their meaning: 少童命 (lit. 'small-child-deity'; in Chinese, *shao tong ming* 'lord of children'), out of the belief that gods of the

sea appear in the form of a small child (*Kojiki*, NST 1:322, supplementary note 20).

21) Aston, *Nihongi*, Vol. 1:110; "是時、運屬㆓鴻荒㆒、時鍾㆓草昧㆒。故蒙以養㆑正、治㆓此西偏㆒。皇祖皇考、乃神乃聖、積㆑慶重㆑暉、" (*Nihonshoki*, Vol. 1, NKBT 67:189, lines 7-8. Sakamoto Tarô et al. state that many of the words in this passage are found in the *Wenxuan* (*Anthology of Literature*), compiled by Xiao Tong (Prince Zhao Ming, A.D. 501-531), and that the passage contains phrases from the *Zhouyi* (*Book of Changes*) as well (*Nihonshoki*, Vol. 1, NKBT 67:189, headnote 19).

22) Aston, *Nihongi*, Vol. 1:151; "詔曰、惟我皇祖、諸天皇等、光㆓臨宸極㆒者豈為㆓一身㆒乎。" (*Nihonshoki*, Vol 1, NKBT 67:237, line 13). Sakamoto et al. note that from this point in the text, there are many imperial decrees which appear to be written in pure classical Chinese. In their view, these were most likely composed by the compilers themselves, and not taken from Chinese documents (*Nihonshoki*, Vol. 1, NKBT 67:237, headnote 34).

23) Aston, *Nihongi*, Vol. 1:124; "戰勝而無㆑驕者、良將之行也。" (*Nihonshoki*, Vol. 1, NKBT 67:205, line 8). Sakamoto et al. note that there is a similar passage in the *Shiji* (*Records of the Historian*) (*Nihonshoki*, Vol. 1, NKBT 67:205, headnote 6).

24) Aston, *Nihongi*, Vol. 1:113; "今我是日神子孫、而向㆑日征㆑虜、此逆㆓天道㆒也。" (*Nihonshoki*, Vol. 1, NKBT 67:193, lines 4-5).

25) "向㆑日而戰不良。" (*Kojiki*, NST 1:118, line 7).

26) Aston, *Nihongi*, Vol. 1:131; "賴以㆓皇天之威㆒、凶徒就戮 . . . 不㆓亦可㆒乎。" (*Nihonshoki*, Vol. 1, NKBT 67:213, lines 2, 6). This is a lengthy passage, of which Motoori gives only the beginning and the end. Sakamoto et al. list similar phrases found in the *Wenxuan* (*Anthology of Literature*), the *Zhouyi* (*Book of Changes*), the *Liji* (*Book of Rites*), and the *Huai-nan tzu*, which may have been taken as models for this section (*Nihonshoki*, Vol. 1, NKBT 67:212, headnotes 6, 7, 8).

27) Aston, *Nihongi*, Vol. 1:138; "天皇風姿岐嶷。少有㆓雄拔之氣㆒。及㆑壯容貌魁偉。武藝過㆑人。而志尚沈毅。" (*Nihonshoki*, Vol. 1, NKBT 67:219, lines 12-13). Sakamoto et al. note that the word 沈毅 (*ogogosi* 'resolute in the extreme') is found in the *Wei zhi* (*History of the Kingdom of*

Wei, one of the *San guo zhi*, <*Standard History of the Three Kingdoms*>, ca. 297) in a similar context. They also state that passages taken from the *Wei zhi* and the *Han shu* are particularly noticeable in Books Four, Five, and Six of the *Nihonshoki* (*Nihonshoki*, Vol. 1, NKBT 67:218, headnote 19). Book Four begins with the reign of Emperor Suizei (r. 581-549 B.C.), and Book Six ends with the reign of Emperor Suinin (r. 29 B.C.-A.D.70).

28) Aston, *Nihongi*, Vol. 1:150; "天皇 . . . 識性聰敏。幼好二雄略一。既壯寛博謹愼、" (*Nihonshoki*, Vol. 1, NKBT 67:237, lines 4-5). Sakamoto et al. trace several phrases in this passage to the *Jin shu* and the *Han shu* (*Nihonshoki*, Vol. 1, NKBT 67:236, headnotes 8, 9).

29) Aston, *Nihongi*, Vol. 1:266; "峯巖紛錯、陵谷相續。芳草薈蔚、長瀾潺湲。" (*Nihonshoki*, Vol. 1, NKBT 67:375, line 10).

30) Aston, *Nihongi*, Vol. 1:357-58; "蘐略、而龍翥。欻聳擢、而鴻驚。異體蠭生、殊相逸發。" (*Nihonshoki*, Vol. 1, NKBT 67:485, lines 9-10). Sakamoto et al. note that this entire section is taken from the *Wenxuan*, with the clauses transposed (*Nihonshoki*, Vol. 1, NKBT 67:485, headnote 22).

31) Aston, *Nihongi*, Vol. 1:117-18; " 弟猾大設二牛酒一、以勞二饗皇師一焉。" (*Nihonshoki*, Vol. 1, NKBT 67:197, line 13).

32) Aston, *Nihongi*, Vol. 1:152; "盍下命神龜、以極致レ災之所由上也。" (*Nihonshoki*, Vol. 1, NKBT 67:239, lines 9-10). Sakamoto et al. suggest that the reference to divination by means of tortoise shells may be ornamentation in light of the fact that this type of divination was practiced from antiquity in China. They do note, however, that a diviner was among the chief officials in charge of the worship of the deities of heaven and earth at the time of the Yôrô Code (757), and that the duties of the diviner as defined in the *Ryô no gige* (*Exposition of the Administrative Laws*, 833) included the heating of tortoise shells for divination. Archaeological evidence indicates that divination by means of scapulamancy (*Futomani*), the heating of the shoulder blade of a deer and reading the ensuing cracks, antedates the use of tortoise shells for divination (*kiboku*) in Japan (Carmen Blacker, "Divination," in *Kodansha Encyclopedia of Japan* <Tokyo: Kodansha, 1983>, Vol. 2:121; Philippi, *Kojiki*, 52). The three references to divination in the *Kojiki*

(5:2, 17:10, 73:10) all use the term *Futomani*, and the *Wei zhi* describes the Japanese as practicing divination by means of scapulamancy (Sakamoto et al., *Nihonshoki*, Vol. 1, NKBT 67:239, headnote 21; Philippi, *Kojiki*, 52, footnote 1). Both types of divination are assumed to have been introduced to Japan from China. In China, scapulamancy was being practiced by the Lung-shan Culture periods, and turtle shells came to be used in divination in the Shang and Chou periods (Chang Kwang-chih, *The Archaeology of Ancient China* <New Haven: Yale University Press, 1986, fourth ed.>, 298). The earliest archaeological evidence of divination by turtle shell in Japan dates from around A.D. 200, the Late Yayoi period (Blacker, "Divination," 121).

33) Aston, *Nihongi*, Vol. 1:203; "天皇持二斧鉞一、以授二日本武尊曰、" (*Nihonshoki*, Vol. 1, NKBT 67:301, 303, lines 14, 1). Sakamoto et al. note that the 斧鉞 (*huetu*; *fu yue* in Chinese, 'battle ax') was an instrument used in meting out punishment in China. It was bestowed by the emperor to his general as a sign to carry out the death penalty. Here, it is used merely as a classical Chinese rhetorical flourish, to mark Yamato Takeru's commission to pacify the regions to the east (*Nihonshoki*, Vol. 1, NKBT 67:301, headnote 25).

34) *Kojiki*, NST 1:180. The *FiFiragï*, an oleaceous evergreen, was believed to have the magical power to exorcise evil spirits (*Kojiki*, NST 1:180, headnote *FiFiragï nö ya-Firö Fokö*).

35) Aston, *Nihongi*, Vol. 2:3; "男大迹天皇、西向讓者三。南向讓再。" (*Nihonshoki*, Vol. 2, NKBT 68:21, lines 11-12).

36) Aston, *Nihongi*, Vol. 1:140, "元年春正月壬申朔己卯、. . . 尊二皇后一曰二皇太后一。" (*Nihonshoki*, Vol. 1, NKBT 67:221, lines 11-12). The Empress granted the title of "Grand Empress" (or "Empress Dowager"), is the mother of Emperor Suizei, Fime-tatara-isuzu-Fime-nö-mikötö, and the wife of Emperor Jinmu. As heir-apparent, Jinmu married AFira-tu-Fime, and made her his wife (妃, *mime*) (Aston, *Nihongi*, Vol. 1:110; *Nihonshoki*, Vol. 1, NKBT 67:189). Subsequently, he married Fime-tatara-isuzu-Fime-nö-mikötö, and made her his principal wife (正妃, *mukaFime*). When he ascended the throne and the first year of his reign commenced, he honored his principal wife by making her Empress (皇后, *kisaki*) (Aston, *Nihongi*, Vol. 1:132;

Nihonshoki, Vol. 1, NKBT 67:213). Emperor Suizei is the third son of Emperor Jinmu.

The compilers follow the style of the *Han shu* and other works where it is the custom to give a description of the granting of the title of "皇太后" (*oFokisaki/kôtaikô* 'Empress Dowager') to the Empress of the former Emperor in the section dealing with the first year of the new Emperor's reign. They carry on this practice throughout the *Nihonshoki*. (*Nihonshoki*, Vol. 1, NKBT 67:221, headnote 24). Motoori writes this title with the character 大 ('grand') in place of the character 太 ('noble'); 太 is now the standard character for this term.

37) *Kojiki-den*, MNZ 10:418-20. Motoori discusses the title 大后 which occurs in the section in the *Kojiki* narrating Emperor Jinmu's desire to find a maiden to become his 大后 (*oFogisaki* 'chief-empress'), after he has already married AFira-Fime. Motoori states that in antiquity, the wives of the emperor were called *kisaki* (后), and the principal wife among them was honored with the title of *oFogisaki* (大后). The *Nihonshoki* uses the Chinese term 皇后 (Chinese *huang hou*) to refer to the principal wife or chief-empress, and Motoori argues that it should, therefore, be read *oFogisaki*. It also uses the Chinese term 皇太后 (Chinese *huang tai hou*) to refer to the mother of the emperor, and Motoori argues that it should be read with the Japanese term for 'mother of the emperor', *oFomioya*.

Aoki et al. identify the term 大后 as a title in use prior to the term 皇后 (*kôgô*), which was a term established in the *ritsuryô* system to refer to the principal consort of an emperor. They note that calling the chief empress 大后 (*oFokisaki*) corresponds to calling the emperor 大王 (*oFokimi*). The term 大后 is first seen in the *Nihonshoki* in the entry for the twentieth year of Emperor Yûryaku's reign (r. 456-479); the entry includes a quotation from the *Paekchegi* (*Record of Paekche*) in which 大后 refers to the principal wife of the King of Paekche. They conclude that the terms 大后 and 大王 both appear to have been borrowed from Korean (*Kojiki*, NST 1:128-129, headnote *oFokisaki*; *Nihonshoki*, Vol. 1, NKBT 67:497).

Aoki et al. also note that in the *Kojiki*, the term *oFokisaki* is ordinarily written as 大后, although there are two instances where it is written as 皇后

(*Kojiki*, NST 1:261, headnote *oFokisaki*).

[38] One such place is in the *Kojiki zakkô* (*Miscellaneous Studies on the Kojiki*), Motoori's draft text of the first chapters of *Kojiki-den*, where he criticizes such practice as occurring after the fact (MNZ 14:59).

3
Discussion of the *Kujiki*

There is a ten-chapter work entitled *Kuji hongi* (*Fundamental Records of Ancient Matters*) which is extant.[1] It is not the original work compiled by Prince Shôtoku [574-622],[2] but rather a forgery created by someone in a later age.[3] <The preface to the work is also something created in a later age based on the section on Empress Suiko [r. 592-628] in the *Nihonshoki*.>[4] The work was not written and created out of nothing, however, but was compiled by selecting passages from the *Kojiki* and the *Nihonshoki*. This will be apparent to someone who simply opens up a chapter and takes a look, but those who still have doubts should give careful scrutiny to the sections which record events from the Age of the Gods. Passages have been taken from the *Kojiki* and the *Nihonshoki* for each event and put together just as they are, so that there is no cohesion to the style; it is as if a piece of bamboo had been grafted onto a tree in a proverb. Events from the *Kojiki* and events from the *Nihonshoki* have been juxtaposed, and there are even cases of overlapping accounts of the same event, which results in a text which is very confusing. Both the style and the graphs used for the names of things are quite different in the *Kojiki* and the *Nihonshoki*, so that even though chunks have been taken from them and mixed together, the distinction between the two is quite apparent.

Here and there things have been taken from the *Kogo shûi* (*Gleanings from the Ancient Language*, 807),[5] but, again, they have been lifted verbatim, so they are easy to spot. <According to the work, it was created after the Daido era [806-809], and that is why Emperor Saga [r. 809-823] also appears in the text.> For the reigns after Emperor Jinmu [r. 660-585 B.C.], the text relies only on the *Nihonshoki* and omits certain items, but here, again, the text is exactly the same as that of the *Nihonshoki*, so it is easy to recognize. All of the songs have been omitted, with the exception of one, for whatever reason, from the chapter on Emperor Jinmu, which does not differ from the same song in the *Nihonshoki* by even a single letter.

Furthermore, there is nothing to inform us of whose or of what "Fundamental Records" it is; in all respects it is a text which is incorrect. There are three sections, however, which are not found in any other text: (1) the account in the third chapter of the descent of Nigi-Faya-Fi-nö-mikötö from heaven,[6] (2) the account in the fifth chapter of the lineages of the Owari no murazi and the Mononobe no murazi, and (3) chapter 10 "The True Account of the Founding of the Nation." Since the above accounts do not appear to be newly created legends, however, there must have been some other ancient work from which they were taken. <In each of these some questionable episodes have been included; therefore, one should weigh them with related accounts.> These sections thus have many things which can be profitably used even now.

There are many places in the existing manuscripts of the *Kojiki* which contain errors, and one occasionally finds these same passages in this text which have been taken from an earlier manuscript of the *Kojiki* which did not contain these errors. These passages can be of some help. Otherwise, it is a text which is unlikely to be of much use. <There is a text titled *Kuji taiseikei*, which is a product of recent times and contains various falsifications.[7] In addition, the extant text titled *Shinbetsu hongi* is a forgery made by someone in recent times.[8] There are many forgeries among other works used by students of Shinto. If one studies antiquity in detail, one will easily be able to distinguish the true document from the forgery.>

Notes

1) Also known as the *Sendai kuji hongi* (*Fundamental Records of the Ancient Matters of Former Ages*), and the *Kujiki* (*Record of Ancient Matters*), it is a work in ten volumes, compiler(s) unknown, covering the period from the "Age of the Gods" to the reign of Empress Suiko (r. 592-628). It appears in Kuroita Katsumi and Kokushi taikei henshû kai, eds., *Kojiki, Sendai kuji hongi, Shintô gobusho*; Kokushi taikei, Vol. 7 (Yoshikawa kôbunkan, 1966).

2) The preface to the *Sendai kuji hongi* links it to the compilations of Prince Shôtoku and Soga no Umako in the 28th year of the reign of Empress Suiko (620), but of the three texts compiled at that time, two were destroyed by fire, and one received no later mention. See chapter 1, endnote 2.

3) It is thought to have been compiled by persons unknown at some time in the first half of the Heian period (794-1185). Source documents include works from the early Heian period (Kuroita Katsumi, "Hanrei," in Kuroita et al. eds., *Kojiki, Sendai kuji hongi, Shintô gobusho*, Kokushi taikei 7:1).

4) The preface is attributed to Soga no Umako and others (Kuroita et al., eds., *Kojiki, Sendai kuji hongi, Shintô gobusho,* Kokushi taikei 7:1). Motoori refers to the entry for the 28th year of the reign of Empress Suiko, which describes the three compilations undertaken by Prince Shôtoku and Soga no Umako. See chapter 1, endnote 2.

[5] A history compiled by Inbe Hironari. He included in the work legends which had been passed down through the Inbe family but omitted from the official histories. The intent of the compilation was to assume a stronger position for the Inbe family vis-a-vis their counterparts in performing the Shinto ceremonies at court, the Nakatomi family.

[6] Nigi-Faya-Fi-nö-mikötö appears before Emperor Jinmu at the end of his pacification of Yamato, and, claiming to have also descended from heaven, presents Emperor Jinmu with "the heavenly emblems" and serves him (Philippi, *Kojiki*, 177; *Kojiki*, NST 1:126). In the version of his story given in the *Nihonshoki*, he is described as a "Child of the Heavenly Deity," who has descended prior to Emperor Jinmu, and is introduced to Emperor Jinmu via a messenger (Aston, *Nihongi*, Vol. 1:127-28; *Nihonshoki*, Vol. 1, NKBT 67:209).

[7] A history covering roughly the same period as that of the *Sendai kuji hongi*, but regarded as a forgery. It was published by the Zen priest Chôon in 1697 (Ueda Masaaki, "Kuji taiseikyô," in Kawade Takao, ed., *Nihon rekishi daijiten*, Vol. 6 <Kawade shobô shinsha, 1964>, 230-31).

[8] A forgery written under the false pretext of being a work of Inbe no sukune Hamanari (Hisamatsu Sen'ichi, *Motoori Norinaga shû*; Koten Nihon bungaku zenshû, Vol. 34 <Chikuma shobô, 1960>, 91, endnote 2).

4
On the Title of the *Kojiki*

The reason for giving the title of *Kojiki* (古事記) to this text is because it is a text (記, *Fumi*) which has recorded the things (事, *koto*) of antiquity (古へ, *inisiFe*). In the *Nihonshoki*, the account of the command to Prince Kawashima and the others to compile a national history in the reign of Emperor Tenmu [r. 672-686] states that the orders were to "commit to writing a chronicle of the Emperors, and also matters of high antiquity."[1] These words, in fact, bear the same meaning as the title of the *Kojiki*.

The fact that the title of the *Kojiki* does not include the name of the country, unlike that of the *Nihonshoki*, and that what it prominently displays is merely "ancient matters," is dignified and quite splendid. This is because it does not seek to ingratiate itself to a foreign country, and conforms only to the meaning of the land at the boundary of heaven and earth ruled by the ancestors of the heavenly deities. <As for the intent of the compilers, it is unlikely that they thought about the title to this extent, but the fact that it naturally corresponds to this meaning is fine indeed.> Those who seek to learn about our country must never forget this mental attitude.

In addition, the naming of the books as "*kami tu maki*" ('upper GENITIVE book'), "*naka tu maki*" ('middle GENITIVE book'), and "*simo tu maki*" ('lower GENITIVE book'), which pays no attention to the example of Chinese writing, is also splendid. <To say "*maki no kami*" ('book GENITIVE upper'), "*maki no naka*" ('book GENITIVE middle'), and "*maki no simo*" ('book GENITIVE lower'), is the Chinese style, as is "*maki no iti*" ('book GENITIVE one') and "*maki dai iti*" (book number one'). It would be preferable to say "*iti no maki*" ('one GENITIVE book'), "*ni no maki*" ('two GENITIVE book'). To read those written in Chinese style as "*maki no tuide Fitotu*" ('book GENITIVE order one'), or "*Fito maki ni ataru maki*" ('one book LOCATIVE corresponding book') would be rather too complicated for our imperial country's way of saying things.>

Despite the fact that even the title of the *Nihonshoki* has a *kun* (Japanese) reading of *Yamatö-bumi*, there seems to have been no *kun* reading for the title of the *Kojiki*. The intention of the compilers seems to have been merely to read it according to the sounds of the characters. If, however, we were to follow the example of *Yamatö-bumi*, then it would be desirable to give the *kun* reading of *Furu-kötö-bumi* to the title of the *Kojiki*. Likewise, we should give the *kun* reading of "*kami tu maki*" ('upper GENITIVE book') for *zyôkan* ('upper book'), "*naka tu maki*" ('middle GENITIVE book') for *tyûkan* ('middle book'), and "simo tu maki" ('lower GENITIVE book') for *gekan* ('lower book').

Notes

[1] Aston, *Nihongi*, Vol. 2:350. "記㆓定帝紀及上古諸事㆒。" (*Nihon-shoki*, Vol. 2, NKBT 68:447, line 8).

5
Manuscripts and Commentaries

At present, there are two manuscripts of the *Kojiki* in circulation. One of these is a manuscript made from a woodblock carved in the Kan'ei era [1624-1630], in which many graphs have been omitted or are mistaken.[1] There are also places where readings supplied in erroneous graphs have been copied as is, and in general, it is a very bad edition. The second manuscript is one inscribed by a Shinto priest from Ise named Watarai no Nobuyoshi, who compared several old editions and corrected and revised them.[2] In this manuscript, he has corrected most of the omissions and mistakes of the first manuscript and added readings which seem reasonable. At the same time, however, he has ventured to add his own unfounded opinions and seems to have changed some graphs, resulting in some questionable passages. He did not have any knowledge of the ancient language, and since he merely read through the text trying to grasp the essentials of it, his readings run quite contrary to antiquity in both form and meaning. They are either those of a later period, or Chinese. This edition is not one to use.

Aside from the two manuscripts above, old editions are extremely rare, and are quite difficult to obtain now. I was fortunate enough to acquire a copy of one, but when I read over it, the mistakes were legion. Recently, I had the chance to take a second look at a manuscript copied from the one on which Nobuyoshi had written many comments after first comparing various different editions, and also to view the old manuscript in the possession of Mr. Murai Takayoshi of Kyoto.[3] Neither of these had any outstanding features, and both had many errors. The Murai manuscript was close to the old printed book.[4]

Subsequently, in looking at a manuscript copied from a book that had been handed down from ancient times located in the Shinpukuji Temple <commonly known as Ôzu Kannon> in Nagoya in Owari Province, I discovered that it had some valuable features that were different from the other editions.[5] Omitted graphs and mistakes, however, were quite numerous. Given this state of affairs, it has become difficult to find an edition from ancient times with no errors. At any rate, the manuscripts mentioned above each have their good and bad points, and if used in comparison, can be quite profitable.[6]

One does not hear of there having been any commentary on the *Kojiki* from ancient times. Yet, the fact that there are two references to a commentary in the *Gengenshû* (*Collection of Origins*, 1337-1338),[7] viz., "according to the *Kojiki* <*Commentary on the Kojiki*>," and "according to the commentary on the *Kojiki*," is evidence that there may have existed a commentary in ancient times. As to who the commentator might have been, not even his name appears elsewhere; we could not possibly hear of it today. <In a forgery, there is a reference to a commentary on the *Kojiki*, citing a false name, but as it is a forgery, it is not worth mentioning.>

Notes

[1] This edition of the *Kojiki* is known as the *Kan'ei Kojiki*, and was printed in Kyoto in 1644, the first time for the *Kojiki* to appear in public in printed form (Philippi, *Kojiki*, 30). The thirty-two odd existing manuscripts of the *Kojiki* fall under two traditions: the first is that of the Shinpukuji and related manuscripts (see endnote 5 below), and the second, that of the manuscripts in the tradition of the Urabe family. The *Kan'ei Kojiki* was based on a manuscript of the Urabe type. See Philippi, *Kojiki*, 30; Kurano Kenji and Takeda Yûkichi, eds., *Kojiki, Norito*, NKBT, 1:30-31; and Kuroita Katsumi, "Hanrei," in *Kojiki, Sendai kuji hongi, Shintô gobusho;* Kokushi taikei, Vol. 7 (Yoshikawa kôbunkan, 1966), 1-8 for discussion of these manuscript traditions.

When quoted from in the *Kojiki-den*, this edition is referred to as 舊印本 (*huruki erimaki* 'old printed manuscript') (Sasazuki Kiyomi, *Motoori Norinaga no kenkyû* <Iwanami shoten, 1944>, 130). See Sasazuki (p. 138-145) for a discussion of Motoori's opinion given elsewhere of this edition and the others mentioned below.

Motoori first bought a copy of the *Kojiki* in Kyoto in 1754, at the age of 24 (Muraoka Tsunetsugu, *Motoori Norinaga* <Iwanami shoten, 1928>, 224-225), but the record apparently does not indicate which edition.

[2] Also a printed edition, known as the *Gôtô Kojiki*, and published at Ise in 1687. Watarai Nobuyoshi (1615-1690) is thought to have used manuscripts of both traditions in the preparation of this edition (Kurano Kenji and Takeda Yûkichi, *Kojiki, Norito*, NKBT 1:31). When quoted from in the *Kojiki-den*, this edition is referred to as 延佳本 (Nobuyoshi-bon). Motoori obtained his copy of this edition in 1764 (Muraoka Tsunetsugu, *Motoori Norinaga*, 225).

Watarai Nobuyoshi, a priest at the Outer Shrine of Ise Shrine, is regarded as the most important Tokugawa theorist of Ise Shinto. See Peter Nosco, "Masuho Zanko (1655-1742): A Shinto Popularizer Between Nativism and National Learning," in Peter Nosco, ed., *Confucianism and Tokugawa*

Culture (Princeton: Princeton University Press, 1984), 174-76, for a discussion of Watarai Nobuyoshi's thought.

[3] The three manuscripts discussed in this paragraph are referred to collectively as 一本 ('one manuscript') when quoted from in the *Kojiki-den* (Sasazuki, *Motoori Norinaga no kenkyû*, 131). Sasazuki names each, respectively, as "One manuscript," the "Nobuyoshi annotated manuscript," and the "Murai Takayoshi private old manuscript" (p. 131).

[4] I.e., the *Kan'ei Kojiki*. See endnote 1 above.

[5] The Shinpukuji manuscript, the oldest extant manuscript of the *Kojiki*, was copied in 1371-1372 by Ken'yû, a priest in the Shinpukuji Temple (Philippi, *Kojiki*, 30). Motoori completed a careful reading of his own copy of the manuscript in 1787 (Sasazuki, *Motoori Norinaga no kenkyû*, 132). A photographic reproduction of the Shinpukuji manuscript is provided in Hôsei'in shozô, rep.; Introduction by Kojima Noriyuki, *Kojiki: Kokuhô Shinpukuji-bon* (Ôfûsha, 1978). An annotated edition of the manuscript can be found in Nishimiya Kazutami, ed., *Kojiki* (Ôfûsha, 1979).

[6] One additional source used in writing the *Kojiki-den* came from his teacher, Kamo no Mabuchi. Motoori began his work on the *Kojiki-den* in 1764, at which time he began to collect and compare manuscripts (Muraoka, *Motoori Norinaga*, 225). In 1765, he asked Kamo for his copy of the *Kojiki*, in which his notes and readings were inscribed (Matsumoto Shigeru, *Motoori Norinaga, 1730-1801* <Cambridge: Harvard University Press, 1970>, 70). In late 1767 or early 1768, Motoori obtained a copy in which one of Kamo's disciples had written down readings taught in class, and in 1768 and 1769 obtained the latter two-thirds of Kamo's own copy (Matsumoto, *Motoori Norinaga, 1730-1801*, 212, endnote 7). When quoted from in the *Kojiki-den*, these manuscripts are referred to collectively as 師の説 ('my teacher's theory') (Sasazuki, *Motoori Norinaga no kenkyû*, 131).

In addition to these manuscripts of the *Kojiki*, Motoori also referred to quotations from the *Kojiki* found in other texts such as the *Kujiki*, discussed above in Chapter 3, and the *Shaku Nihongi*, the oldest surviving commentary on the *Nihonshoki*, written by Urabe Kanekata in the late thirteenth century (Sasazuki, *Motoori Norinaga no kenkyû*, 132).

[7] An anthology of accounts of the origin of Japan, attributed to Kitabatake Chikafusa (1293-1354). It is based on the *Ruijû jingi hongen* (1332) by Watarai Ieyuki, one of the major works in the Ise Shinto school (H. Paul Varley, trans., *A Chronicle of Gods and Sovereigns: Jinnô Shôtôki of Kitabatake Chikafusa* <New York: Columbia University Press, 1980>, 13).

6
On the Style of Writing

All of the sentences in the *Kojiki* are written in the style of classical Chinese.[1] Since the *Kojiki* is a work whose main purpose is to transmit the language of antiquity, one would expect that it would have been written in the language of our imperial country, not deviating from it even by a single letter, and using syllabic script like the language found in the *monogatari* ('narrative tales') of the past. I will discuss the question of why it was written in classical Chinese in detail below.

Since we did not originally have a writing system in our august country <needless to say, the syllabary in existence now which is called "*zindai mozi*" ('god-age script') is the forgery of a person in a later era>,[2] ancient things were transmitted merely by speech in human mouths, which was heard by human ears. Subsequently, books came across from foreign lands. <The initial arrival of a writing system from western lands was, according to the *Kojiki*, in the reign of Emperor Ôjin [r. 270-310],[3] when a person from Kudara named Wani Kishi[4] came bearing the *Lunyu* (J. *Rongo*, *Analects of Confucius*) and the *Qianzi wen* (J. *Senjimon*, *Thousand Character Classic*)[5] as tribute, so it must have been from this time. Furthermore, this same information is also seen in the preface to

the *Kaifû sô* (*Yearnings for the Ancient Chinese Style*, 751), so it must have been something that was transmitted in the Nara period [710-794] as well.

There is mention of foreigners visiting Japan prior to this: in the *Nihonshoki*, it states that in the reign of Emperor Sujin [r. 97-30 B.C.], a person came from the country of Mimana for the first time,[6)] and in the reign of Emperor Suinin [r. 29 B.C.-A.D. 70], a prince from the country of Siragï named Amë-nö-Fibokö is mentioned,[7)] but it is likely that a writing system had yet to be transmitted to Japan.

As for communication with foreign countries, it is written in Chinese records that beginning with the Han dynasty [206 B.C.-A.D. 220], envoys from Japan had reached China,[8)] but there is no recognition of this in the Japanese court. There are various discussions regarding this, and I have written about them elsewhere.[9)] The first time that Japan sent an official envoy to China was much later, in the reign of Empress Suiko [592-628].[10)] The kingdoms of Korea began to pay tribute to Japan after the subjugation of these kingdoms by Empress Jingû [Regent, r. 201-269],[11)] so the arrival of books into Japan must have begun at the time of Wani's coming to Japan.[12)]

There are those who think that there must already have been a writing system in existence from the time of Emperor Jinmu [r. 660-685 B.C.], but this is merely their impression from having gone through the *Nihonshoki* without acknowledging its numerous ornamentations, taking the writing at face value.>

We read and learned those texts through our own language, and understood their meaning. <In the *Nihonshoki*, we see that in the fifteenth year of Emperor Ôjin [A.D. 285], the Crown Prince

studied the classics with Atiki and Wani of Kudara, and understood them well.> [13] We adopted their writing system, borrowed the words of those writings, and began to write down and record Japanese things as well <as is noted in the fourth year of the reign of Emperor Richû [404] in the *Nihonshoki*>.[14]

Those texts, however, were all in the words of another country, and that language was quite different from our language in its grammar and in other respects. Therefore, it was quite difficult to borrow that language and write down things about Japan in the manner of our native idiom alone. This is why we came to record everything in the style of classical Chinese. Even into the Nara Period [710-794], there is nothing to be found written purely in Japanese. One can discover this by observing that even in an anthology of poetry such as the *Man'yôshû*, the headnotes and other matters are all written in classical Chinese. It was only in the Heian period [794-1185], after *hiragana* appeared, that people were able to write purely in Japanese, in genres such as the *monogatari*. The only exceptions to this were songs, *norito* (Shinto ritual prayers), and *senmyô* (imperial edicts), which had been transmitted from very ancient times and written down solely in the language of antiquity. These were exceptions in that the words had a design to them, they were finely tuned, and people recited them aloud, causing the gods and men as well to marvel at their beauty. Songs were read aloud, and if even one letter was wrong, it would spoil the effect. For this reason, it was difficult to write them in classical Chinese.

Songs, like those in the *Kojiki* and the *Nihonshoki*, were written using only the sound of a graph, and these letters were called *kana* (假字). <Kana are "*karina*" ('provisional letters'); people borrowed

only the sound of a graph without utilizing any of its meaning, as in writing *sakura* (桜, 'cherry blossom') as 佐久羅 (*sa-ku-ra*), and *yuki (*雪, 'snow') as 由伎 (*yu-ki*). The *na* of *karina* means "letter;" in antiquity, letters were called *na.*[15] The kana of antiquity were all kana like those illustrated in the examples 佐久羅 and 由伎 above.

Subsequently, *katakana* ('partial kana') were invented to make writing more convenient. It is not clear who created katakana; perhaps Kibi no Makibi.[16] The reason why this syllabary was called katakana was because it was written by omitting one side of the original kana, and using the remaining side, as in イ for 伊 (*i*) and リ for 利 (*ri*). The term "katakana" appears in the "Kurabiraki" and "Kuniyuzuri" chapters of *Utsuho monogatari* (*The Tale of the Hollow Tree*, late 10th C.),[17] and in *Sagoromo monogatari* (*The Tale of Sagoromo*, 11th C.).[18]

Katakana, a square syllabary, was too stiff for women and young people, and the writing of poetry. Thus, the cursive style of writing was further loosened, and *hiragana* ('plain kana') was created. Here, again, it is uncertain who created hiragana, but the *Kachô yojô* (*Atmosphere of Blossoms and Birds*, 1472)[19] attributes the invention to Kôbô Daishi,[20] and this is what had been generally assumed. It may be true.[21] This syllabary is termed hiragana, in contrast to katakana, but the term hiragana is not attested in older texts.> [22]

For *norito* and *senmyô*, there was another method of writing, known as *senmyô-gaki.*[23] <Many *norito* are to be found in the *Engi shiki* (*Procedures of the Engi Era*, 927), particularly in chapter eight. Many imperial edicts appear in the *Shoku Nihongi* (*The

Nihongi Continued, 797), and in the chronicles of successive generations.>

In general, other types of text, i.e., those which did not require a special design, were all written in classical Chinese. <As the habit of using classical Chinese spread, there were many places where the Japanese language itself came to resemble classical Chinese in its phraseology. Even *senmyô* and *norito* in later ages retained only the style of writing of antiquity; in terms of vocabulary, they were distinctly Chinese. The fact that in later periods the phraseology of classical Chinese came to sound refined, and people no longer strived to achieve the elegance (*miyabigoto*) of our imperial country is very sad indeed.> Therefore, when the *Kojiki* was compiled, since the method of writing in katakana did not exist at that time, it was written in classical Chinese, with the exception of songs, *norito*, and *senmyô*, as was the custom for all documents of the time.

In those days, the study of Chinese things was flourishing, and people in Japan were able to write skillfully in classical Chinese. Therefore, one would expect the *Kojiki*, like the *Nihonshoki*, to have its sentences embellished, but this is not the case. The reason why the classical Chinese of the *Kojiki* appears inferior is that things are represented simply as is. With his main purpose being to transmit the language of antiquity, the compiler did not direct much attention to classical Chinese. <The compiler was not inferior at writing in classical Chinese; one has only to look at the preface, which amply demonstrates his proficiency in classical Chinese.> This is why there are many places where it seems that he did not give much concern to either the meaning or the position of the characters. In fact, given his statements in the preface: "when I relate the events through the use of Chinese graphs for their sound values only, the account becomes too lengthy. For this reason, I have related some passages with some graphs used for their meaning and others for their sound, and other passages with the graphs used only for their meaning;"[24] we can see that his true desire must have been to write it all down in syllabic script.

Although most of the *Kojiki* is written in classical Chinese, it is not pure classical Chinese alone; there are various styles of writing, and many places written in syllabic script, as in 久羅下那洲多陀用幣流 (*kurage nasu tadayoFeru* "drifting like a jellyfish").[25] There are also passages written in *senmyô-gaki*, as in 在祁理 (*arikeri* "have [been]"),[26] and 吐散登許曾 (*Faki-tirasu tö kösö* "must be [what my brother] has vomited and strewn about").[27] There are also passages which do not differ at all from the language of antiquity, as in 立㆓天浮橋㆒而指㆓下其沼矛㆒ (*ama nö ukiFasi ni tatasite sönö nuFokö wo sasi-orösi* "[the two deities] stood on the Heavenly Floating Bridge, and, lowering the jeweled spear, [stirred with it])."[28] <In classical Chinese, one ordinarily puts the graphs "stand (立)" and "lower (指下)" at the head of their respective phrases, but if one reads the graphs just as they are in their usual order, it is no different from the language of antiquity.>

There are a good many passages, however, where the style has been influenced by classical Chinese, and differs from the language of antiquity. For example, passages such as: 名㆓其子㆒云㆓木俣神㆒ (*sönö ko wo nadukëte Kï-nö-mata-nö-kamï tö iFu* 'naming that child they called him Kï-nö-mata-nö-kamï')[29] should be written as 其子名云㆓木俣神㆒ (*sönö ko nö na wo Kï-nö-mata-nö-kamï tö iFu* 'that child's name was called Kï-nö-mata-nö-kamï') or 其子名㆓木俣神㆒ (*sönö ko wo Kï-nö-mata-nö-kamï tö naduku* 'they named the child Kï-nö-mata-nö-kamï'), if they are to be written in the language of antiquity.[30] In another example, inserting the graph 之 (*nö* 'GENITIVE') in the passage 此謂㆓之神語㆒也 (*köre* [之] *wo kamu-gatari tö iFu* "this is called Kamu-gatari") differs from the language of antiquity.[31] The placement of the words 如㆑先 (*saki nö götösi* 'as before') in the passage 更往㆓廻其天之御柱㆒如㆑先 (*sara ni sönö amë nö miFasira wo saki nö götösi yuki-mëguri-tamaFu* "they . . . walked once more in a circle around the heavenly pillar as [they had done] before"),[32] differs from the usual word order in Japanese. The normal word order would be 更 其天之御柱如㆑先 往廻 . One must be attentive to such types of expressions; otherwise, one is likely to become captivated by classical Chinese.

The following passages are pure classical Chinese, and do not correspond at all to the language of antiquity: 懐妊臨㆑産 (*Fara-maseru mi-ko are-masamu tö situ* "[the child which she] was carrying was about to be born"),[33] 不㆑得㆑成㆑婚 (*e me sezu* 'he was not able to make her his wife'),[34] 足㆑示㆓後世㆒ (*nöti nö yö ni simesu ni mö aFënamu* "[this dishonor] will suffice to show to future generations"),[35] and 不㆑得㆑忍㆓其兄㆒ (*sönö iröse wo ömö-Fösi-kanete* "hopelessly yearning for her brother").[36] People did not write in this style because they particularly liked it. Rather, they had become accustomed in those days to writing things only in classical Chinese, and therefore, it was only natural that lapses in attention to the language of antiquity should occur, with the result that passages such as those just listed above became blended in as well. <This is due to the fact that there are no examples of writing with kana in antiquity; it was the custom to record things in classical Chinese. One can understand this in light of the fact that

after people began to write in kana, there were no examples of classical Chinese phraseology to be found in the style of the *monogatari*.>

Moreover, expressions (文字) such as 庶兄 (*syokei* 'illegitimate elder brother'), 嫡妻 (*tyakusai* 'legitimate wife'), 人民 (*zinmin* 'the people'), and 国家 (*kokka* 'national polity') are concepts which are alien to our language, yet, as people had become accustomed to using them, they appear as is. Similarly, expressions such as 山海(*sankai* 'mountains and seas'), and 晝夜 (*tyûya* 'day and night') appear as is, due to habit of writing, despite the fact that in our language we say *umi-yama* (海山, 'sea and mountains'), and *yoru-hiru* (夜晝, 'night and day').

There are four types of writing used to record the language of antiquity. The first of these is writing in kana, and since kana represents a word in its entirety without the slightest deviation, it is the most accurate of the four. The second type of writing is in *masamozi* (正字, 'correct graphs'),[37] where, for example, 阿米 (*amë*) is written as 天 'heaven', and 都知 (*tuti*) is written as 地 'earth', and the meaning of the graph corresponds to the meaning of the word. This type is also accurate. <There are instances, however, when one should read 天 as 阿麻 (*ama* 'heaven') or 曾良 (*sora* 'sky'), and 地 as 久爾 (*kuni* 'earth') or 登許呂 (*tökörö* 'place'), so there is lack of certainty at times as to how a word should be read. *Masamozi*, therefore, cannot compare with kana when it comes to accuracy, but when it comes to furnishing the meaning of a word, *masamozi* are superior to kana.>

Then we have graphs which, though *masamozi*, are exceptions: for example, for 股 (*mata* 'groin'), we write 俣 (*mata* 'groin') <this is a graph which does not exist in Chinese>; for 橋 (*hasi* 'bridge'), we use the graph 椅 <this is a graph which does not have the meaning of 'bridge'>, and for 蜈蚣 (*mukade* 'centipede') we write 呉公 <this is an example of omitting the left-hand radical>. Each one of these forms one subclass. <I will explain the origins of these in their respective places.>

The third type is *karimozi* (借字, 'borrowed graphs'), where no attention is paid to the meaning of a word, and the reading of a graph is simply "borrowed" to represent a word with a different meaning.[38] The passage from the preface to the *Kojiki* which states: "when I use Chinese graphs for their meanings alone, the words will not correspond exactly with the meaning" refers to this type of writing.[39] This type is particularly common in names of deities, personal names, and place names, but it is also used here and there with ordinary words as well. Up until the Nara period [710-794], it was common practice to write everything in *karimozi*, and the *karimozi* performed the same function as kana, but in later ages, as people focused their attention solely on the form of writing, they seem to have had some doubt about the validity of this style. In antiquity, however, they were mainly concerned with meaning, and not with the writing system, so they wrote making use of whatever they could.

The fourth method of writing was to write in a hybrid mixture of the three styles mentioned above. There is also one additional style people used in writing: this is the method whereby one writes *Kusaka* as 日下, *Kasuga* as 春日, *Asuka* as 飛鳥, *OFomiwa* as 大神, *Hatuse* as 長谷, *Wosada* as 他田, and *Sakikusa* as 三枝.[40]

Notes

[1)] This statement is a generalization. As Motoori illustrates later in this chapter, the *Kojiki* is written in a variety of styles. The three basic styles are classical Chinese (漢文, *kanbun*), hybrid classical Chinese, and Japanese written in phonogram notation. The preface is written in classical Chinese, as are a few sections in the main body of the work (Philippi, *Kojiki*, 27). The main body of the work is written primarily in hybrid classical Chinese.

Hybrid classical Chinese, which is thought to have developed as native Japanese began to join their teachers from the continent in the act of reading and writing, is a mixture of classical Chinese with some elements of Japanese syntax and lexicon interspersed (see Christopher Seeley, *A History of Writing in Japan* <Leiden: E.J. Brill, 1991>, 25 ff. for a discussion of the hybrid classical Chinese style illustrated by examples from the *Kojiki* and elsewhere).

It is assumed that texts written in hybrid classical Chinese style were meant to represent Japanese language and to be read as Japanese. Motoori discusses various examples of hybrid Chinese and the problems involved in assigning a Japanese reading later in this chapter.

The third style, that of writing in Japanese by means of phonogram notation, is used primarily in songs and other specialized passages where close attention is given to precise representation of the Japanese words. A phonogram is a Chinese graph which is used for its sound value alone, and meaning plays no part. Phonograms which use the Japanese approximation of the Chinese reading are termed *on* phonograms, while phonograms which use the Japanese reading of the Chinese graph are termed *kun* phonograms (terms taken from Seeley, *A History of Writing in Japan*, 189, 191). Both types of phonogram are included in the term *man'yôgana*.

[2)] The earliest reference to an indigenous writing system having been in existence since the "Age of the Gods" is found in Urabe Kanekata's *Shaku Nihongi* (late 13th C.) (Fukuda Ryôsuke, "Zindai mozi," in Kokugogakkai, eds., *Kokugogaku daijiten* <Tôkyôdô, 1980>, 531-32 ; Seeley, *A History of Writing in Japan*, 3). Earlier texts from the Heian period (794-1185) such as the *Kogo shûi* (*Gleanings from the Ancient Language*, 807) by Inbe Hironari, however, state that there had been no writing system in Japan prior to the introduction of Chinese graphs and the invention of the Japanese kana (syllabary). The notion of a "god age script" is viewed as a fabrication created by Shinto theorists of the Kamakura period (1185-1333), chief among them members of the Urabe family. Ban Nobutomo (1773-1846) pointed out that one version of the script was quite similar to the Korean han-geul script, and others demonstrated that the inventory of syllables represented by the various versions of the script was too small to represent the number of sounds differentiated in the texts prior to the tenth century.

3) Modern scholars agree that the chronology given in the *Nihonshoki* for the founding emperor, Emperor Jinmu (r. 660-685 B.C.), up to Emperor Yûryaku (r. 456-479) cannot be considered accurate. One reason is that the earliest emperors are given impossible life spans and reigns of great duration; another is that it is only from the reign of Emperor Yûryaku that the chronology tends to agree with that of the Korean and Chinese histories (*Nihonshoki*, Vol. 1, NKBT 68:580, supplementary note 18). The *Kojiki* gives the death dates, but not the dates of accession, for fifteen of the thirty-four emperors it covers, and these dates differ from those given in the *Nihonshoki* for all but four of the later emperors (Philippi, *Kojiki*, 18-19). The dates given in the *Kojiki* may be more reliable, but the problem is that the dates are recorded in Chinese-style sixty-year cycles, which means that a given death date may be any one of a series of years. In the case of Emperor Sujin, the first emperor whose death date is recorded in the *Kojiki*, the year of his death was the "fifth year of the Tiger," which occurred in the years 43 B.C., A.D. 18, 78, 138, 198, 258, 318 (Philippi, *Kojiki*, 209, note 11). Some scholars have argued in favor of 258, and others in favor of 318. Thus, while the *Kojiki* death dates are viewed as presenting a more probable chronology than the *Nihonshoki*, there remains the problem of determining in which round of the sixty-year cycle the death occurred.

Prince Shôtoku (574-622) is believed to have established the date of 660 B.C. as the beginning of imperial reign when he compiled the *Tennôki* and the *Kokki* in 620 (see chapter 2 endnote 2) (Mayuzumi Hiromichi, "Kigen," in *Kodansha Encyclopedia of Japan* <Kodansha, 1983>, Vol. 4:203-04). Prince Shôtoku determined that the year 601 (Suiko 9) was auspicious in accordance with Chinese beliefs. The Chinese believed such a year to come only once every 1,260 years, so the supposition is that he simply counted back 1,260 years and fixed that year, 660 B.C., as the coronation of Emperor Jinmu (Robert Karl Reischauer, *Early Japanese History, Part A* <Gloucester, Mass.: Peter Smith, 1967, reprint of 1937 edition>, 13.)

It is the current convention to fix Emperor Sujin's death at either 258 or 318, and give each of the nine previous emperors an arbitrary regnal span of thirty years. This gives a coronation date for Emperor Jinmu of either late first century B.C., or early A.D. first century.

Scholars have determined that the reign of Emperor Ôjin, which is given as 270-310 in the *Nihonshoki*, should instead be placed 120 years later to compensate for the artificial stretching of the imperial chronology imposed by the framework of Prince Shôtoku.

4) *Kojiki*, NST 1: 214; Philippi, *Kojiki*, 285. Seeley (*A History of Writing in Japan*, 4-5) translates the passage as follows:

> Also the king of the land of Paekche, King Shôko, presented a stallion and a mare, which he sent accompanied by Atikísi. This Atikísi is the ancestor of the scribe families of Achiki. The king also presented a sword and a large mirror.
>
> The emperor commanded the land of Paekche, saying: 'If there be a wise man, present him!' Therefore, in response to this command, one Wanikísi was presented. The *Lunyu* (*Confucian Analects*) in ten volumes and the *Qianziwen* (*Thousand-Character Classic*) in one volume were presented along with this man. This Wanikísi is the ancestor of the Fumi no Obito (Chiefs of Writing).

The *Nihonshoki* version of these events differs in that Ati-kisi also instructed the heir apparent, Udi-nö-Waka-iratuko, after accompanying the horses to Japan. It notes the arrival of Wani-kisi, but there is no mention of any texts accompanying him. He also serves as teacher to the heir apparent (*Nihonshoki*, Vol.1, NKBT 67:371, 373; Aston, *Nihongi*, Vol. 1:261-62).

The revised chronology discussed in endnote 3 above would put the arrival of Ati-kisi and Wani-kisi in Japan at 404-405, rather than 284-285, the dates given in the *Nihonshoki*. This would be in accordance with what is known of Korean history; at the beginning of the fifth century many immigrants from the Korean peninsula arrived in Japan (Seeley, *A History of Writing in Japan*, 5-6.) Seeley notes that while not all Japanese scholars agree that Atikí and Wani were historical individuals, "they may be taken as at least being symbolic of the process by which knowledge of writing was actively transmitted to Japan" (6, footnote 10).

[5] The *Qianzi wen* (*Thousand-Character Classic*) known today was compiled by Zhou Xingsi (d. 521), so the so-named *Thousand-Character Classic* which appears here cannot be this text which is known today. It was possibly an earlier text with the same name (*Kojiki*, NST 1:215, headnote *Senjimon* <*Qianzi wen*>).

[6] *Nihonshoki*, Vol. 1, NKBT 67: 253,255; Aston, *Nihongi*, Vol. 1:164. Aston's translation is as follows: "65th year, Autumn, 7th month. The land of Imna [Mimana] sent Sonaka-cheulchi and offered tribute. Imna is more than 2000 ri to the north of Tsukushi, from which it is separated by the sea. It lies to the south-west of Ké-rin [Shiragi]." This is the first mention of contact with a foreign country (*Nihonshoki*, Vol. 1, NKBT 67:253, headnote 24).

[7] *Nihonshoki*, Vol. 1, NKBT 67:261; Aston, *Nihongi*, Vol. 1:168. Two versions of the arrival of Amë-nö-Fi-Fokö are given. Aston's translation of the first is as follows: "3rd year, Spring, 3rd month. The Silla prince, Ama no hi-hoko, arrived. The objects which he brought were—one Ha-buto gem, one Ashi-daka gem, one red-stone Ukaka gem, one Idzushi short sword, one Idzushi spear, one sun-mirror, and one Kuma-himorogi, seven things in all. These were stored in the Land of Tajima, and made divine things forever." The story of this Silla prince coming to Japan is also narrated in the *Kojiki*, in a section from the reign of Emperor Ôjin where it states that it took place in "ancient times" (*mukasi*) (*Kojiki*, NST 1: 220; Philippi, *Kojiki*, 291).

8) The first record of an envoy to China appears in the entry for A.D. 57 in the *Hou Han shu* (*History of the Later Han Dynasty*): "the Wa country Nu sent an envoy with tribute who called himself *ta-fu*. This country is located in the southern extremity of the Wa country. Kuang-wu bestowed on him a seal" (Tsunoda Ryûsaku, trans., and L. Carrington Goodrich, ed., *Japan in the Chinese Dynastic Histories: Later Han Through Ming Dynasties* <South Pasadena: P. D. and Ione Perkins, 1951>, 2).

9) *Kara osame no ureta migoto* (馭戎慨言, *Sorrowful Words on Suppressing Barbarians*), written in 1777 and published in 1796. An analysis of diplomatic relations up until the early Tokugawa (1603-1867), written from the perspective of revering the internal and despising the foreign (Hisamatsu Sen'ichi, *Motoori Norinaga shû*; Koten Nihon bungaku zenshû, Vol. 34. <Chikuma Shobô, 1960>, 96, endnote 2).

10) *Nihonshoki*, Vol. 2, NKBT 68:189; Aston, *Nihongi*, Vol. 2:136. Aston's translation reads: "Autumn, 7th month, 3rd day. The Dairai, Imoko Wono no Omi, was sent to the land of the Great Thang." In fact, this embassy of 607 was to the Sui court, not the T'ang court, and is recorded in the *Sui shu* (*History of the Sui*), which covers the years 581-617 (Tsunoda and Goodrich, *Japan in the Dynastic Histories*, 32). As endnote 8 above indicates, this was not the first official embassy to China. There were other official embassies which preceded the embassy recorded here. The *Wei zhi* (*History of the Kingdom of Wei*), which covers the years 221-265, records an official mission to the Wei kingdom in 238 (Tsunoda and Goodrich, *Japan in the Dynastic Histories*, 14), and the *Song shu* (*History of the Song*), which covers the years 420-479, records the visits of several official envoys from Japan.

11) According to the *Kojiki* and the *Nihonshoki*, Empress Jingû led an expedition to Korea in the year 200, and landed in the kingdom of Silla. The king of Silla, awed by her impressive forces, agreed to submit to the empress' country. In the *Kojiki* account, the land of Paekche also submits (*Kojiki*, NST 1:198; Philippi, *Kojiki*, 262-263); in the *Nihonshoki* account, the lands of Paekche and Kôkuli also submit (*Nihonshoki*, Vol. 1, NKBT 67:337, 339; Aston, *Nihongi*, 230-232). There is no record of these

events in the Korean or Chinese histories, and modern scholars regard them as legend (*Nihonshoki*, Vol. 1, NKBT 67:337, headnote 26; Philippi, *Kojiki*, 263, footnote 10). Large-scale Japanese advancement into the Korean peninsula began in the fourth century: in a major expedition of 391, Japanese forces fought against the forces of the king of Kôkuli, and reduced the states of Silla, Paekche, and part of Imna to tributary status (Reischauer, *Early Japanese History*, Part A, 17).

[12)] See endnote 4 above.

[13)] *Nihonshoki*, Vol. 1, NKB, 67:373; Aston, *Nihongi*, Vol. 1:262-263. Aston's translation reads as follows: "16th year, Spring, 2nd month. Wang-in [Wani] arrived, and straightaway the Heir Apparent, Uji no Waka-iratsuko, took him as teacher, and learnt various books from him. There was none which he did not thoroughly understand. Therefore the man called Wang-in [Wani] was the first ancestor of the Fumi no Obito."

[14)] See chapter 1, endnote 1.

[15)] For a discussion of textual evidence in substantiation of the validity of Motoori's definition, see pages 211-212 in Tsuru Hisashi, "Man'yôgana," in Ôno Susumu and Shibata Takesi, eds., *Monji*; Iwanami kôza Nihongo 8 (Iwanami shoten, 1977), 209-248.

[16)] The theory that Kibi no Makibi (693-775) created katakana is one that circulated after Fujiwara no Nakachika (d. 1429) suggested it in his work *Yamato katakana hansetsu gige* (Nanbokuchô period, 1336-1392). Kibi no Makibi was a scholar of the late Nara period (710-794), who twice visited Tang dynasty (618-906) China. He introduced Chinese culture to Japan, founded a ceremonial festival to honor Confucius and his disciples, and participated in the revision of the ancient legal codes. Perhaps these activities made him a likely candidate for the inventor of katakana (Ôno Susumu, ed., *Kojiki-den*, MNZ 9:517, supplementary note "page 18, line 10").

Existing documents, however, indicate that katakana were not created by a single individual or single group effort, but rather developed as a result of the expanding practice of writing down *man'yôgana* in abbreviated form at the beginning of the Heian period (794-1185). Buddhist scholars and disciples in Nara seem to have been the first to use katakana, sometime in the early

800s, as they wrote down notes in texts written in classical Chinese, either between the lines or in the margins of the graphs. The first attested use of katakana is in a document titled *Jôjitsuron* (828), held in the Shôsôin and Tôdaiji Temple Library. The katakana written in this text are in the form of *kunten*: reading glosses and marks to indicate how the text is to be read in Japanese (Ôno Susumu, ed., Ibid; Seeley, *A History of Writing in Japan*, 62 ff.).

[17] Utsuho monogatari kenkyû kai, Sasabuchi Tomoichi, rep., eds., Chapter 14, "Kurabiraki," *Utsuho monogatari: honbun to sakuin, honbun hen* (Kasama shoin, 1943), 275, and Chapter 16, "Kuniyuzuri," 331. In the former, it appears as *katakanna*, the first attested appearance of the term (Nakada Norio, "Katakana," in Kokugogakkai, eds., *Kokugogaku daijiten* <Tôkyôdô, 1980>, 152), and in the latter, it is written as *katakana*. See Seeley, *A History of Writing in Japan*, 77-78, for a translation and discussion of the latter passage.

[18] Matsumura Hiroji and Ishikawa Tôru, eds., *Sagoromo monogatari;* Nihon koten zensho (Asahi shinbunsha, Vol. 1, 1965; Vol. 2, 1967), Vol. 1:196, Vol. 2:101, 160.

[19] A commentary on the *Tale of Genji* by Ichijô Kanera (1402-1481).

[20] Kôbô Daishi, posthumous title of the Buddhist monk Kûkai (773 or 774-835), founder of the Shingon sect in Japan. From the end of the Heian period (794-1185), Kôbô Daishi was credited with the creation of the *Iroha uta*, a poem using each sign of the syllabary once only. The *Iroha uta*, written in hiragana, was the first step used in practicing the syllabary. This is possibly the link which associated Kôbô Daishi with the creation of hiragana. The *Iroha uta*, however, consists of forty-seven syllables; had Kôbô Daishi written the *Iroha uta*, he would have created a poem consisting of forty-nine, rather than forty-seven, syllables. In Kôbô Daishi's age a distinction was still maintained between the syllables *e* and *ye*, and *ko* and *kö*, which had merged into the single syllables *e* and *ko* by the time the *Iroha uta* was composed. Therefore, the *Iroha uta* cannot have been written by Kôbô Daishi. In addition, while cursive style phonograms were in use during his

age, hiragana were developed much later, so he cannot have created hiragana (Ôno Susumu, ed., *Kojiki-den*, MNZ 9:517, note "page 18, line 13").

[21] Hiragana, like katakana, are thought to have been developed over time, and not to have been the creation of a single individual. In the earliest stages, *man'yôgana* were written in the "square" style; later, they came to be written in the "running" and "cursive" styles as well. Further cursivization of the *man'yô gana* written in cursive style led to the creation of hiragana. People seem to have used this cursivized phonogram script in private or informal documents: there is little textual evidence of the earliest stages of the development of hiragana that remains. For discussion of the earliest known documents containing hiragana-like phonograms, see Seeley, *A History of Writing in Japan*, 70-75, and Roy Andrew Miller, *The Japanese Language* (Chicago: University of Chicago Press, 1967), 125.

Scholars point to the appearance of the *Kokin wakashû* (*Collection of Ancient and Modern Japanese Poems*, ca. 905), the first of the anthologies to be compiled by royal decree (by Emperor Daigo <r. 897-930>, in 905), as marking official recognition of a hiragana-type script (Seeley, *A History of Writing in Japan*, 74-75). The original manuscript of the *Kokin wakashû* is lost, but all extant manuscripts are in hiragana-like phonogram script, and it is assumed that the original was written in such a script as well.

[22] The earliest attestation of the term hiragana appears to be in the *Vocabulario da Lingoa de Iapam* (a Portuguese-Japanese dictionary compiled by Portuguese missionaries in Japan, published in 1603) (Seeley, *A History of Writing in Japan*, 78). In the Heian period (794-1185), the terms used to denote the hiragana-type phonogram script were *onnade* 'women's hand', and *onna mozi* 'women's graphs'. The term *otoko mozi* 'men's graphs', in contrast, referred to Chinese graphs used as logograms, and *man'yôgana* written in the square Chinese style. Both Seeley (*A History of Writing in Japan*, 78, footnote 61) and Miller (*The Japanese Language*, 124) caution against interpreting these terms too literally: those who learned to read and write in the Heian period began with the hiragana-type phonogram script, and then went on to learn classical Chinese. Women's education generally stopped after the

learning of the script, while men proceeded to the second stage and learned classical Chinese.

[23] In *senmyô-gaki*, the 'written format of imperial edicts', the language written down is Japanese, rather than classical Chinese, in a combination of Chinese graphs used as logograms and as *man'yôgana*. Nouns, adverbs, and verbal and adjectival stems were written primarily in logograms appearing in large script, written in Japanese word order, and particles and suffixes were written in *man'yôgana* appearing in small script offset to the right of the large script. An example is the verb form 謀家利, where the stem form *Fakari-* 'plot' is written in large script (謀), and the past tense suffix *-keri* is written in small script (家利) which, in a vertical text, would appear below and to the right of the large script graph (example is from *senmyô* number thirty, Empress Shôtoku <r. 764-770> in Kaneko Takeo, *Shoku Nihongi senmyô kô* <Kôka shoten, 1989, reprinting of original 1941 Hakuteisha edition>, 268). Some *man'yôgana* also appear which are not particles or suffixes, and are written in large script: this was done in the case of proper names, in places where there are two possible Japanese readings for a given logogram and the context does not make it apparent which is the desired reading, and when the appropriate logogram did not correspond to the intended sense in Japanese (Tsukishima Hiroshi, "Senmyôgaki," in Kokugogakkai, eds., *Kokugogaku daijiten*, 561- 562). See also Seeley, *A History of Writing in Japan*, 54-55, for a discussion of the earliest examples of *senmyô-gaki*.

[24] *Kojiki*, NST 1:16, lines 3-4.

[25] *Kojiki*, NST 1:18, line 4; Philippi, *Kojiki*, 47.

[26] *Kojiki*, NST 1:36, line 13; Philippi, *Kojiki*, 68.

[27] *Kojiki*, NST 1:48, line 14; Philippi, *Kojiki*, 79.

[28] *Kojiki*, NST,1:20, line 6; Philippi, *Kojiki*, 49. Aoki et al. read *amë* for *ama* (天), and *nupokö* for *nuFokö* (沼矛) (*Kojiki*, NST 1:21).

[29] *Kojiki*, NST 1:70, line 1. Aoki et al. read Kïmata-nö-kamï for Kï-nö-mata-nö-kamï (木俣神) . See Philippi (*Kojiki*, 103) for his translation.

[30] Word order in classical Chinese is SVO; the revised versions given here have (S)OV word order.

31) *Kojiki*, NST 1:74, line 10; Philippi, *Kojiki*, 112. Aoki et al. do not include the ACCUSATIVE particle *wo* in their reading.

32) *Kojiki*, NST 1:22, line 11; Philippi, *Kojiki*, 52. Aoki et al. read the passage as: *sara ni sönö amë nö miFasira wo yuki-mëguri-masu kötö saki nö götösi.*

33) *Kojiki*, NST 1:198, line 14; Philippi, *Kojiki*, 264. Motoori does not give a reading here for this example. The reading is that supplied by Motoori in the body of the *Kojiki-den* (*Kojiki-den*, MNZ 11:391). Aoki et. al. read the passage as: *Farami-maseru ga umu töki ni mukaFu.* By analogy with a previous passage in a similar context which contains the graph 時 (*töki* 'time'): 臨二産時一 *umu töki ni mukaFinu* 'it is nearing the time I shall give birth' (*Kojiki*, NST 1:112; Philippi's translation appears on p. 156), they have added *töki* to this passage (p. 198, footnote 14). Rather than reading 臨 as *-mu tö su* (PRESUMPTIVE) as in Motoori's reading, Aoki et al. read it as *mukaFu* 'to draw near'.

34) *Kojiki*, NST 1:272, line 7. Motoori does not give a reading here for this example. The reading is that supplied by Motoori in the body of the *Kojiki-den* (*Kojiki-den*, MNZ 12:272). Aoki et al. read the passage as: *maki wo nasi enu kötö*. Philippi's translation appears on p. 354.

35) *Kojiki*, NST 1:292, line 7; Philippi, *Kojiki*, 381. Motoori does not give a reading here. The reading is that supplied by Motoori in the body of the *Kojiki-den* (*Kojiki-den*, MNZ 12:371). Aoki et al. read the passage as: *nöti nö yö ni simesu ni taramu.*

36) *Kojiki*, NST 1:160, line 12; Philippi, *Kojiki*, 214. Aoki et al. read the passage as: *sönö iröye ni sinöbï ezu* (p. 161).

37) *Masamozi*, a term coined by Motoori, is the method whereby Chinese graphs are used as logograms to write down native Japanese words. It is now customary to refer to this method as *kun* ("<semantic> gloss," Miller, *The Japanese Language*, p. 97). Habein terms it *shôkun* "regular *kun*" (Yaeko Sato Habein, *The History of the Japanese Written Language* <Tokyo: University of Tokyo Press, 1984>, 12).

38) Miller uses the term "rebus script" to refer to this method, and notes that *ateji*, which he defines as "[Chinese] characters aligned [in rebus fashion

with the sound of their Japanese semantic equivalents]," is the Japanese term for this method (*The Japanese Language*, 99). An example is the use of the graph 庭 with a native *kun* reading of *niwa* 'garden' to write the grammatical particle sequence *ni wa* 'in TOPIC' (Miller, *The Japanese Language*, 98). Habein uses the term *shakukun* "*kun*-borrowing" (*The History of the Japanese Written Language*, 12), while Seeley uses the term *kun* phonograms (*kungana*) (*A History of Writing in Japan*, 50) to refer to this method.

[39] *Kojiki*, NST 1:16. Modern interpretation of this passage differs from Motoori's: it is viewed as referring to the fact that Chinese graphs used for their meaning alone will result in the writing of classical Chinese, and this classical Chinese cannot fully express the original meaning contained in the native oral tradition (Aoki et al., *Kojiki*, NST 1:16 headnote *kötoba-kökörö ni oyöbazu*; Philippi, *Kojiki*, 43, footnote 58; David Pollack, *The Fracture of Meaning: Japan's Synthesis of China from the Eighth through the Eighteenth Centuries* <Princeton: Princeton University Press, 1986>, 42).

[40] These are all place names or surnames, or both. The writing of some of them derives through association with a pillow word (*makura kotoba*): for example, the place name *Kasuga* was written with the graphs 春日 through association with the pillow word *Faru Fi* 'spring day', as in *Farubi wo Kasuga nö yama nö* "Among the hills of Kasuga, where the spring sun is dimmed" (*Man'yôshû* 372) (Ôno Susumu et al., *Iwanami kogo jiten* <Iwanami, 1974>, 292, *Kasuga* entry; translation of *Man'yôshû* 372 is from Ian Hideo Levy, *The Ten Thousand Leaves: A Translation of the Man'yôshû, Japan's Premier Anthology of Classical Poetry*, Vol. 1 <Princeton: Princeton University Press, 1981>, 196). In like fashion, the place name/river name *Asuka* was written with the graphs 飛鳥 through association with the pillow word *töbu töri* 'flying birds', as in *töbu töri nö Asuka nö kawa nö* "the Asuka, where the birds fly" (*Man'yôshû* 194) (Ôno Susumu et al., *Iwanami kogo jiten*, 292, *Kasuga* entry; Levy, *The Ten Thousand Leaves*, 123).

7

On Kana

I list the kana used in the *Kojiki* below:

〔ア〕 *a* 阿

In addition, there is the sequence 亞亞[1] in the section on the palace at KasiFara[2] in the Nobuyoshi edition of the *Kojiki*, but this seems to be a mistake, as can be determined by looking at the manuscript.

〔イ〕 *i* 伊

〔ウ〕 *u* 宇，汚

There is only one example of 汚, in a passage in Book One which is found in the section on the "heavenly rock-cave door": 伏二汚氣一 (*ukë Fusete* "overturning a bucket").[3]

〔エ〕 *ye*,[4] *e* 延，愛

The kana 愛 appears only in Book One, in the expressions 愛袁登古, 愛袁登賣 (*e wotöko*, *e wotöme* "how good a lad!", "how good a maiden!"),[5] and in the name of the deity 愛比賣 (EFime).[6]

〔オ〕 *o* 淤，意，隱

In addition to the above kana, there is one instance of 於 in a song in the section on Emperor Nintoku at Takatu Palace: 於志弖流 (*ositeru* 'glittering'),[7] but another edition has the kana 淤, so this

於 must be a later mistake. The kana 隱 appears only in the name of the province 隱伎 (Oki).[8]

〔カ〕*ka* 加，迦，訶，甲，可；<voiced> *ga* 賀，何，我
Of the above, 甲 is used only in the sequence 甲斐 *kaFï*. <This kana is used not only for the name of the province, but also to write all instances of the sequence *kaFi*>.[9]

The kana 可 appears only in the phrase 阿可良氣美 (*akarakë-mi* "too reddish") in the song of Emperor Ôjin at the palace in Ka-rusima in Book Two.[10] <The Nobuyoshi manuscript has 可豆良 (*kadura*) in a song from the section on the palace at Asakura in Book Three, but this is a mistake.>[11]

There are those who say that the kana 賀 *ga* is also used to represent its voiceless counterpart (*ka*), but such is not the case; it is always the voiced sound (*ga*). <Of the approximately 130 times that this kana appears in the songs of the *Kojiki*, there are only five instances where it must represent the voiceless sound; the some 120-odd other instances are all representations of the voiced sound.>

The kana 何 *ga* appears in the phrase 和何 (*wa ga* 'I NOM-INATIVE or GENITIVE') three times in the songs of Book One,[12] and also in the phrase 岐美何 (*kimi ga* 'you-MASCULINE GEN-ITIVE').[13]

The kana 我 (*ga*) appears only in the *kabane* 蘇我 (Soga) found in Book Two.[14] <In Book Three, this *kabane* appears as 宗賀.>[15]

〔キ〕*ki* 伎，吉；*kï* 紀，貴，幾；<used as both voiceless and voiced> *ki, gi* 岐；<voiced> *gi* 藝，棄；*gï* 疑
Of these, there is something unclear about the distinction in usage between the kana 伎 *ki* and the kana 岐 *ki/gi*. In the first part of

Book One, there is distinction between voiceless and voiced, with the use of 伎 for the voiceless (*ki*), and 岐 for the voiced (*gi*) only. Subsequently, only 岐 is used for both the voiceless and voiced (sounds), and 伎 is found only in the following examples: 伎許志弖 (*kikösite* "hearing-HONORIFIC") in the song of Ya-ti-Föko-nö-kamï in Book One,[16] 那伎 (*naki* "sang"),[17] 伊須々岐伎 (*isusugi-ki* "in great confusion") in the section from the palace at KasiFara in Book Two,[18] 迦豆伎 *(kaduki* "diving into the water") from the palace at Karusima in Book Two,[19] and in Book Three, 伊波迦伎加泥弖 (*iFa kaki-kanete* "losing hold of the rocks") in the section on the palace at Takatu,[20] 由々斯伎 (*yuyusiki* "awesome") in the section on the palace at Asakura.[21] If we proceed on the assumption that throughout the *Kojiki,* there are no instances of one kana being used to represent both the voiceless and the voiced sounds, then we must conclude that the places which contain the voiceless sound (*ki*) should have been represented by the kana 伎 throughout the work, and that since the shapes of the two graphs (伎 and 岐) resemble one another, errors were made later on in the text and 岐 was also used to represent the voiceless sound. <In addition, there are places where the 岐 *gi* of Izanagi-nö-mikötö is written with 伎, which is another instance of the two being confused.>[22] As the matter is difficult to resolve at this point, I will list 岐 provisionally as being used to represent both the voiceless and voiced sounds.

The kana 貴 *kï* is found only in the name of the deity 阿遅志貴 (Adi-sikï).[23] <His name is written with this kana in a song as well.>[24]

The kana 幾 *kï* is found only in the place name 志幾 (Sikï) in KaFuti.[25] <The Sikï of Yamatö is in all instances written as 師木.>

The kana 吉 *ki* is found only in the province name 吉備 (Ki-bï);[26] <[in the only instance] in a song, it is written as 岐備>,[27] and in the *kabane* 吉師 (Kisi).[28]

The kana 疑 *gï* is found only in 佐疑理 (*sagïri* "mist") in Book One,[29] in three instances of 泥疑 (*negï* "entreat") in Book Two,[30] and in three instances of 須疑 (*sugï* "pass by").[31]

The kana 棄 *gi* appears only in 奴棄宇弖 (*nugiute* "I throw it off") in Book One.[32] <The other instance of *nugiute* in this same passage is written as 奴岐 *nugi*.>

〔ク〕 *ku* 久, 玖; <voiced> *gu* 具

〔ケ〕 *ke* 祁; *kë* 氣, <voiced> *ge* 下, 牙; *gë* 宜

Of these, the kana 下 *ge* is found only in 久羅下 (*kurage* "jellyfish") in Book One.[33] The kana 牙 *ge* is found only in 佐夜牙流 (*sayageru* "are rustling") in Book Two.[34]

〔コ〕 *ko* 古, 故, 胡, 高; *kö* 許, 去; <voiced> *gö* 碁, 其

Of these, the kana 故 *ko* is found only once, in the place name 故志能久爾 (Kosi nö kuni "land of Kosi") in a song in Book One.[35] <In the text itself, Kosi is written as 高志.>[36]

There are just three examples of the kana 胡 *ko*: in the passage 盈盈志夜胡志夜 (*ee si ya ko si ya*) from the section on the palace at KasiFara in Book Two [two examples],[37] and in the phrase 宇良胡本斯 (*urakoFosi* 'will miss') in a song from the section on the palace at Mikakuri in Book Three.[38]

The kana 去 *kö* is found only in 志祁去岐 (*sikeköki* 'dirty') from the section on the palace at KasiFara.[39] <If this is a mistake for the kana 古 *ko*, then there is no instance at all of the kana 去.>[40] The kana 高 *ko* is found only in the place name 高志 (Kosi),[41] and in the personal name 高目郎女丸高王 (Komuku-nö-Iratume-marö-ko-nö-miko).[42]

The kana 碁 *gö* is, in places, written with the graph 基. The various manuscripts differ with respect to these two graphs to such an extent that one wonders whether there were in fact originally two different kana. Since there is no definite pattern of usage, it is likely that originally these two graphs constituted a single kana, and that, subsequently, errors were made in writing, and it split off into two separate kana. At this point, it is difficult to say which is the correct one, so, for the time being, we will establish the one that is more numerous [碁 *gö*] as the correct one, and regard 基 as an error.

There is only one instance of the kana 其 *gö* in a song in Book One.[43] <The numerous examples of this same word prior to and subsequent to this example are all written with the kana 碁/基, so this instance of 其 must be a mistake for the kana 碁/基.>

〔サ〕 *sa* 佐, 沙, 左; <voiced> *za* 邪, 奢

Of these, the kana 沙 *sa* is used often in the names of deities, personal names, and place names. The only other instance of it is in 沙庭 (*saniFa* "ceremonial palace") in Book Two.[44]

The kana 左 *sa* is found only in the name of the province 土左 (Tosa).[45] There are manuscripts which write the kana 佐 *sa* as 作 in two places, both in Book One: 麻都夫作爾 (*matubusa-ni* "all"),[46] and 岐作理持 (*kisari-möti* "bearer of the burial offerings");[47] these are errors.

The kana 邪 *za* is often written as 耶, and, while it is not a mistake <in Chinese writing, as well, these two graphs are often used interchangeably; in the *Yu Pian* [543],[48] it states that 耶 is the common way of writing 邪>, we should treat 邪 as correct.

The kana 奢 *za* is found in the names of the deities 久比奢母知 (KuFiza-möti),[49] 奥奢加流 (Oki-zakaru),[50] 伊奢沙和氣 (Izasawakë);[51] in personal names such as 伊奢之眞若 (Iza-nö-mawa-ka),[52] and in the word 伊奢 (*iza* "come . . . !"), found twice in Book Two.[53]

〔シ〕 *si* 斯, 志, 師, 色, 紫, 芝; <voiced> *zi* 士, 自

Of these, the kana 師 *si* appears only in [the place name] 壹師 (Itisi),[54] and in [the title] 吉師 (Kisi).[55] <The 師 *si* of examples such as 師木 (Sikï, place name),[56] and 味師 (Umasi, part of a name) are to be taken as *kun*, and are examples of *karimozi*; they are not examples of kana.>[57]

The kana 色 *si* is found only in the elements 色許男 (*sikö-wo*) and 色許男 (*sikö-me*) in personal names.[58] The kana 紫 *si* is found only in 筑紫 (Tukusi, place name).[59] There is only one example of the kana 芝 *si* in 芝賀 (*si ga* "its") in a song from the section on the palace at Takatu in Book Three.[60]

The kana 自 *zi* is found only in the place name 伊自牟 (Izi-mu), [61] and in the personal name 志自牟 (Sizimu).[62]

There are, in addition to the above, one instance of the kana 式 *si* in the song from the section on the palace at Midugaki in Book Two,[63] one instance of the kana 支 *si* in a song from the section on the palace at Karusima in Book Two,[64] and one instance of the kana 之 *si* in a song from the section on the palace at Takatu in Book Three,[65] but these are quite doubtful and may well be mistakes. They will be addressed in their respective sections of the commentary.

〔ス〕 *su* 須, 洲, 州, 周; <voiced> *zu* 受

Of these, the kana 洲 *su* is found only in 久羅下那洲 (*kurage nasu* "like a jellyfish") in Book One.[66] <The 洲 *su* in examples such as 堅洲国 (Kata-su-kuni),[67] and 洲羽海 (SuFa *nö umi* 'lake

of Suwa'),[68] are instances of the use of 洲 su in its *kun* reading, and are thus not examples of kana.>

The kana 州 *su* is found only in 州須 (*susu* 'soot') in Book One.[69] Perhaps either one of the kana 洲 *su* or 州 *su* is a mistake for the other.

The kana 周 *su* appears only in the name of the province 周芳 (SuFa).[70] There is one instance of the kana 素 *su* in the song in the section on the palace at Midugaki in Book Two, but this is a mistake for the kana 袁 *wo*.[71]

〔セ〕 *se* 勢, 世; <voiced> *ze* 是

〔ソ〕 *so* 蘇, 宗; *sö* 曾; <voiced> *zö* 叙[72]

Of these, the kana 曾 *sö* is ordinarily used only for the voiceless sound, yet it is always used to represent the *teniwoha zö*.[73] <The same is true in the *Nihonshoki* and the *Man'yô shû* as well.> One might, therefore, be tempted to conclude that the *teniwoha zö* was in fact voiceless *sö* in antiquity, but the kana 叙 *zö* is used three times for this *teniwoha* in the songs from the section on the palace at Karusima in Book Two. Furthermore, as the kana 叙 *zö* is most often used for the closing (*iitozimuru*) *zö*,[74] this particle could likewise not have been the voiceless *sö*. Nevertheless, there are one or two instances of 曾 *sö* being used to write the closing *zö*, so one might be lead to conclude that the kana 曾 *sö* may well have been used to represent both voiceless *sö* and voiced *zö*. There are, however, no such examples in the *Kojiki*, and as there are, with the exception of the *teniwoha zö*, no other places where 曾 is used to represent the voiced *zö*, we will establish it as voiceless *sö* for the time being. We should also give further consideration to the matter of this kana 曾 being used to represent the voiced sound *zö* only in the case of the *teniwoha zö*.[75]

The kana 宗 *so* is used only in the *kabane* names 阿宗 (Aso),[76] and 宗賀 (Soga).[77]

〔タ〕 *ta* 多, 當, 他; <voiced> *da* 陀, 太

Of these, the kana 當 *ta* is found only in such examples as 當藝志美々命 (Tagisi-mimi-nö-mikötö),[78] 當藝斯 (*tagisi*, 'rudder'),[79] 當藝野 (Tagi-*nu*, "plain of Tagi"),[80] and 當岐麻 (Tagima-[*ti*], 'Tagima road').[81]

The kana 他 *ta* is found only in the place name 多他那美 (Tatanami),[82] and in the phrase 他賀 (*ta ga* 'whose') in a song from the section on the palace at Takatu in Book Three.[83]

The kana 太 *da* is found in the name 品太天皇 (Fomuda-nö-oFokimi) in the section on the palace of Namiki in Book Three.[84] <This august name is written as 品陀 (Fomuda) in all other instances.> The appearance of 太陀理 (*tadari* 'fine sake flask') in a song from the section on the palace at Asakura in the Nobuyoshi manuscript is a clever attempt at revision which is a mistake. All other manuscripts have 本陀理 (*Fodari* "soaring flagon"), which is correct.[85] <I will treat the matter of *Fodari* itself later in detail in the commentary on this particular song.>[86] In Book Two, there is also the *kabane* 阿太之別 (Ada-nö-wakë), but there is some doubt as to whether in fact 太 *da* may be a mistake for the kana 本 *Fo*.[87]

〔チ〕 *ti* 知, 智; (voiced) *di* 遅, 治, 地

Of these, the kana 地 appears only in the names of the deities 宇比地邇 (U-Fidi-ni),[88] and 意富斗能地 (OFo-to-nö-di).[89]

〔ツ〕 *tu* 都; <voiced> *du* 豆

〔テ〕 *te* 弖, 帝; <voiced> *de* 傳, 殿

The kana 帝 *te* is found only in the name of the deity 布帝耳 (Fute-mimi),[90] and in the phrase 佐夜藝帝 (*sayagite* "in an uproar").[91] The kana 殿 *de* is found only in the phrase 志殿 (*side* "suspended") in Book One.[92]

〔ト〕 *to* 斗, 刀, 土; *tö* 登, 等; <voiced> *do* 度; *dö* 杼, 縢, 騰 Of these, the kana 等 *tö* appears only in 袁等古 (*wotöko* "lad"),[93] 美許等 (*mikötö* "beloved") in Book One,[94] and 等母邇 (*tömö ni* "together with").[95] The kana 土 *to* appears only in the name of the province 土左 (Tosa).[96]

The kana 縢 *dö* appears only in the name of the deity 淤縢山津見 (Odö-yama-tu-mi).[97] The kana 騰 *dö* appears only in 曾富騰 (*söFodö* "scarecrow").[98] <The writing of Kati-dö-Fime (name of a rock) as 勝騰門比賣 must be a mistake.>[99] It may well be that of the two kana 縢 *dö* and 騰 *dö,* one is a mistake for the other.

〔ナ〕 *na* 那

〔ニ〕 *ni* 邇, 爾

〔ヌ〕 *nu* 奴, 怒, 濃, 努[100]

The kana 濃 *nu* is found only in the province name 美濃 (Mi-nu).[101] <In ancient works, the graphs 農 and 濃 were consistently used to represent the kana *nu*, and not the sound *no*. The province 美濃 (Minu) came to be called Mino only from the period of Late Old Japanese.> The kana 努 *nu* appears only in the place name 美努村 (Minu *nö mura* 'village of Minu') in Book Two.[102]

〔ネ〕 *ne* 泥, 尼, 禰

The kana 尼 *ne* is found only in 加尼 (*kane* '*kun* reading for 金, metal') in Book One,[103] and in the phrase 阿多尼都岐 (*atane tuki* "pounded *atane* plants").[104] The kana 禰 *ne* is found only in 宿禰 (*sukune*, title),[105] and in the name 沙禰王 (Sane-nö-miko) from the section on the palace at Karusima.[106] <Perhaps this instance is an error for the kana 彌 *mi*.>

〔ノ〕*nö* 能, 乃

Of these, the kana 乃 *nö* is found only in the name of the deity 大斗乃辨神 (OFo-to-nö-be-nö-kami),[107] and in the phrases 余能那賀乃比登 (*yö nö naga nö Fitö* "person of a long life-span"),[108] 加流乃袁登賣 (Karu *nö wotöme* 'maiden of Karu'),[109] and 比志呂乃美夜 (Fisirö *nö miya* 'the palace of Fisiro') in Book Three.[110]

〔ハ〕*Fa* 波; <voiced> *ba* 婆

〔ヒ〕*Fi* 比, 卑; *Fï* 肥, 斐; <voiced> *bi* 毘; *bï* 備

Of these, the kana 卑 *Fi* is found only in the name of the deity 天之菩卑命 (Amë-nö-Fo-Fi-nö-mikötö)[111] <the name of this deity is also written with 比 *Fi*>.[112]

〔フ〕*Fu* 布, 賦; <voiced> *bu* 夫, 服

Of these, the kana 賦 *Fu* is found only in [the names] 賦登麻和訶比賣 (Futö-ma-waka-Fime)[113] and 日子賦斗邇命 (Fiko-Futoni-nö-mikötö),[114] and in the place names 伊賦夜坂 (IFuya-zaka)[115] and 波邇賦坂 (FaniFu-zaka).[116] The kana 服 *bu* is found only in the place name 伊服岐 (Ibuki).[117]

〔ヘ〕*Fe* 幣, 平; *Fë* 閉; <voiced> *be* 辨; *bë* 倍

The kana 平 *Fe* is found only in the place name 平群 (Feguri).[118] There are places where the kana 幣 *Fe* is written with 弊; these should be regarded as a mistake. The explanation for this is the same as that given for 碁 *gö* and 基 *gö* above. There are also places where the kana 辨 *Fe* is written with 弁; these are errors in copying and should be regarded in like fashion. <This parallels the writing of 釋 as 尺, and 慧 as 恵. These are examples of borrowing a graph of fewer strokes and equivalent sound to write a graph of many strokes. Since people were accustomed to writing 辨 as 弁 all the time, this should be interpreted as precisely the same thing. It was not that this graph (弁) was being used in addition [to 辨].

There would be no problem with making 弁 a separate kana from the start, but such was not the case.>

〔ホ〕 *Fo* 富, 本, 菩, 番, 蕃, 品; <voiced> *bo* 煩

There is no instance of the kana 本 *Fo* in Book One, but it is used widely in Books Two and Three. The kana 菩 *Fo* is found only in [the name of the deity] 天之菩卑命 (Amë-nö-FoFi-nö-mikötö),[119] and in 加牟菩岐 (*kamuFogi* "divinely blessed") in Book Two.[120] The kana 番 *Fo* is found only in [the name of the deity] 番能邇々藝命 (Fo-nö-ninigi-nö-mikötö),[121] and in 番登 (*Foto* "genitals").[122] The kana 蕃 *Fo* occurs only in 蕃登 (*Foto* "genitals").[123] Of the two kana 番 *Fo* and 蕃 *Fo*, one must be a mistake for the other. The kana 品 *Fo* appears only in [the name of the deity] 品牟智和氣命 (Fo-muti-wakë-nö-mikötö) in Book Two.[124] <In subsequent text, the same name is written with the kana 本 *Fo*.>[125] Elsewhere, 品 is used to represent the two syllables ホム *Fomu* in various contexts.

〔マ〕 *ma* 麻, 摩

〔ミ〕 *mi* 美, 彌; *mï* 微, 味

The kana 彌 *mi* is found in the name of the deities 彌都波能賣 (Mitu-Fa-nö-me)[126] and 彌豆麻岐 (Midu-magi),[127] and in 意富岐彌 (*OFokimi* "lord") from the section on the palace at Takatu in Book Three.[128] <Other instances are written with 美 *mi*.> The sole remaining use of the kana 彌 *mi* is 和賀多々彌 (*wa ga tatami* "my sitting-mat") from the section on the palace of TöFo-tu-Asuka in Book Three.[129] There is only one instance of the kana 味 *mï*, in 佐味那志爾 (*samï nasi ni* "no blade inside") in Book Two.[130]

〔ム〕 *mu* 牟, 无, 武

The kana 无 *mu* appears only in the name of the province 无邪志 (Muzasi),[131] and the kana 武 *mu* appears only in the name of the province 相武 (Sagamu).[132] <There are manuscripts which write it as 相模, and in a song it is written with the kana 牟 *mu*.>[133]

〔メ〕*me* 賣, 咩; *më* 米

The kana 咩 *me* appears only in the name 當麻之咩斐 (Tagima-nö-meFï) at the end of the section on the palace at Karushima.[134] <The correct writing for this kana is 咩.>

〔モ〕*mo* 毛; *mö* 母

There is also one instance of the kana 文 *mo* in a song from the section on the palace of Takatu in Book Three, but this is likely a mistake.[135]

〔ヤ〕*ya* 夜, 也

There is only one instance of the kana 也 *ya*, at the end of a song in Book One, in 曾也 (*zoya*, compound emphatic particle).[136] This is doubtful, but I have listed it provisionally <I will discuss it later in the commentary on this song.>[137]

〔ユ〕*yu* 由

〔ヨ〕*yo* 用; *yö* 余, 與, 豫

The kana 豫 *yö* appears only in the province name 伊豫 (Iyö)[138] <in Books Two and Three it is written as 伊余>,[139] and in the phrase 豫母都志許賣 (Yömö tu sikö-me "the hags of Yömi").[140]

〔ラ〕*ra* 羅, 良

〔リ〕*ri* 理

〔ル〕*ru* 琉, 流, 留

〔レ〕*re* 禮

〔ロ〕*ro* 路, 漏, 盧, 樓; *rö* 呂, 侶

The kana 路 *ro* appears only in Book One in the words 斯路岐 (*siroki* 'white,' two examples),[141] and 久路岐 (*kuroki* 'black');[142] in Books Two and Three, the *ro* of *siro/kuro* ('white/black') is written with 漏 *ro*. The only example of 侶 *rö* is 佐久々斯侶 (*saku-kusirö* "bell-bracelets").[143] The only example of 盧 *ro* is 意富牟盧夜 (*oFo-muroya* "large pit dwelling").[144] The kana 樓 *ro* appears only in 摩都樓波奴 (*maturoFanu* "unsubmissive")[145] <in the other instance of the word, it is written with 漏>.[146]

〔ワ〕 *wa* 和, 丸

The kana 丸 *wa* appears only in the place name 丸邇 (Wani) <this is not a *kun* reading but rather an *on* reading>.[147]

〔ヰ〕 *wi* 韋

〔ヱ〕 *we* 惠

〔ヲ〕 *wo* 袁, 遠

In addition to the above, the following are also found used as kana in some manuscripts, but they are all errors in copying: 記, 氾, 游, 劒, 梯, 之, 天, 未, 末, 且, 徵, 彼, 衣, 召, 此, 忌, 計, 酒, 河, 被, 友, 申, 祀, 表, 存, 在, 又.

Texts prior to the Tenryaku era [947-957] are for the most part correct in the use of kana: there was no confusion as to the sounds 伊韋延惠於袁 (*i/wi*, *e/we*, *o/wo*),[148] nor to those sounds which occur word-internally, 波比布閇本 (*Fa*, *Fi*, *Fu*, *Fe*, *Fo*),[149] or the sounds 阿伊宇延於和韋宇惠袁 (*a*, *i*, *u*, *e*, *o*, *wa*, *wi*, *u*, *we*, *wo*). This is because people made a distinction in these sounds when speaking; therefore, it was only natural that they should make a distinction when writing things down. <To assume that in antiquity as well there was no distinction in these sounds, and that people differentiated between them only when writing things down in kana is a grave error. If there were no distinctions in the sound of words, by what means could they possibly have made a distinction in kana? In light of the fact that the *Kojiki* and the *Nihonshoki* do not differ in terms of their usage of kana, and that they used the

same kana as a matter of course, we can determine that there was originally a distinction in the sounds of words.

From mid-antiquity, the sounds discussed above finally blended in with one another, resulting in one single sound, and when people wrote things down, there was no longer a basis for distinction of kana in terms of sound, with the result that two different kana were used to represent a single sound. Thus, it reached the point where there seemed to be no reason for the use of different kana. Subsequently, Fujiwara Teika [1162-1241] established a system for the use of kana in poetry, and this resulted in the practice of "*kanazukai*."[150] At that time, however, people had ceased to make a distinction in these sounds in words, and did not rely on the texts of antiquity. Rather, such matters were decided subjectively, with the result that the *kanazukai* of this period differs a great deal from the conventions of antiquity. What poets of a later age must have thought was that in antiquity, there were no distinctions between kana, and that it was only with Fujiwara Teika that kana usage came to be fixed for the first time. In recent times there are theories which maintain that kana should be determined solely on the basis of the "lightness" or the "heaviness" of the sound,[151] but such theories are all the misconceptions of those who do not know antiquity. It was the monk Keichû [1640-1701] of Naniwa who, in thinking carefully about the old texts, was able to see for the first time that the *kanazukai* of antiquity was correct.[152] All matters in the path to the study of antiquity first came to be revealed bit by bit through the extremely meritorious efforts of this priest.>

Of those texts which are correct, i.e. the *Kojiki* [712], the *Nihonshoki* [720], and the *Man'yôshû* [ca. 759], the *Kojiki* is particularly accurate. To explain this state of affairs in some detail, first of all, texts from the *Shoku Nihongi* [797] onwards do not make a distinction between voiceless and voiced sounds. <Not only do they use voiceless kana in the place of voiced sounds, they also mix voiced kana in the place of voiceless sounds.> Furthermore, they mix *on* and *kun* indiscriminately. The *Kojiki*, the *Nihonshoki*, and the *Man'yôshû*, however, make a distinction between voiceless and voiced sounds. <Some still doubt whether in fact a distinction between voiceless and voiced sounds is made in the kana of the *Kojiki*, the *Nihonshoki*, and the *Man'yôshû*; now, they should consider this carefully. It seems that many of the words containing voiced sounds in later ages were pronounced with voiceless sounds in antiquity. For example, the older texts use only voiceless kana to represent syllables like the *Fi* in the *makura-kotoba* ('pillow word') *asiFikï*,[153] and in the word *miyaFitö* ('persons who serve at court'),[154] and the *tö* in *simatutöri* ('island bird') and *iFetutöri* ('house-bird');[155] there are no instances of voiced kana. There are many of this type. There are also many examples where, in words which in later ages contain voiceless sounds, only voiced kana have been used. This is not due to a confusion with regard to *kanazakai*. Rather, since the voiceless/voiced sounds in the words of antiquity and in the words of later ages differ, it will not do to rush in doubt about this matter based upon one's intuitions of today.

There are also rare instances when a voiced kana has been used in a place where one would surely expect to find a voiceless sound, such as word-initially; these are to be regarded as careless mistakes, or later errors in copying. This type of error is quite rare in the *Kojiki*: no more than approximately twenty are to be found in its entirety. Ten of these involve the kana 婆 *ba*. One manuscript, however, has the kana 波 *Fa* for eight of these, and therefore one can surmise that the remaining two to three instances of 婆 *ba* were originally 波 *Fa*. Thus, of those places in the *Kojiki* which appear at first to be errors with respect to voiceless versus voiced kana, only ten of them are indeed so. The hundreds of other voiceless and voiced sounds are all distinguished correctly, so what is the use in fretting about one very rare aspect of it, and calling the whole thing into doubt?

Compared to the *Kojiki*, the *Nihonshoki* has many discrepancies in voiceless and voiced sounds, and I would indeed like to know the reason for this.[156)] It is not, however, a text which mixes them up indiscriminately with no distinctions whatsoever. For the most part, distinctions are made correctly, and it is therefore not a text of the sort to be found in later ages where everything is all mixed together.

The *Man'yôshû*, when compared to the *Kojiki*, also has quite a few errors, but when compared to the *Nihonshoki*, the errors are quite few in number and the voiceless and voiced sounds are correctly differentiated.[157)] One can draw conclusions about these distinctions only after thinking about and comparing carefully each kana which is used. One will have difficulty knowing anything in detail if one merely takes a general overview of things.>

The kana of the *Man'yôshû* are a mixture of *on* and *kun*. <There are instances where it is difficult to say that kana are being used as proper kana, and there are many passages of aberrant writing styles.> Both the *Kojiki* and the *Nihonshoki* use only *on*: there is no instance where they make use of a *kun*. This is the correct kana usage. <By "use of *kun*," I mean kana such as 木 *kï*, 止 *tö*, 三 *mi*, 女 *me*, and 井 *wi*. There are no such kana to be found in the *Kojiki* or the *Nihonshoki*. The two [*kun*] kana 迹 *to* and 津 *tu* in

the song in the chapter on Emperor Ingyô [412-453] in the *Nihon-shoki* are both errors in copying. The wide use of the kana 苫 *to* is also a mistake for 苔 *tai*. This example of the use of a graph with the sound *tai* to represent the syllable *tö* corresponds to the use of 廼 *nai* for *nö*, 廼 *dai* for *dö*, and 耐 *dai* for *dö*. There are many other instances of this sort of thing in other sounds. Extant manu-scripts of the *Nihonshoki* contain many errors in kana and many misreadings; I will discuss this in detail elsewhere.> [158]

The *Nihonshoki* blends together both *kan'on* and *go'on*,[159] and since it uses one graph to represent three or even four sounds, it is quite vexing, and there are always many misreadings. The *Ko-jiki*, on the other hand, uses only *go'on*, and there is not a single in-stance of a *kan'on*. <The use of 帝 for *te*, and of 禮 for *re* re-presents not the *kan'on tei* and *rei* but rather the *go'on tai* and *rai*. This is the same method as the use of 愛 *ai* for *e*, and 賣 *mai* /米 *mai* for *me*.[160] This sort of kana is found in the *Nihonshoki* as well, as in 開 *kai*/ 階 *kai* for *kë*, 細 *sai* for *se*, and 珮 *Fai*/ 背 *Fai* for *Fë*. The graph 用 had the *go'on yû*, and the *kan'on yô*; its use to represent the kana *yo* may perhaps reflect the possibility that the *go'on* of this graph in antiquity was also *yô*. In both the *Nihonshoki* and the *Man'yôshû*, it is used only as the kana *yo*, and there are no examples of it used to represent *yu*.>

In addition, in the *Kojiki*, a single kana represents just one sin-gle sound; there are no instances where a kana is used to represent two or three sounds. <To read 宜 *gë* as *gï*, and 用 *yo* as *yu* is a mistake.>[161] Furthermore, there are hardly any instances of the use of a kana from the *nissyô* group;[162] the use of the kana 意 to represent *o* is the only such example. <This is a case where the left-hand radical of 億 *oku* has been omitted; in antiquity there are

many examples which are written down with the left-hand radical omitted. I discuss this in detail in Book Ten of this work in the section on 呉公 (*mukade* 'centipede').[163] Both 億 and 憶, among others, are used to represent the kana *o* in the *Nihonshoki*, and the graph 意 also has the *on* reading of 億 *oku*. It is used to represent 臆 *oku* as well; it will not do, however, to disregard the true reading of the graph and adopt the reading of the right-hand phonetic element. One should merely regard it as an example where the left-hand radical of 億 has been omitted.> [164]

Quite rarely, there are instances of 色 used to write *si*, 甲 used to write *ka*, and 服 used to write *bu*, but there is a logic behind this: the sound which immediately follows must be a sound which corresponds to the same rime. <The kana 色 is used only in the 色許 (*sikö*) of personal names; the final or rime of 色 *siki* is *ki*, and 許 *kö* is a corresponding sound. The kana 甲 is used only in the place name 甲斐 (KaFï); the final or rime of 甲 *kaFu* is *Fu*, and 斐 *Fï* is a corresponding sound. The kana 服 is found only in the place name 伊服岐 (Ibuki); the final or rime of 服 *buku* is *ku*, and 岐 *ki* is a corresponding sound. One should be able to understand for the most part just from these examples how very impressive was the kana usage of the people of antiquity.>

In addition, the kana 吉 is found in 吉備 (Kibï) and 吉師 (Kisi), but as these are the names of a province and of a *kabane*, respectively, they differ slightly from the examples of kana proper. <That is why the name of the province 吉備 (Kibï) is written in the songs as 岐備 (Kibï); all of the songs and all of the notes on readings are examples of kana proper.>

It is also the case that use of kana representing the same sound depends upon the word in which they are used; there are many whose use is determined according to individual word.[165] To give an example, of the two kana 許 *kö* and 古 *ko* which are generally used to write the kana *ko*, only 古 is used to write 子 *ko* ('child'); 許 is never used. <The same holds true for the *ko* of 彦 *Fiko* ('sun-child; prince') and 壮士 *wötöko* 'man in his prime'>. Of the two kana 米 *më* and 賣 *me* which are generally used to represent the kana *me*, only 賣 is used to write 女 *me* ('woman; female'); 米 is never used. <The same holds true for the *me* of 姫 *Fime* ('sun-girl; princess'), 處女 *wötöme* ('young woman'), and others.> Of the three kana 伎 *ki*, 岐 *ki*, and 紀 *kï* which are ordinarily used to write the kana *ki*, only 紀 is used to write 木 *kï* ('tree') and 城 *kï* ('fortress'); 伎 and 岐 are not used. Of the three kana 登 *tö*, 斗 *to*, and 刀 *to* which are used to write the kana *to*, only 斗 and 刀 are used to write the *to* of 戸 *to* ('door'), 太 *Futo* ('of wide girth'), and 問ふ *toFu* ('to ask'); 登 is not used.[166] Of the two kana 美 *mi* and 微 *mï* which are used to write the kana *mi*, only 微 is used to write the *mï* of 神 *kamï* ('deity') and the 實 *mï* ('seed') of trees and grasses; 美 is not used. Of the two kana 毛 *mo* and 母 *mö* which are ordinarily used to write the kana *mo*, only 毛 is used to write the *mo* of 妹 *imo* ('sister'), 百 *momo* ('one-hundred'), 雲 *kumo* ('cloud'), and others; 母 is not used. Of the two kana 比 *Fi* and 肥 *Fï* which are ordinarily used to write the kana *Fi*, only 肥 is used to write 火 *Fï* ('fire'); 比 is never used. Only the kana 斐 *Fï*, however, is used to write the *Fï* of 生 *oFï* ('to grow'); neither 比 nor 肥 is used. Of the two kana 備 *bï* and 毘 *bi* which are used to write the kana *bi*, only 毘 is used to write the voiced sound *bi* when it appears in 彦 *Fiko* ('sun-child; prince') and 姫 *Fime* ('sun-girl; princess'); 備 is not used. Of the two kana 氣 *kë* and 祁 *ke* which are used to write the kana *ke*, only 氣 is used to write the *kë* of 別 *wakë* ('difference'); 祁

is not used. Only 祁 is used to write the *ke* in the verbal suffix *-keri* (EVIDENTIAL/OBJECTIVE); 氣 is not used. Although 藝 *gi* is ordinarily used to write the kana *gi*, the *gï* of 過 *sugï* ('to pass through') and the *gï* of 祷 *negï* ('to pray') are written only with the kana 疑 *gï*; 藝 is not written. Of the two kana 曾 *sö* and 蘇 *so* which are used to write the kana *so*, only 蘇 is used to write the *so* of 虚空 *sora* ('space'); 曾 is not written. Of the kana 余 *yö*, 與 *yö*, and 用 *yo* which are used for the kana *yo*, only 用 is used to write the *yo* of 自 *yori* ('from'); neither 余 or 與 is used. Of the kana 奴 *nu* and 怒 *nu* which are ordinarily used to write the kana *nu*, only 怒 is used to write the *nu* which became *no* in later ages in words such as 野 *nu* ('plain'), 角 *tunu* ('horn'), 忍 *sinubu* ('to endure'), 篠 *sinu* ('a small variety of bamboo'), and 樂 *tanusi* ('satisfied'); 奴 is not used.[167)]

What I have attempted to do above is to list some examples of recurrent patterns of the same words throughout the *Kojiki*. There are many other examples of this fixed pattern of kana usage. These conventions hold true not only for the *Kojiki*, but can also be perceived to some extent in the kana of the *Nihonshoki*, the *Man'yôshû*, and other works. For the most part, however, attempts at classification have yet to be successful, and it will be necessary to think about this matter in more detail.[168)] No other texts, however, can rival the *Kojiki* in accuracy and detail. There are many things in it which will serve well as an aid to explain the language of antiquity; indeed, there are things which heretofore had remained undetected which I have been able to see for the first time.

Kana representing combinations: these are found only in personal names and in place names.

〔アム〕淹 *amu*: 淹知(アムチ) (Amuti, place name)

〔イニ〕印 *ini*: 印惠命 (Iniwe-nö-mikötö); 印色之入日子命 (Inisiki-nö-iri-biko-nö-mikötö)

〔イチ〕壹 *iti*: 壹比韋 (ItiFiwi, place name); 壹師 (Itisi, place name)

〔カグ〕香 *kagu*: 香山 (Kaguyama, place name); 香用比賣 (Kaguyo-Fime)

〔カゴ〕香 *kago*: 香余理比賣 (Kagoy ö ri-Fime); 香坂王 (Kago-saka-nö-miko)

〔グリ〕群 *guri*: 平群 (Feguri, place name)

〔サガ〕相 *saga*: 相模 (Sagamu, ancient kuni); 相樂 (Sagaraka, place name)

〔サヌ〕讃 *sanu*: 讃岐 (Sanugi, ancient kuni)

〔シキ〕色 *siki*: 印色之入日子命 (Inisiki-nö-iri-biko-nö-mikö-tö)

〔スク〕宿 *suku*: 宿禰 (Sukune, a *kabane*)

〔タニ〕丹, 旦 *tani*: 丹波 (TaniFa, place name); 旦波 (TaniFa, place name)

〔タギ〕當 *tagi*: 當麻 (Tagima, place name)

〔ヂキ〕直 *diki*: 阿直 (Adiki)

〔ツク〕筑, 竺 *tuku*: 筑紫 (Tukusi, place name); 竺紫 (Tukusi, place name)

〔ヅミ〕曇 *dumi*: 阿曇 (Adumi)

〔ナニ〕難 *nani*: 難波 (NaniFa, place name)

〔ハハ〕伯 *FaFa*: 伯伎 (FaFaki, ancient kuni)

〔ハカ〕博 *Faka*: 博多 (Fakata, name of mountain)

〔ホム〕品 *Fomu*: 品遲部 (Fomudi-be); 品夜和氣命 (Fomuya-wakë-nö-mikötö); 品陀和氣命 (Fomuda-wakë-nö-mikötö)

〔マツ〕末 *matu*: 末羅 (Matura, place name)

〔ムク〕目 *muku*: 高目郎女 (Kömuku-nö-iratume)

〔ラカ〕樂 *raka*: 相樂 (Sagaraka, place name)

This type of kana is quite common in the place names found in ancient texts.

Kun phonograms (*karimozi*): these are most numerous in personal names and in place names.

〔ウ〕菟 *u*

〔エ〕江, 枝 *e*

〔カ〕鹿, 蚊 *ka*

〔キ〕木, 寸 *kï, ki*

〔ケ〕毛 *kë*

〔コ〕子 *ko*

〔サ〕狭 *sa*

〔シ〕師 *si* <This is a case where the original *on* reading is made to serve as a *kun* reading as well, and in that capacity serves as a *kun* phonogram (*karimozi*). The character 師 *si* in all of the following examples is a *kun* reading used as a *kun* phonogram (*karimozi*), and not an *on* reading serving as a kana: 師木 (Sikï, place name), 百師木 (Momosikï, personal name), 味師 (Umasi, part of a surname), 時置師神 (Töki-okasi-nö-kamï, name of a deity), 秋津師比賣 (Akidusi-Fime, name of a deity)>.

〔ス〕巣, 洲, 酢 *su*

〔セ〕瀬 *se*

〔タ〕田, 手 *ta*

〔チ〕道, 千, 乳 *ti*

〔ツ〕津 *tu*

〔テ〕手, 代 *te*

〔ト〕戸, 砥 *to*

〔ナ〕名 *na*

〔ニ〕丹 *ni*

〔ヌ〕野, 沼 *nu*

〔ネ〕根 *ne*

〔ハ〕羽, 歯 *Fa*

〔ヒ〕日, 氷 *Fi*

〔ヘ〕戸 *Fë*

〔ホ〕穂, 大 *Fo*

〔マ〕間, 眞, 目 *ma*

〔ミ〕見, 海, 御, 三 *mi*

〔メ〕目 *më*

〔モ〕裳 *mo*

〔ヤ〕屋, 八, 矢 *ya*

〔ユ〕湯 *yu*

〔ヰ〕井 *wi*

〔ヲ〕尾, 小, 男 *wo*

The graphs discussed above were used often as *kun* phonograms (*karimozi*). In listing these graphs, however, I do not intend to imply that they function only as *kun* phonograms (*karimozi*). In many instances they function as *masamozi* (correct graphs). Furthermore, there are many instances where it is difficult to determine whether they are functioning as *kun* phonograms or *masamozi*. *Kun* phonograms are not limited to these graphs alone; here, I have just listed the majority of them in a general fashion. Certain persons hold that *kun* phonograms are simply kana, and that there is no need to speak of them separately as "*kun* phonograms" (*karimozi*). They also maintain that one should not claim that there is no use of *kun* readings in the kana of the texts of antiquity, but this is not precise enough. Although kana and *kun* phonograms are, ultimately speaking, the same thing, there is not a single instance of a *kun* phonogram in any of the songs or the notes on *kun* readings (*kuntyû*) in either the *Kojiki* or the *Nihonshoki*.[169] Therefore, as they are not examples of pure kana, *kun* phonograms (*karimozi*) are to be recognized as a separate class. Accordingly, as they constitute a separate class, I have given them the term "*kun* phonograms" (*karimozi*).

Kun phonograms (*karimozi*) which represent combinations:

〔アナ〕穴 *ana*
〔イク〕活 *iku*
〔イチ〕市 *iti*
〔イナ〕稲 *ina*
〔イハ〕石 *iFa*
〔イヒ〕飯 *iFi*
〔イリ〕入 *iri*
〔オシ〕忍, 押 *osi*
〔カタ〕方 *kata*
〔カネ〕金 *kane*
〔カリ〕刈 *kari*
〔クシ〕櫛 *kusi*
〔クヒ〕杙, 咋 *kuFi*
〔クマ〕熊 *kuma*
〔クラ〕倉 *kura*
〔サカ〕坂, 酒 *saka*
〔シロ〕代 *sirö*
〔スキ〕鋤 *suki*[170]
〔ツチ〕椎 *tuti*
〔ツヌ〕角 *tunu*
〔トリ〕鳥 *töri*
〔ハタ〕幡 *Fata*
〔フル〕振 *Furu*

〔マタ〕俣 *mata*

〔マヘ〕前 *maFe*

〔ミミ〕耳 *mimi*

〔モロ〕諸 *mörö*

〔ヨリ〕依 *yöri*

〔ワケ〕別 *wakë*

〔ヲリ〕折 *wori*

Obviously, these function exactly the same as the *kun* phonograms (*karimozi*) which represent just one sound. In addition to the above, there are many other *kun* phonograms which represent combinations of sounds; what I have done here is simply to list several which were selected from among those that appear frequently in the text.

Notes

[1] 亞々音引。志夜胡 志夜 (*ee* {*köwe Fiku*} *siyago siya*, a *hayasi kotoba* or nonce refrain, with notes in brackets instructing that the graphs are to be recited as one drawn-out sound) (Aoki et. al., *Kojiki*, NST 1:124, line 11). Motoori reads 亞々 as *aa*, but Ôno Susumu provides evidence from Chinese rime tables which indicates that the correct reading for the graph 亞 is *e*, not *a* (*Kojiki-den*, MNZ 9:518, supplementary note "page 20 line 5"). In the *Guan yun* (1013), 亞 has a departing tone, and a *fan qie* spelling of 衣 *y* plus 嫁 *kie*, which would indicate that the sound should be *e* (I am indebted to Liu Le Ning for providing me with these sound values for Medieval Chinese). The same rime group contains 覇, Old Japanese *Fe*, and if even-tone and rising tone syllables are included, the following are members as well: 牙, Old Japanese *ge*; 雅, Old Japanese *ge*; 下, Old Japanese *ge*; 賈, Old Japanese *ke*; and 馬, Old Japanese *me*, which also indicates that the sound value of 亞 should be *e*.

In his edition of the *Kojiki*, Motoori retains the 疊疊 (*ee*) of the Shinpukuji-bon manuscript (*Kojiki-den*, MNZ 10:374), while Aoki et al. take the reading of 亞々 (*ee*) from the alternate version written down in the Ôtono gohon collations to Book Two of the Shinpukuji-bon manuscript (*Kojiki*, NST 1:124, footnote 8). Motoori regards 疊 as a scribal error, a mistake in reading the cursive form of the graph 盈 as 疊 (*Kojiki-den*, MNZ 10:380). In his view, 盈 is used here as a kana for *e*, despite the fact that there are no other examples of its use as a kana. He argues that this may have been done because the passage contains words which differ from ordinary language (*Kojiki-den*, MNZ 10:380-81). Hashimoto Shinkichi discusses this theory of Motoori's, but ultimately rejects it, noting that there are no other examples of the use of 盈 as a kana in any document from the time, while there is ample evidence of the use of 亞 as the kana *e* in texts of the time which have resurfaced in recent years ("Kodai kokugo no *e* no kana ni tsuite," 1942, in *Moji oyobi kanazukai no kenkyû* <Iwanami shoten, 1949>, 206-208).

2) After the sections having to do with the "Age of the Gods," Motoori organizes his commentary according to the location of the imperial court.

3) *Kojiki*, NST 1:52, line 6; Philippi, *Kojiki*, 84. Books 3 through 17 of the *Kojiki-den* deal with material pertaining to the "Age of the Gods," and the sections are subdivided according to narrative event.

4) Subsequent research has revealed that two types of syllabic *e* were distinguished in early Old Japanese. Motoori's pupil Ishizuka Tatsumaro (1764-1823) appears to have been the first to notice this distinction, in his *Kanazukai oku no yamamichi* (ca. 1798) (Hashimoto Shinkichi, "Kodai kokugo no *e* no kana ni tsuite," p. 192). The two are commonly referred to in the Japanese literature as the "*ya-gyo e*" (*y*-line *e*) and the "*a-gyo e*" (*a*-line *e*). Mabuchi Kazuo assigns a phonetic value of {ie} to the *y*-line *e* , and { ɛ } or {e} to the *a*-line *e* (*Kokugo on'inron* <Kasama shoin, 1971>, 32-33). Samuel Martin labels them as *e*1 and *e*2 , with the phonetic values of {ye} and {e}, respectively (*The Japanese Language Through Time* <New Haven and London: Yale University Press, 1987>, 49). He notes that the distinction was no longer observed by 938 (Ibid.).

5) *Kojiki*, NST 1:22, lines 4-5; Philippi, *Kojiki*, 51.

6) *Kojiki*, NST 1:24, lines 1-2; Philippi, *Kojiki*, 53. A region of the island of Iyö (present-day Shikoku), which was born of Izanagi and Izanami, and now forms present-day Ehime prefecture.

7) *Kojiki*, NST 1:232, line 3; Philippi, *Kojiki*, 306.

8) *Kojiki*, NST 1:24, line 3; Philippi, *Kojiki*, 53.

9) Ôno Susumu suggests that although it is possible to interpret this passage to mean that all instances of the sound sequence *kaFï* are written as 甲斐, the examples Motoori has in mind are those of the type 甲斐郎女 (KaFï- nö-iratume, female name, lit. 'Maiden of KaFï', *Kojiki*, NST 1:252, lines 1-2; Philippi, *Kojiki*, 330) (*Kojiki-den*, MNZ 9:518, supplementary note "page 21, line 4"). He notes that other sequences of the sounds *kaFi*, such as 貝 (kaFi 'shellfish'), 飼ひ (kaFi 'to feed'), and 峡 (kaFi 'ravine'), are written as 加比 or 賀比.

10) *Kojiki*, NST 1:210, line 9; Philippi, *Kojiki*, 278.

11) The other manuscripts have 宇豆良 (*udura* 'quail') (Takagi Ichinosuke and Tomiyama Tamizo, eds. *Kojiki sôsakuin*, Vol. 1: *Honbun hen* <Heibonsha, 1974>, 334).

12) The first two examples are in the repeated line 和何多々勢礼婆 (*wa ga tatasereba* "I stood there", *Kojiki*, NST 1:70, lines 9-10; Philippi, *Kojiki*, 105), and the third in the phrase 和何許々呂 (*wa ga kökörö* "my heart", *Kojiki*, NST 1:70, line 15; Philippi, *Kojiki*, 106).

13) *Kojiki*, NST 1:114, line 6; Philippi, *Kojiki*, 158.

14) *Kojiki*, NST 1:142, line 1, two examples; Philippi, *Kojiki*, 194.

15) *Kojiki*, NST 1:298, lines 5-6, two examples; Philippi, *Kojiki*, 388.

16) *Kojiki*, NST 1:70, line 7; Philippi, *Kojiki*, 104.

17) *Kojiki*, NST 1:70, line 11. Aoki et al. follow the Shinpukuji manuscript which adds the perfective suffix *-nu* (那伎奴). Philippi, *Kojiki*, 105.

18) *Kojiki*, NST 1:128, line 12. Aoki et al. read it as *isusukiki*. Philippi, *Kojiki*, 178.

19) *Kojiki*, NST 1:210, line 6; Philippi, *Kojiki*, 277.

20) *Kojiki*, NST 1:240, line 15; Philippi, *Kojiki*, 318.

21) *Kojiki*, NST 1:272, line 9; Philippi, *Kojiki*, 354.

[22] Takagi and Tomiyama do not list any variants containing the kana 伎, rather than 岐, in their index (*Kojiki sôsakuin*, Vol. 2: *Sakuin hen*, 35-36). Aoki et al. read this deity's name as Izanaki.

[23] *Kojiki*, NST 1:86, line 12; Philippi, *Kojiki*, 127.

[24] *Kojiki*, NST 1:88, line 4; Philippi, *Kojiki*, 128.

[25] *Kojiki*, NST 1:190, line 15; Philippi, *Kojiki*, 252.

[26] *Kojiki*, NST 1:116, line 7; Philippi, *Kojiki*, 164; one of several instances.

[27] *Kojiki*, NST 1:232, line 8; Philippi, *Kojiki*, 306.

[28] *Kojiki*, NST 1:200, line 12; Philippi, *Kojiki*, 266.

[29] *Kojiki*, NST 1:72, line 18. Aoki et al. follow the Shinpukuji-bon manuscript, which does not have 佐. They note that while 疑 represents the voiced kana *gï*, in the example in question, 疑理 (*kïri* 'mist'), it is to be read *kï* (footnote 11, 72). Philippi, *Kojiki*, 109.

[30] *Kojiki*, NST 1:174, line 14; 176, line 1; Philippi, *Kojiki*, 232.

[31] *Kojiki*, NST 1:234, line 14 (two instances); Philippi, *Kojiki*, 310. The other instances occur in the *-te* (弖) form.

[32] *Kojiki*, NST 1:72, line 13. Aoki et al. regard 棄 as the voiceless kana *ki*, and read the verb as *nukiute* (p. 72, footnote 9). Philippi, *Kojiki*, 108-109.

[33] *Kojiki*, NST 1:18, line 4; Philippi, *Kojiki*, 47.

[34] *Kojiki*, NST 1:132, line 13; Philippi, *Kojiki*, 183.

[35] *Kojiki*, NST 1:70, line 6; Philippi, *Kojiki*, 104.

[36] Ibid., line 3.

[37] *Kojiki*, NST 1:124, lines 11-12. Aoki et al. read this kana as *go*. Philippi, *Kojiki*, 173.

[38] *Kojiki*, NST 1:286, line 14. Aoki et al. read this kana as *go*. Philippi's translation of the passage appears on p. 375.

[39] *Kojiki*, NST 1:132, line 2; Philippi's translation of this passage appears on p. 181.

[40] Ôno Susumu notes that while this is the only instance of the use of 去 as the kana *ko* in the *Kojiki*, there are four instances where it is used in the

songs of the *Nihonshoki*, and it is also found in the *Man'yôshû*. Therefore, it is not a totally spurious kana, in his view. The word *sikeköki* itself, however, is problematic in that there are no other attestations of its use. Ôno prefers, therefore, not to regard 去 as a mistake for 古, but rather as a mistake for 志, the kana *si*, which would yield the word *sikesiki* ('dirty-ATTRIBUTIVE'). The word *sikesi* appears under the entry for 蕪, along with 穢 'filth' and 荒 'unkempt' in the *Shinsenjikyô* (892, 898-901, a Chinese-Japanese dictionary). The word 蕪 is also defined as *sikesi*, and *aretari* ('in disarray') in the *Ruijumyôgishô* (12th C., a Chinese-Japanese dictionary) (Ôno Susumu, ed., *Kojiki-den*, MNZ 9:518, supplementary note "page 22, line 6"). Aoki et al. also read 志 *si* instead of 去, and note that 去 is used to represent the *kun* readings of *tu* and *yaru* in the *Kojiki*, but is not used as an *on-gana* (*Kojiki*, NST 1:132, footnote 1). Nishimiya also regards 去 as an error, and replaces it with 志 (*Kojiki*, 99, headnote 4).

41) *Kojiki*, NST 1:70, line 3; Philippi, *Kojiki*, 104.

42) *Kojiki*, NST 1:206, line 2. The texts in Aoki et al., Nishimiya (*Kojiki*, 148) and Takagi and Tomiyama (*Kojiki sôsakuin*, Vol. 1 *Honbun hen*, 237) lack the latter three graphs 丸高王 and their assigned readings, therefore, of "Komuku-nö-iratume" are a reflection of this. Philippi, *Kojiki*, 272 reads it as "Takamuku-nö-iratume."

43) *Kojiki*, NST 1:70 (加多理其登母 *katari-gÖtö mö* "the words handed down"), line 13. Aoki et al. note that this is the only instance of the use of 其 as the *on* phonogram *go*, and that when the same phrase appears several lines later, it is written with 碁 (Ibid., footnote 5). Philippi, *Kojiki*, 105.

44) There are two instances: *Kojiki*, NST 1:194, line 17; 196, line 11; Philippi, *Kojiki*, 257, 260.

45) *Kojiki*, NST 1:24, line 3; Philippi, *Kojiki*, 53.

46) There are two instances, and in each case, Aoki et al. have 佐 rather than 作. *Kojiki*, NST 1:72, lines 9, 11; Philippi, *Kojiki*, 108.

47) Aoki et al. have 佐 for 作. *Kojiki*, NST 1:86, line 5; Philippi, *Kojiki*, 126.

48) *Yu Pian* (*Gyoku-hen* in Japanese), a character dictionary compiled by Gu Yewang (519-581), completed in 543.

49) There is no deity named KuFiza-möti; rather, a pair of deities, Amë-nö-kuFiza-möti-nö-kamï and Kuni-nö-kuFiza-möti-nö-kamï, contain this segment, the etymology of which is unclear, in their names. Motoori derives it from 汲匏持 (*kumi-Fisago moti* 'bearing a gourd scoop'), with *-Fi-* as a contraction of *-mi Fi-*, and the elision of *go*, with the voicing of "*go*" transferred back onto *-sa-* to form *-za* (*Kojiki-den*, MNZ 9:210). The names appear in *Kojiki*, NST 1:26, lines 10, 11; Philippi, *Kojiki*, 56.

50) *Kojiki*, NST 1:38, lines 4-5; Philippi, *Kojiki*, 69. The name Okizakaru is written as 奥疎 in the main text, with the reading of 奢加留 (*-zakaru*) given in small print below.

51) *Kojiki*, NST 1:202, line 10; Philippi, *Kojiki*, 268.

52) *Kojiki*, NST 1:206, line 1; Philippi, *Kojiki*, 272.

53) The first instance is found in *Kojiki*, NST 1:178, line 13; Philippi, *Kojiki*, 236, and the second in *Kojiki*, NST 1:202, line 5; Philippi, *Kojiki*, 267.

54) *Kojiki*, NST 1:136, line 16; Philippi, *Kojiki*, 189.

55) As in 吉師部 (Kisibe), *Kojiki*, NST 1:200, line 12; Philippi, *Kojiki*, 266. See Philippi, *Kojiki*, 499, note "Kishibe" for a discussion of the term.

56) *Kojiki*, NST 1:146, line 12; Philippi, *Kojiki*, 199.

57) As in 味師内宿禰 (Umasi-uti-nö-sukune), *Kojiki*, NST 1:140, line 14; Philippi, *Kojiki*, 193. These examples are discussed in the section on *kun* phonograms under the entry "シ si " below.

58) Two examples are 内色許男命 (Utu-sikö-wo-nö-mikötö) and 内色許賣命 (Utu-sikö-me-nö-mikötö), *Kojiki*, NST 1:140, lines 5-6; Philippi, *Kojiki*, 193.

59) *Kojiki*, NST 1:116, line 3; Philippi, *Kojiki*, 163.

60) *Kojiki*, NST 1:234, line 11; Philippi, *Kojiki*, 309.

61) *Kojiki*, NST 1:48, line 7; Philippi, *Kojiki*, 78.

62) *Kojiki*, NST 1:268, line 1; Philippi, *Kojiki*, 348. The name derives from a place name (*Kojiki*, NST 1:268, headnote "Sizimu").

63) The song appears in *Kojiki*, NST 1:152, and Philippi, *Kojiki*, 205-206, but Aoki et al. do not show the kana 式 in this song, nor do Takagi and

Tomiya (*Kojiki sôsakuin*, Vol. 1: *Honbun hen*, 173-174). Motoori himself has it in neither his text nor his commentary (*Kojiki-den*, MNZ 11:43).

64) Takagi and Tomiyama list 支 as a variant for 志 in two manuscripts (支豆延 for 志豆延, *siduye* "lower branches," *Kojiki sôsakuin*, Vol. 1: *Honbun hen*, 246). The song appears in *Kojiki*, NST 1:212; Philippi, *Kojiki*, 280.

65) Neither Aoki et al. (*Kojiki*, NST 1:228-244) or Takagi and Tomiyama (*Kojiki sôsakuin*, Vol. 1: *Honbun hen*, 267-290) show the kana 之 as variant for any of the kana *si* in the songs found in this section.

66) *Kojiki*, NST 1: 18, line 4; Philippi, *Kojiki*, 47.

67) A fragment of the land name Ne-nö-kata-su-kuni, *Kojiki*, NST 1:42, line 9; Philippi, *Kojiki*, 73.

68) *Kojiki*, NST 1:90, line 15; Philippi, *Kojiki*, 133.

69) The reading of "州須" *susu* is given in small print immediately following 凝烟 in the text (*Kojiki*, NST 1:94, line 1; Philippi, *Kojiki*, 136).

70) *Kojiki*, NST 1:48, line 8; Philippi, *Kojiki*, 78.

71) Takagi and Tomiyama list 素 as a variant for 袁 (= 緒 *wo* 'life') in two manuscripts (*Kojiki sôsakuin*, Vol. 1: *Honbun hen*, 173). The song appears in *Kojiki*, NST 1:152; Philippi, *Kojiki*, 205.

72) Ôno points out that there is one other graph used to represent the kana *zö*, that of 存, found in a song from the section on Emperor Ingyô in Book Three in the Shinpukuji-bon and other manuscripts: *közö* (許存) *kösö Fa yasuku Fada Fure* "Tonight at last I caress her body with ease" (Ôno, *Kojiki-den*, MNZ 9:518, note "page 23, line 6"; passage found in *Kojiki*, NST, 1: 254, line 11; Philippi, *Kojiki*, 333). Ôno notes that 存 begins with a voiced sound, and assigns it a Middle Chinese reading of *dzuən*. The Kan'ei-bon and other manuscripts, however, have 在 rather than 存 in this example, and Ôno surmises that this is the reason for Motoori's omission of it from his list.

73) The term *teniwoha* (辭) is first seen in treatises on poetry from the Kamakura period (1185-1333) (Inoue Seinosuke, "Teniwoha," in Kokugogakkai, eds., *Kokugogaku daijiten*, <Tôkyôdô, 1980>, 617-619). Inoue suggests that the most convincing theory as to the origin of the term *teniwoha* is that of Togami Michitoshi, who argues in his *Teniha abikizuna* (1770)

that it derives from the symbols found in the four corners of the *okoto-ten* schema used in the Hakaseke-no-ten ('court scholars' system') method of assigning Japanese readings to Chinese texts. The *okoto-ten* were special diacritics in the form of dots marked to the side of or on graphs to indicate particles and inflectional endings (Seeley, *A History of Writing in Japan*, 62 ff., also 201-202). Reading the four corners of the Hakase-ke-no-ten system, represented below, from the lower left corner clockwise yields " teniwoha."

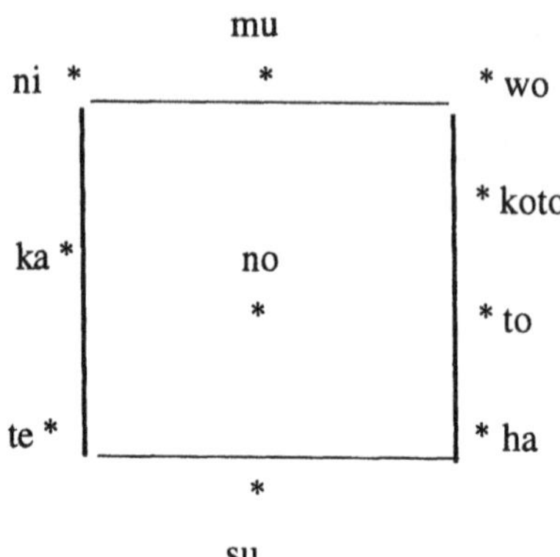

This explanation of the origin of the term *teniwoha* would account for the fact that the category itself seems to represent a miscellaneous assortment of both particles and inflectional endings, and would also perhaps account for what Bedell notes as the term *teniwoha* having been used ambiguously: at times it refers to grammatical relations and their phonological representations, while at other times it refers to grammar as a whole (George Dudley Bedell, *Kokugaku Grammatical Theory* <MIT Ph.D. Dissertation, 1968>, 44).

Modern Japanese scholarship now recognizes two categories of speech, *zyosi* ('particles') and *zyodôsi* ('auxiliaries'), for those items originally subsumed under the category of *teniwoha*. The particle *zö* in question here is termed an "emotive particle" (*kakari zyosi*) (Ikeda Tadashi, *Classical Japanese Grammar Illustrated with Texts* <Tôhô gakkai, 1975>, 218, 221).

74) The particle *zö* in question here is termed a "final particle" (*syû-zyosi*), with the function of "assertion" (Ikeda, 236).

[75] Ôno agrees that since the kana 曾 is used to represent the voiceless sound *sö* in the *Man'yôshû*, *Kojiki*, and *Nihonshoki*, one might be tempted to conclude that only in the case of the emotive particle *zö* and the final particle *zö* is it used to represent the voiced, and not the voiceless, sound. He cites textual evidence which suggests, however, that these particles may in fact have been voiceless *sö* and *sö* in earlier Japanese. He notes that in the case of postpositions, there is a general tendency in Japanese to voice initial sounds which were originally voiceless, as in *bakari* from *Fakari*, *gurai* from *kurai*, and suggests that this same process was taking place in the case of the emotive and final particles, from *sö* to *zö*. He locates the change as taking place in the Nara (710-794) to Heian periods (794-1185), with the voiced version gradually being used more frequently, and suggests that what we find in the Nara period, and in the *Kojiki*, is the use of both the voiceless and the voiced versions. His conclusion, therefore, is that use of the voiceless kana 曾 does indeed indicate the original voiceless version of the particles in question, *sö*, while use of the voiced kana indicates the voiced version of these same particles, *zö* (Ôno, Kojiki-den, MNZ 9:518-519, note "page 23, line 11").

[76] *Kojiki*, NST 1:146, line 8; Philippi, *Kojiki*, 197.

[77] *Kojiki*, NST 1:298, line 6; Philippi, *Kojiki*, 388.

[78] *Kojiki*, NST 1:132, line 6; Philippi, *Kojiki*, 183.

[79] *Kojiki*, NST 1:186, line 15. Aoki et al. follow the Shinpukuji-bon manuscript for this passage, which has "成二当藝当藝斯玖一" (*tagitagisiku narinu* "have become wobbly"). In other manuscripts, the same passage reads "成二当藝斯形一" (*tagisi nö katati ni narinu* 'have taken the form of rudders') (see Takagi and Tomiyama, *Kojiki sôsakuin*, Vol. 1: *Honbun hen*, 214, for this version, and Nakada Norio et al., *Kogo daijiten* <Shôgakukan, 1983>, 988, entry "*tagisi*" for a discussion of both versions). Philippi, *Kojiki*, 247.

[80] *Kojiki*, NST 1:186, line 14; Philippi, *Kojiki*, 246. See note 100 below with respect to the reading of "Tagi-nu" for "Tagi-no."

[81] *Kojiki*, NST 1:246, line 16; Philippi, *Kojiki*, 325.

[82] *Kojiki*, NST 1:194, line 7; Philippi, *Kojiki*, 255.

83) *Kojiki*, NST 1:240, line 6; Philippi, *Kojiki*, 317.

84) *Kojiki*, NST 1:294, line 4; Philippi, *Kojiki*, 383.

85) *Kojiki*, NST 1:282, line 4; Philippi, *Kojiki*, 367.

86) *Kojiki-den*, MNZ 12:323.

87) *Kojiki*, NST 1:168. Aoki et al. read 阿太 as "Ata". Philippi, *Kojiki*, 211. Motoori concludes that 太 is a mistake for 本 *Fo*, but also considers the possibility of assigning 太 the reading of *Fo* rather than *da*, as he has done elsewhere. He rejects this possibility due to the incompatibility of the combination of an *on-kana*, 阿 *a*, with the *kun* reading of *Fo* for 太 (*Kojiki-den*, MNZ 11:82).

88) *Kojiki*, NST 1:18, line 11; Philippi, *Kojiki*, 48.

89) *Kojiki*, NST 1:18, line 12; Philippi, *Kojiki*, 48.

90) *Kojiki*, NST 1:60, line 3; Philippi, *Kojiki*, 92.

91) *Kojiki*, NST 1:120, line 4; Philippi, *Kojiki*, 168.

92) *Kojiki*, NST 1:52, line 2; Philippi, *Kojiki*, 83.

93) *Kojiki*, NST 1:22, lines 4, 13, two instances. All of the manuscripts appear to have 登 *tö* rather than 等 *tö*. Philippi, *Kojiki*, 51-52.

94) *Kojiki*, NST 1:72, line 16; Philippi, *Kojiki*, 109.

95) *Kojiki*, NST 1:232, line 8; Philippi, *Kojiki*, 306.

96) *Kojiki*, NST 1:24, line 3; Philippi, *Kojiki*, 53.

97) *Kojiki*, NST 1:32, line 4; Philippi, *Kojiki*, 60.

98) *Kojiki*, NST 1:78, line 5; Philippi, *Kojiki*, 116.

99) *Kojiki*, NST 1:200, line 3. Aoki et al. have "勝門比売" (Kati-to-Fime). Takagi and Tomiyama note that some manuscripts also contain the graph 騰 (*Kojiki sôsakuin*, Vol. 1: *Honbun hen*, 230, headnote 3). Philippi, *Kojiki*, 264.

100) Scholars have determined that three distinct sets of kana were used in the *Kojiki* and *Man'yôshû* to represent what became in later Japanese just the two kana symbols *nu* and *no*. Ôno lists the three sets as follows, and presents several representative examples that each set of kana was used to write (*Kojiki-den*, MNZ 9:519-520, note "page 24, line 7").

1. 奴・濃・農 and others. Used to write: *-nu* 'PERFECTIVE', *nuki* 'to remove', *nusi* 'husband', *nusumi* 'to steal', *inu* 'dog', *kinu* 'clothing', *nanuka* 'seventh day', etc.
2. 怒・努 and others. Used to write: *no* 'field', *sino* 'a small type of bamboo', *tuno* 'horn', *sinogu* 'to get through', *tanosi* 'enjoyable', etc.
3. 乃・能 and others. Used to write: *no* 'GENITIVE', *sono* 'garden', *tono* 'lord', *nokoru* 'to remain', *konomu* 'to enjoy', *onore* 'oneself', etc.

Edo period (1603-1867) *kokugakusha* chose to group the kana in (1) and (2) together, as representing one sound, *nu*, based on the reasoning that the sound value of the graphs in (1) and (2) was the same. The readings they assigned the words in (2), therefore, contained *nu* rather than *no*. Hashimoto Shinkichi argued that since the three types seem to have been clearly differentiated in use, they must have represented three different syllables, and proposed that the kana in group (1) represent *nu*, the kana in group (2) represent *no* (*kô*-type), and the kana in group (3) represent *nö* (*otsu*-type). After the Heian period (794-1185), the sounds of groups (2) and (3) merged into one syllable, *no*. Subsequent scholarship takes the interpretation proposed by Hashimoto. Ôno points out that the value of all of the graphs in the Chinese language of that time was *no*, as Chinese had no syllable which corresponded to *nu*. Since the Japanese language distinguished both *no* and *nu*, a graph had to be arbitrarily selected to represent the syllable *nu*. The most natural choice would be one from the group having a sound value of *no*, and he suggests that the graph 奴 was selected to represent *nu* because it had the fewest number of strokes, and the syllable *nu* had a much higher frequency of occurrence than the syllable *no*.

The graphs 怒 and 努, then, with a greater number of strokes, were selected to represent the less frequent *no*. As an arbitrary convention, however, it seems not to have been strictly observed; there are many exceptions with indiscriminate use of these graphs, even as early as the *Man'yôshû*. See also Roland A. Lange, *The Phonology of Eighth-Century Japanese* (Tokyo: Sophia University, 1973), 25-26, for a discussion of this issue.

[101] *Kojiki*, NST 1:86, line 14. Aoki et al. assign the reading "Mino". Philippi, *Kojiki*, 127.

[102] *Kojiki*, NST 1:148, line 13. Aoki et al. assign the reading "Mino". Philippi, *Kojiki*, 201.

[103] *Kojiki*, NST 1:50, line 9.

[104] *Kojiki*, NST 1:72, line 13. Philippi, *Kojiki*, 109. Aoki et al. follow the Shinpukuji-bon manuscript, which has a repetition symbol following the syllable 多 *ta*, yielding the reading of "*ata tane*" 'other seeds', instead of "*atane*", 'a type of plant used for dyeing' (footnote 10), or, perhaps, a mistake for "*akane*" 'madder', a plant used for its crimson dye (Kurano and Takeda, *Kojiki*, *Norito*, NKBT 1:103, headnote 22).

[105] There are numerous examples. One such is 葦田宿禰 Asida-nö-sukune, *Kojiki*, NST 1:246, line 1; Philippi, *Kojiki*, 324.

[106] *Kojiki*, NST 1:226, line 9. Aoki at al. assign the reading of "*oFo-kimi*", rather than that of "*miko*", to 王. Philippi, *Kojiki*, 297.

[107] *Kojiki*, NST 1:18, lines 12-13; Philippi, *Kojiki*, 48.

[108] *Kojiki*, NST 1:242, line 15; 244, line 2, two instances. Aoki et al. omit 乃 in accordance with the Shinpukuji-bon manuscript, which lacks it, yielding the reading "*yö nö nagaFitö*". Several manuscripts contain it (Kurano and Takeda, *Kojiki*, *Norito*, NKBT 1:280, footnote 2-3). Philippi, *Kojiki*, 320.

[109] *Kojiki*, NST 1:256, line 14; Philippi, *Kojiki*, 336.

[110] *Kojiki*, NST 1:280, line 1; Philippi, *Kojiki*, 363.

[111] *Kojiki*, NST 1:46, line 10; Philippi, *Kojiki*, 77.

112) *Kojiki*, NST 1:48, lines 6-7; Philippi, *Kojiki*, 78.

113) *Kojiki*, NST 1:136, line 7; Philippi, *Kojiki*, 188.

114) The indexes in Takagi and Tomiyama (*Kojiki sôsakuin*, Vol. 2: *Sakuin hen*), Ôno (*Kojiki-den*, MNZ 12), and Philippi (*Kojiki*) failed to yield the name of this deity.

115) *Kojiki*, NST 1:36, lines 10-11; Philippi, *Kojiki*, 67.

116) *Kojiki*, NST 1:246, line 12; Philippi, *Kojiki*, 325.

117) *Kojiki*, NST 1:186, line 7. Aoki et al. assign the reading of "IFuki". Philippi, *Kojiki*, 245.

[118] *Kojiki*, NST 1:142, line 2; Philippi, *Kojiki*, 194.

[119] *Kojiki*, NST 1:46, line 10; Philippi, *Kojiki*, 77.

[120] *Kojiki*, NST 1:204, line 4. Aoki et al. assign the reading "*kamu-Foki*".

Philippi, *Kojiki*, 270.

[121] *Kojiki*, NST 1:94, line 10; Philippi, *Kojiki*, 137.

[122] *Kojiki*, NST 1:52, line 7; Philippi, *Kojiki*, 84.

[123] *Kojiki*, NST 1:28, line 9; Philippi, *Kojiki*, 57.

[124] *Kojiki*, NST 1:156, lines 3-4. The name of the deity appears as 品牟都和氣命 Fo-mutu-wakë-nö-mikötö, with 都 *tu* rather than 智 *ti*. Philippi, *Kojiki*, 210.

[125] *Kojiki*, NST 1:164, line 3. The name appears as 本牟智和氣 Fo-muti-wakë. Philippi, *Kojiki*, 217.

[126] *Kojiki*, NST 1:28, line 12; Philippi, *Kojiki*, 57.

[127] *Kojiki*, NST 1:80, line 9. Aoki et al. assign the reading "Midu-maki". Philippi, *Kojiki*, 119.

[128] *Kojiki*, NST 1:238, line 16; Philippi, *Kojiki*, 315.

[129] *Kojiki*, NST 1:258, line 6; Philippi, *Kojiki*, 337.

[130] *Kojiki*, NST 1:180, line 2; Philippi, *Kojiki*, 237.

[131] *Kojiki*, NST 1:48, line 7. Aoki et al. have 无耶志 rather than 无邪志. Philippi, *Kojiki*, 78.

[132] *Kojiki*, NST 1:180, line 16; Philippi, *Kojiki*, 240.

[133] 佐賀牟 Sagamu, *Kojiki*, NST 1:182, line 12; Philippi, *Kojiki*, 242.

[134] *Kojiki*, NST 1:222, line 9; Philippi, *Kojiki*, 293. 咩 and its variant form 哶 is a graph no longer used in Japanese. Ôno defines its meaning as the bleating of a sheep, with a sound value of *mei*, *me*, or *mi*, based on its entry in the *Ruijumyôgishô* (*Kojiki-den*, MNZ 9:520, note "page 25, line 12").

[135] Takagi and Tomiyama do not list 文 as appearing in the body of the *Kojiki* (*Kojiki sôsakuin*, Vol. 2: *Sakuin hen*).

[136] *Kojiki*, NST 1:88, line 5. Aoki et al. assign the reading "*so*". Kurano et al. state that 也 is not the kana *ya*, but rather a graph used as punctuation

at the end of a phrase (*Kojiki, Norito*, NKBT 1:118, footnote 1). Philippi, *Kojiki*, 128.

137) Motoori notes that "*zoya*", while common in the language of his time, is not found in the language of antiquity or in the archaic songs. Furthermore, there are no instances in the *Kojiki* of 也 being used as a kana. He argues, therefore, that perhaps it is best to end the song with "*zo*", and to regard 也 as a graph placed as punctuation to denote the end of a song. Observing, however, that there are no other such examples of graphs placed as punctuation at the end of a song, he leaves the reading as "*zoya*" (*Kojiki-den*, MNZ 10:86-87).

138) *Kojiki*, NST 1:22, line 14; Philippi, *Kojiki*, 53.

139) For Book Two: *Kojiki*, NST,1:134, line 5; Philippi, *Kojiki*, 184, and for Book Three: *Kojiki*, NST 1:258, line 1; Philippi, *Kojiki*, 337.

140) *Kojiki,* NST 1:34, line 8; Philippi, *Kojiki*, 64.

141) *Kojiki*, NST 1:72, line 1; 74, lines 6-7; Philippi, *Kojiki*, 107, 112.

142) *Kojiki*, NST 1:72, line 9; Philippi, *Kojiki*, 108.

143) *Kojiki*, NST 1:96, line 11; Philippi, *Kojiki*, 140.

144) *Kojiki*, NST 1:126, line 2; Philippi, *Kojiki*, 174.

145) *Kojiki*, NST 1:180, line 5; Philippi, *Kojiki*, 238.

146) *Kojiki*, NST 1:152, line 5; Philippi, *Kojiki*, 205.

147) There are many examples of this place name. One such occurs in 丸邇池 (Wani nö ikë "the Wani pond"), *Kojiki*, NST 1:230, line 2; Philippi, *Kojiki*, 302.

148) In Old Japanese, each member of the pairs /i/ and /wi/, /e/ and /we/, and /o/ and /wo/ constituted a distinct syllable (Martin, *The Japanese Language Through Time*, 38). Around the year 1000, however, the distinction between /o/ and /wo/ began to break down, as is evidenced in notes written down by monks in the margins to sutras where, for example, the verb *wosamu* 'rule' is written as *osamu*. The merging of /o/ and /wo/ to /wo/ began with a fixed number of words, and gradually spread throughout the language. A similar breakdown in the distinctions between /i/ and /wi/, and /e/ and /we/ occurred as well (Ôno Susumu, "Kanazukai no rekishi," in Ôno Susumu and Shibata Takeshi, eds., *Monji*; Iwanami kôza: Nihongo, Vol. 8: <Iwanami

shoten, 1977>, 303-304). /i/ amd /wi/ merged as /i/, and /e/ and /we/ merged as /e/, with /e/ later taking on a "prothetic y-" to become /ye/ (Martin, Ibid., 38).

149) The /h/ of Modern Japanese was the voiceless bilabial fricative /F/, and sometime around the middle of the Heian period (794-1185) it underwent lenition intervocalically to become /w/, so that the syllables /Fa, Fi, Fu, Fe, Fo/ became /wa, wi, u, we, wo/ following a vowel (Miller, *The Japanese Language*, 201, and Ôno, "Kanazukai no rekishi," 304). As an illustration, the verb *omoFu* 'think' which had taken the inflectional forms of *omoFa*, *omoFi*, *omoFu*, and *omoFe* came to be pronounced as *omowa*, *omowi*, *omou*, and *omowe*. A further change occurred when the /w/ was dropped from the syllables /wi/ and /we/, and the pronunciation of these syllables changed to /i/ and /ye/. Then, the verbal inflections of *omou* changed to *omowa*, *omoi*, *omou*, and *omoye*. There was considerable confusion as to which kana should be used to write down those syllables which had undergone a sound change (Ôno, Ibid., 304-305).

150) *Kanazukai* is the proper use of a fixed number of kana which are thought to be distinct from one another (Ôno, "Kanazukai no rekishi," 303). For Fujiwara Teika (1162-1241), who was the first to establish a method for the use of kana, it was the correct differentiation of the forty-seven kana contained in the *Iroha uta*, a poem in which each kana is used only once. The poem contained kana for each of the syllables /i, wi/, /e, we/, and /o, wo/, even though these sounds had merged by Teika's time (see note 148 above). Teika wished to establish a standard to differentiate their use so that he would be able to write down poetry and copy older texts properly. In the only text of Teika remaining concerning *kanazukai*, the *Hekian* (later known as the *Gekanshû*), he did two things: (1) distinguished between /o/ and /wo/ on the basis of accent, with the sound with a high, level accent being written as /wo/, and the sound with a low, level accent being written as /o/, and (2) determined that the use of the kana for /i, wi, hi/ and /e, we, he/ were to be decided on the basis of individual words, which he listed as illustration (Ôno, Ibid., 308).

151) The term Motoori uses here is *karuki-omoki* (軽き重き), which is not a technical term. The same graphs in Sino-Japanese, however, *keizyû* (軽重) represent a technical term found in Chinese and Japanese linguistics which has been used to refer to various phenomena at different points in time. In the work of scholars in Edo period (1600-1868) Japan, it is used in two basic senses: (1) to distinguish between "light" accent and "heavy" accent, and (2) to characterize the /o/ of the *a*-line of the syllabary as "light," and the /wo/ of the *wa*-line of the syllabary as "heavy" (Maeda Tomiyoshi, "Keizyû," in Kokugogakkai, eds., *Kokugogaku daijiten* <Tôkyôdô, 1980>, 267). Motoori himself uses the terms "light" and "heavy" in the latter sense in his *Mojigoe no kanazukai* (1776) where he states that "/o/ is light and belongs in the *a*-line, while /wo/ is heavy and belongs in the *wa*-line" (Ôno Susumu, ed., *Mojigoe no kanazukai*, MNZ 5:331). Kaibara Ekiken (1630-1714), a Neo-Confucianist who also did work in philology, uses the term in the former sense in his *Wajikai* (1699), where he suggests that "light" accent, that which starts high, and "heavy" accent, that which starts low, is the distinguishing factor for the homophonous triplets /i, wi, hi/, and /o, wo, ho/ (Hachiya Kiyohito, "*Wajikai*," in Satô Kiyoji, ed., *Kokugogaku kenkyû jiten* <Meiji shoin, 1977>, 693). Perhaps Motoori's criticism is directed toward this type of analysis. See also Günther Wenck's discussion of the history of this term, wherein he points to its origin in the Sanskrit phonetic tradition (*Japanische Phonetik*, Band I <Wiesbaden: Otto Harrassowitz, 1954>,197).

152) Keichû (1640-1701), in a close examination of many of Japan's earliest texts (eighth to tenth centuries), found many discrepancies in the use of kana when compared to writing based on Fujiwara Teika's method of kana usage (see note 150 above). He wrote his major work on kana, *Wajishô-ranshô* (1693, published 1695), to correct the defects in Teika's system (Nakada Norio, "*Wajishô ranshô*," in Kokugogakkai, eds., *Kokugogaku daijiten* <Tôkyôdô, 1980>, 941). In the *Wajishô ranshô*, he deals with kana from the *a*-line, the *ya*-line, the *wa*-line, and the *ha*-line of the syllabary, from the *za*-line and *da*-line of the syllabary, and with the writing of /u/ and /mu/ (Nakada, Ibid.) His system, which was based on examples culled from

the early texts, is called "*rekishiteki kanazukai*" ('historical kana usage'), and was adopted as the standard system of kana usage until 1946 (Seeley, *A History of Writing in Japan*, 125).

153) The pillow word *asiFikï* was paired with words such as *yama* ('mountain') and *mine* ('peak'), but its original sense has become obscure. It is often interpreted as "foot-dragging", but Ôno Susumu et al. state that Heian poets seem to have read *asi* as 'reed', and suggests that *Fikï* is 'cramp' (*Iwanami kogo jiten* <Iwanami shoten, 1974>, 27). Subsequently, the initial consonant of the second member of this compound word became voiced, i.e. *asibiki*.

154) Subsequently, *miyabito*.

155) Subsequently, *simatudori*, and *iFetudori*, respectively.

156) According to Ôno, the *Nihonshoki* does not contain numerous examples of indiscriminate use of voiced and voiceless kana (*Kojiki-den*, MNZ 9:521, supplementary note "page 27, line 6"). In his view, Motoori apparently assumed that each *man'yôgana* in use in the Nara period (710-794) should have a uniform sound value. Therefore, he found it puzzling that kana which were used consistently to indicate voiced sounds in the *Kojiki* and the *Man'yôshû* were used to indicate voiceless sounds in the *Nihonshoki*. For example, one finds 波 for *Fa* and 婆 for *ba* in the *Kojiki* and the *Man'yôshû*, but in the *Nihonshoki*, both 波 and 婆 are used to write *Fa*, while *ba* is written with 磨, 魔, or 麼.

Motoori appears not to have been fully aware of the fact that the *man'yôgana* in the *Man'yôshû* and the *Kojiki* were meant to be read with the Six Dynasties *go'on* system of sound values, while the *man'yôgana* in the *Nihonshoki* were to be read with the T'ang dynasty *kan'on* system of sound values. The *go'on* system had sound values which were based on Chinese pronunciation during the Six Dynasties period, which Roy Andrew Miller describes as "northern Chinese down to about the end of the sixth century" (*The Japanese Language*, 102). The *kan'on* system had sound values which were based on "the Chinese language of Ch'ang-an at the peak of the T'ang dynasty, as it reached Japan, *mutatis mutandis*, from the end of the seventh and into the eighth century" (Miller, Ibid., 103). What had been voiced initials in the *go-on* system became voiceless initials in the *kan'on* system (Miller, Ibid., p. 105), which accounts for the fact that kana which are used to indicate voiced sounds in the *Kojiki* and *Man'yôshû* are used to indicate voiceless sounds in the *Nihonshoki*.

157) Ôno Susumu notes that in a survey of the three texts, it is the *Man'-yôshû* which has the greatest number of irregularities in the representation of voiced versus voiceless sounds, with the *Nihonshoki* having the second highest number of irregularities, and the *Kojiki*, the least (*Kojiki-den*, MNZ 9:521, supplementary note "page 27, line 18"). He argues that the greater number of irregularities in the *Man'yôshû* may be due to the fact that the hands of the compilers were not as tightly constrained as the hands of the compilers of the other texts; the *Man'yôshû* is the longest of the three, its compilation extended over the longest time period, and a greater number of persons was involved in the compilation.

158) Motoori discusses this issue in his "*Nihonshoki tsûshô*," a piece included in his miscellaneous writings (*Nihonshoki tsûshô*, MNZ 13:79-86).

159) See note 156 above for discussion of *kan'on*, *go'on*, and the *Nihonshoki*.

160) The latter kana, 米, represents the *otsu* syllable *më*.

161) Ôno notes that it cannot be said that the reading of 宜 as *gï* is a mistake, due to the sound value for this graph in Archaic Chinese, which was *nia*, subsequently changing to ŋi̯ɐ --> ŋi̯ə --> ŋi̯ï (*Kojiki-den*, MNZ 9:521, supplementary note "page 28, line 11"). He explains that an example from the Suiko period (552-646) in Japan where the name "Soga" is written as 巻宜, with 宜 used as a phonogram for *ga*, represents the earlier pronunciation, while 宜 used as a phonogram for *gë* in the *Kojiki* represents the pronunciation of the next period, and the use of 宜 as a phonogram for both *gë* and *gï* in the *Man'yôshû* reflects the later stage of Chinese pronunciation. Ôno also notes that there is no instance in the early texts of 用 being used to represent both *yo* and *yu*.

162) Literary Chinese morphemes having an "entering tone" and ending in the consonants /-p/, /-t/, and /-k/ are termed *nissyô* (入声). In Old Japanese, which lacked syllable-final consonants, the segments /-p/, /-t/, and /-k/ were

regarded as syllables (Tôdô Akiyasu, "Kanji gaisetsu," in Ôno Susumu and Shibata Takeshi, eds., *Monji*; Iwanami Koza: Nihongo, Vol. 8 <Iwanami shoten, 1977>, 125), and rendered as *-Fu* (*-p*); *-ti* (*-t*), *-tu* (*-t*); *-ki* (*-k*), *-ku* (*-k*) in *go'on* borrowings, and *-Fu* (*-p*); *-tu* (*-t*); *-ki* (*-k*), *-ku* (*-k*) in *kan'on* borrowings (Hayashi Chikafumi, "Nihon no kanji-on," in Nakada Norio, ed., *Nihon no kanji;* Nihongo no sekai, Vol. 4 <Chûô kôronsha, 1982>, 390).

163) 呉公 'centipede' is written with the left-hand insect radicals omitted, found elsewhere as 蜈蚣. Motoori's subsequent discussion lists other examples of abbreviations taken from various texts (*Kojiki-den*, MNZ 9:449-450).

164) Ôno argues that it was a natural choice to use 意 as a phonogram for *o*, since it has the same rime as the phonograms 其 *gö* and 碁 *gö* found in the *Kojiki*, and a number of additional phonograms with the value of *kö* or *gö* used in the *Man'yôshû*. He suggests that Motoori assumed the value of 意 must have been *i*, and that is why he looked for an explanation of its use to write *o*, and arrived at the erroneous conclusion given here (*Kojiki-den*, MNZ 9:521, supplementary note "page 28, line 12"). Scholars are not in agreement with respect to whether or not the *kô-otsu* distinction was found in the syllable /o/; see Martin (*The Japanese Language Through Time*, 49-50), for discussion.

165) Motoori was the first to notice that there were two distinct sets of phonograms used in the *Kojiki*, but he did not assume that they represented any phonetic distinctions. He notices the distinction for these syllables in the following passage: *ki*, *gi*, *Fi*, *bi*, *mi*, *ke*, *me*, *ko*, *so*, *to*, *no*, *mo*, *yo*. See also note 168 below.

166) Ôno notes that there is one instance in the *Kojiki*, in a song from the chapter on the reign of Emperor Ingyô (412-453), where the *to* of the verb *toFu* 'to ask' is written with the *otsu* phonogram 登 *tö*. There are no such instances in the *Nihonshoki*. The same is true for the verb *toru* 'to take' as well (*Kojiki-den*, MNZ 9:521-522, supplementary note "page 29 line 4").

167) For a discussion of this issue, see note 100 above.

[168)] Motoori's pupil, Ishizuka Tatsumaro (1764-1823) investigated the matter in detail, and presented the results in *Kanazukai oku no yamamichi* (1798) (Ôno Susumu, "Kaidai," *Kojiki-den*, MNZ 9:23). In this work, Ishizuka demonstrated that such distinctions were not limited to the *Kojiki*, but were found also in the *Nihonshoki* and *Man'yôshû*. He was unable to see into the essence of the issue, however, and the arguments in the work were inconsistent, with the result that he failed to gain an understanding of his views (Ôno, *Kojiki-den*, MNZ 9:522, supplementary note "page 29, line 13"). Hashimoto Shinkichi (1882-1945) rediscovered these same distinctions while working on the *Man'yôshû*, and reintroduced the work of Motoori and Ishizuka, at which point the value of Ishizuka's work was acknowledged. Hashimoto is credited with being the first to propose that the two distinct sets of phonograms represented a distinction in the sound system of Old Japanese, although Kusakado Nobutaka is also said to have proposed this in a commentary to Ishizuka's work titled *Kogen betsuon shô* written some time before 1849 (Lange, *The Phonology of Eighth-Century Japanese*, 23, footnote 11). Hashimoto coined the terms that have subsequently been used in discussions of this issue, calling one set of phonograms *kô-rui* 'type A', and the other set *otsu-rui* 'type B' (Lange, Ibid.).

The two sets of phonograms involve only the vowels *i*, *e*, and *o*, and these vowels are limited in their distribution. For this reason, recent scholarship has begun to indicate these distinctions with subscript$_1$ for the type-A series, and subscript$_2$ for the type-B series, leaving the non-subscripted vowels to indicate lack of possibility of showing the type-A/type B distinction (Shibatani, *The Languages of Japan*, 134-135). Shibatani indicates the possible distinctions in the following table, with note added by translator.

"Distribution of the Old Japanese 'vowels' in terms of syllable units (exclusive of voiced versions), arranged in order of place of articulation from left to right."

a	pa	ma	wa	ta	na	sa	ra	ja	ka
u	pu	mu		tu	nu	su	ru	ju	ku
	pi_1	mi_1							ki_1
i			wi	ti	ni	si	ri		
	pi_2	mi_2							ki_2
	pe_1	me_1							ke_1
e			we	te	ne	se	re	je	
	pe_2	me_2							ke_2
				to_1	no_1	so_1	ro_1	jo_1	ko_1
o	po	mo*	wo						
				to_2	no_2	so_2	ro_2	jo_2	ko_2

(Shibatani, *The Languages of Japan*, 1990:134, Table 6.4)

**Kojiki* contains mo_1 and mo_2, with a total of 88 different syllables, while the *Nihonshoki* and the *Man'yôshû*, which do not have this distinction, contain 87.

These distinctions in phonograms led to the hypothesis that there were eight vowels in Old Japanese "which were at least phonetically distinguished" (Shibatani, Ibid., 132). Ôno Susumu's system, for example, assumes eight vowel phonemes, and views i_2 and e_2 as centralized forms of *i* and *e*, and o_2 as a centralized form of *o*. Thus, he proposes front vowels /i/, /e/, central vowels /ï/, /ë/, /ö/, and back vowels /u/, /o/, and /a/ (Shibatani, Ibid.).

Another hypothesis is that the distinction in phonograms has to do with some sort of palatalization of the preceding consonant. Matsumoto Katsumi's vocalic system, for example, has only five vowel phonemes, /i/, /e/, /a/, /o/, /u/. Based on internal reconstruction, he proposes that e_2 derived from the combination of *a-i*, and i_2 from the sequences *o/u-i*. He views e_1 as deriving from an *i-a* sequence, and i_1 as the original *i*. e_1 and i_1 would, therefore have had a "palatalizing effect on the preceding consonant," while e_2 , deriving from *a-i*, and i_2 , deriving from *o/u-i*, would not. The type-A syllables are given a phonetic realization of [CjV], and the type-B syllables, [CV]. He treats o_1 and o_2 as a single phoneme /o/, and ascribes a phonetic value of [ɔ] to o_2 (Shibatani, Ibid., 133-135).

There are other competing hypotheses as to the type of phonetic distinctions represented by the two series of phonograms. See the following for discussion of research done in this area: Shibatani, Ibid.; Lange, *The Phonology of Eighth-Century Japanese*; Miller, *The Japanese Language;* Timothy J. Vance, *An Introduction to Japanese Phonology* (Albany: State University of New York Press, 1987); and Wenck, *Japanische Phonetik*, Band II.

169) *Kuntyû* are notes written in the text in *on* phonogram notation, providing a gloss to indicate a Japanese reading or to specify an accent.

170) The text here has the graph 鉏 , which also means 'plow', but is apparently no longer used in Modern Japanese.

8
On the Method of Reading

One should treat the language of the texts of antiquity with respect, and there is a reason why this is particularly true of the *Kojiki*. One should carefully consider the language of antiquity contained therein, and value the Japanese readings. Close attention to the words of Emperor Tenmu [r. 672-686] will reveal why this should be so. He states that the *Teiki* (*Imperial Chronicles*) and *Honji* (*Fundamental Dicta*) of the various houses have come to deviate from the truth and are filled with falsehoods, such that if these errors are not corrected immediately, the essential elements of the texts will be lost before long. Therefore, he wishes to take up the *Teiki* and consider the *Honji*, and, after ridding the texts of falsehoods, to pass only what is true on to future generations. The Emperor then commands directly a person named Fiyeda nö Are to recite the *Sumera-mikötö nö Fi-tugi* (*The Imperial Sun Lineage*) and the *Saki-nö-yö nö Furu-götö* (*Ancient Dicta of Former Ages*) and commit them to memory.[1] He mentions specifically not only the *Teiki*, but also the *Kuji* and the *Hongi*, and again later, when the compilation of the *Kojiki* itself by Yasumarö is described, the reason why he is to record the *Kuji* which Are recited by imperial command is because the language of antiquity was viewed as essential.

In close scrutiny of this imperial command, it is apparent that the Emperor was well aware that as it was the custom in antiquity to record and transmit everything in classical Chinese, each time this was done the language of the original would gradually come to differ due to the influence of the Chinese language, and he was saddened at the thought that at some point the language of antiquity might simply fade away. The Emperor must have thought that it was absolutely necessary to remedy the texts at this time, due to the fact that in his reign, the world was undergoing a process of change. The reason why he commanded Are to recite the texts and commit them to memory had to do with the fact that, in many instances, it is difficult to commit to paper that which has been expressed only in the spoken word, and that, quite often, that which is written down does not adequately express what is conveyed via the spoken word. The whole endeavor becomes all the more difficult when the goal is not to deviate from the language of antiquity, yet the convention of the times is to write in classical Chinese. It was his august intent to first of all have the text carefully recited orally, and then to have those exact words recorded faithfully. <At that time, the language of antiquity still survived in narratives (*katari*) of the people, although these narratives did not exist in written documents. As it was an age in which the language of antiquity had yet to die out completely, it was the Emperor's intent that in having Are recite and commit them to memory, even though he would be basing his recitation on old documents recorded in classical Chinese, he would capture the style of the narratives (*katari*) and express it in the language of antiquity still current at the time, thereby

seeking the essence of the transmission through oral recitation. To not do so, and to merely copy in writing from one text to another, would make it difficult to deviate from the classical Chinese of the original text. Some people raise the issue of which text Are could have used as a basis for his recitation of and memorization of the true language of antiquity, if by this time already the records of the various families contained many errors. One must assume that, at that time, documents without errors still survived, and they must have chosen carefully from among them.> After careful evaluation of this august aim of the Emperor, one can realize their efforts not to treat the language of antiquity lightly.

This is the basis for the study of our august country. If such were not the case, and the purpose of compiling a narrative had nothing to do with language, but only to do with principles of logic, would not the act of oral recitation and committing to memory simply be a waste of time?

In the section which narrates the compilation of the *Kojiki*, the Empress deplores the areas where the *Kuji* departs from the truth, and, in an effort to correct the mistakes of the *Senki*, she commands Yasumarö to edit the *Kuji* which Are had recited from memory. One should acknowledge with respect the august solicitude of the august reign of this Empress in light of the mention here, as well, of the *Kuji*. As Emperor Tenmu [r. 672-686] died before the recording was completed, it was not until the Nara period [710-794] that the ultimate plan for the *Kuji*, which Are had kept preserved orally, was brought to completion. Just as in the endeavor initiated by the previous Emperor, the intent to value the language of antiquity as the essential element is readily apparent in the editing and recording by Yasumarö. Detailed instructions are given throughout: for example, the notes to 高天原 (Takama-nö-Fara, place name) indicate that the character 天 is to be read "*ama*;"[2] the notes to 天比登津柱 (Amë-Fitötu-Fasira, place name) state that 天 is to be read "*amë*,"[3] and elsewhere, even indications of rising and falling pitch accent are given.[4] Therefore, when reading the text today, one should clearly grasp the meaning of what was explained above, and not confuse the issue by adhering too strictly to the idea of one character representing one word.

In regard to treating the text with care and respect, reading the *Kojiki* is a very difficult endeavor which differs from reading the Chinese classics or the texts of later ages. To explain why this is so, since all of the chronicles of antiquity are written in classical Chinese, when one reads a text just as it is, even if each single word is in fact a word of the language of antiquity, the syntax and the phraseology are in the style of classical Chinese, and are not those of the imperial country. In older readings of the *Nihonshoki*, there are many places where words are strung together in the style of the language of antiquity, without regard to their order in the text. These readings, however, would seem to reflect the blending in of the efforts of later generations; that the greater part of it is read in the Chinese style is as I have discussed above.

Generally speaking, up until the Nara period [710-794], people knew the style of the language of antiquity quite well, and, as the language of those times was also of an archaic form, they were easily able to make the distinction between reading in the style of antiquity and reading in the Chinese style. People of later ages, however, having eyes for nothing other than Chinese writings, acquired habits whereby their ears became accustomed to nothing but the Chinese readings, and when it came to matters of style of language, were not able to distinguish between the Chinese style and the Japanese style. <People of the modern age for the most part do not know how to use the language of antiquity; if they were to try to write an example, they would put it all in the style of Chinese, as if they were writing classical Chinese in kana, which is quite unsightly. I have discussed the style of composition in high antiquity and mid antiquity in detail elsewhere.> [5]

One should be aware of this type of error, and read the text seeking the pure language of antiquity, without any contamination by the Chinese style. To wash off and rid oneself of these Chinese customs is part of the undertaking of the study of antiquity. Nonetheless, the method of generations of scholars of interpreting the *Nihonshoki* has merely been to focus on the passages of Chinese ornamentation, and get caught up in nothing but principles. Their easy willingness to let the language of antiquity which lies at the basis of the work pass by almost unnoticed is quite deplorable. To ignore language and to emphasize principle alone is what is found in the texts of the exhortations of Confucianism and Buddhism in foreign countries; the ancient texts of the imperial country do not contain a bit of writing about the teachings of such people, or discussions about the principles of things. No hidden meanings or principles lie beyond the words, which are simply used to record antiquity. <To say that they include teachings which lie beyond the narrative is to adulate the Chinese.>

Furthermore, as the characters themselves are makeshift items which were simply attached to the text, what possible sort of deep reality could they represent? It is only through working through and clarifying for oneself the language of antiquity time and again that one will come to understand the customs of antiquity and thereby realize the true purpose of study. One measures the conditions and character of a people in their way of expressing themselves, and the myriad of things in antiquity is no exception: it is in elucidating and comprehending the language of antiquity that one achieves an understanding. How can one possibly understand the language of antiquity or the conditions of that age if one simply reads, as is, a text that is written in the style of classical Chinese? In looking at the songs of antiquity, one should be able to discern how very different the language and mind of our imperial country is from that of China.

To be sure, it is no easy task to read a text using nothing but the language of antiquity. The reason for this is that all of the old texts are written in classical Chinese, and since there is not a single one written entirely in the language of antiquity, it seems as if there is nothing to grasp onto for assistance, no matter which text one may select. There are, however, places here and there in the chronicles of antiquity where things have been recorded solely in the language of antiquity. The language in the imperial edicts (*mikötö-nöri*) in the *Shoku Nihongi* [797] and in the various *norito* ('Shinto ritual prayers') to be found in Book Eight of the *Engi-shiki* [927] is for the most part pure Japanese, in syntax and in all other aspects, so that one should first of all study these texts to learn the style of the language of antiquity.

One should also read and learn the songs to be found in the *Kojiki*, the *Nihonshoki*, and the *Man'yôshû*. The songs of the *Kojiki* and the *Nihonshoki* are particularly precious and valuable, as they contain not even a droplet of Chinese style and are a reflection of the words and mind of antiquity. <If one looks closely at these songs, one will find that things are not stated to excess, and that the

ways of the world and the inner thoughts of people are known by intuition. They only make the discord of the people of later generations who vocalized everything in theories filled with principles of apparent profundity all the more apparent.> The number of songs is limited, however, and their subject matter is not broad, so they are lacking in some respects, but the *Man'yôshû* has a great number of poems which for the most part are in the language of antiquity. <The readings for this anthology are also the work of people of later generations, and there are many places which contain errors and do not correspond to the language of antiquity. Nonetheless, one should take the poems that are written in kana and compare them with examples from other poems in order to determine the language of antiquity.>

In taking the above mentioned texts as the linguistic norm, one must be aware of several things. First of all, although the archaic language contained in the chronicles of antiquity is very old and refined, there are places where the meaning is uncertain due to particles, auxiliaries, and inflections having been omitted. Next, one occasionally encounters passages written in the style of classical Chinese in the words of the imperial edicts since they were issued from the Nara court. <Until the Nara period [710-794], the spoken language had not adopted any classical Chinese-style expressions, but from rather early on, people were attracted to classical Chinese, and the style of classical Chinese is reflected to some extent in what they wrote down in texts. As Prince Shôtoku [574-622] was very fond of Chinese studies, and since, subsequently, in the reigns of Emperor Kôtoku [r. 645-654] and Emperor Tenji [r. 668-671], China was used as the model for all things, it is only natural that the style of classical Chinese should be reflected in the language of

antiquity which was used for transmission. As the imperial edicts in the *Nihonshoki* are later, they contain words which are also pronounced according to their Chinese sounds. In this respect as well the proclamations of antiquity are very curious. The edicts in the *Nihonshoki* are not those of antiquity; many of them are fabrications which were added at a later date. As they are essentially Chinese, they are very troublesome.>

The various ceremonial *norito* ('Shinto ritual prayers') consist for the most part of language that is quite old, but they have not been handed down to us just as they were in antiquity. The *norito* seem to have been fixed at the AFumi and KiyomiFara courts,[6] and are not entirely devoid of words which reflect the influence of Chinese. <The commonly held belief that the *OFoFaraFë no kötöba* (*Ritual of Exorcism for the Great Purification*)[7] is precisely the same ritual that was created in the reign of Emperor Jinmu [r. 660-585 B.C.] shows an ignorance of antiquity: it contains phraseology from a later period and appears to have been set down much later.[8] The oldest *norito* is that of the *Idumo nö kuni-nö-miyatuko nö kamuFogi* (*Laudatory Ritual to the Kami Offered by the Local Chieftain of Izumo*)>.[9] Therefore, when studying these texts as well one must cull out and discard those passages which are cloaked in the Chinese style.

The language of the songs in the *Kojiki* and the *Nihonshoki* represents the language of antiquity in unadulterated form, but one should take them up with an awareness of the fact that there is a difference between the language of song and the language of prose, so that there will be places in the songs where the language is a bit different. The poems in the *Man'yôshû* represent various styles, and there are many which are quite old. One should be aware, however, of the fact that one occasionally encounters among the songs composed in the Nara period [710-794] a song which, in both spirit and word, is derived from Chinese.

Not all differences in the songs composed in the Nara period [710-794], however, may be attributed to the influence of Chinese. The style of the language of antiquity and the style of the language of subsequent ages differ in many respects. We should define the language of antiquity (*hurukoto*) as the language of the pre-Nara through the Nara periods.[10)] The language of subsequent periods, beginning with the founding of the capital of today, differs in many respects from the language of antiquity, and there are many words which have undergone euphonic change. <The concept of *onbin* ('sound euphony'), whereby one reads examples such as 大御神 *oFomikamï* ('august deity') as *oFongami*, and 臣 *omi* (a *kabane*) as *on*, probably should not be applied in all instances to the Japanese readings of the texts of antiquity. There are many examples of this type of *onbin* in the Japanese readings assigned to the *Nihonshoki*.

Works beginning with the *Kokinshû* [ca. 905], and works written in the *monogatari* prose style are written in the refined style (*miyabigoto*) of mid-antiquity.[11)] Since *monogatari* such as the *Ise monogatari* (*Tales of Ise*) and the *Genji monogatari* (*The Tale of Genji*) were originally written in kana ('syllabary'), they do not reflect the influence of the spirit of Chinese to the same extent as the texts of antiquity, and are thus superior in some respects. To be sure, they contain many words borrowed from Chinese, and many words which retain the Chinese pronunciation, but as they are written in the style of the language of the imperial country, they are not Chinese. I have discussed the style of the texts of mid-antiquity in detail elsewhere.> [12]

It is not the case, however, that all of the words in the language of antiquity differ from the words of the language of subsequent periods; there are many words which remain exactly the same from the age of the gods to mid-antiquity to the present. Therefore, one should not discard a reading simply because one concludes that the pronunciation of the word is the same as that of later ages. <In this respect, when people have a distaste for words which are exactly the same in the later language and try to manipulate such words to make them appear archaic, most such attempts are rather forced and incorrect. In recent times, those who study antiquity make the mistake of assuming that words which they are accustomed to hearing must be words from later ages, and conclude that only unusual words which are strange to their ears are from the language of antiquity.>

There are passages in the texts of antiquity which are difficult to read purely in the archaic language no matter how one conceives it. Since what was originally transmitted in the archaic language was later written down with Chinese characters, one might expect that it would not be a difficult matter to restore the language of the text to the original archaic language. Yet, it is also likely that the archaic language underlying texts which have been copied into classical Chinese and transmitted that way has faded away and not been transmitted.

In antiquity, people in our imperial land did not keenly discriminate between various things or various events and give them names. Ordinarily, verbalization was minimal, yet this was sufficient. China and other countries, however, have the noisome habit of breaking things down in fine detail and naming to the point of excess. It is, therefore, only to be expected that when those texts which convey the gist of a matter are copied down with characters, there will be occasion for people to write things down in accordance with the names for various things. In such instances, even though there were no such words in the archaic language of the original, since it was the custom not to read the characters with their Chinese pronunciation, people must have created new readings in accordance with this custom. <It is most likely that, up until the Nara period [710-794], the practice of reading the various terms for everything with their Chinese pronunciation hardly existed, and people used the Japanese readings, to the extent that this was possible, in reading the Chinese classics as well.>[13] We will therefore define anything which appears prior to the Nara period as the "language of antiquity" (*hurukoto*) even though what is represented in a given text may not necessarily be the pure, unadulterated form of the language of antiquity, and make use of such texts when it is unavoidable.

Many of the words in the *Kojiki*, which was recorded from Are's verbal recitation, sound as if they have been transmitted from antiquity unchanged; at the same time, much of the phraseology seems to reflect the idiom of the times, so that it is difficult to assign a reading in the language of antiquity in all instances. One should, therefore, determine what were the words of Are, and assign a reading based on the sensibilities of antiquity. One should also take note of the fact that the same word appearing in different places may in some cases be completely written out, and in other cases be written in abbreviated form with the omission of one or more characters. In such cases, one should compare the abbreviated forms with those that are fully written out, and read the abbreviated forms in the same way as those that are fully written out. To give an example, the phrase 成坐流神之御名者 *nari-maseru kamï nö mi na Fa* ('the name of the god who came into existence') is written as 成神名,[14] 所成坐神名,[15] and 所成神御名,[16] in which the characters 所, 御 (*mi-*), and 坐 (*-mas-*) have been omitted, respectively, yet each represents the same phrase. <This principle is illustrated in the section where even the coming into existence of the deity Yaso-maga-tu-Fi-nö-kamï, who originated in the pollution of the land of Yömï, is described as 所成坐 *nari-maseru* ('came into existence'), with the honorific verbal suffix 座 (*-mase-*),[17] while the coming into existence of those deities who immediately follow is described merely as 所成, with the honorific 坐 omitted even for Ama-terasu-oFo-mi-kamï.[18] When the same phrase is repeated in succession, one is to give the full reading of the initial expression to all of the abbreviated forms. To be unaware of this convention, and to conclude rashly that the text is in disorder with mistakes is an error.> From the examples 如レ拜二吾前一 *a ga mi-maFe wo ituku ga götö* ("just as you would worship in my very presence"), in the decree spoken by Ama-terasu-oFo-mi-kamï in Book One,[19] and 令レ祭二我御前一者 *a ga mi-maFe wo ituka simëba* ("if [OFo-tata-neko] is made to worship before me"), in the words spoken by OFo-mönö-nusi-nö-kamï in Book Two,[20] we know that the honorific prefix 御 *mi-* is to be read in the first example, even though it has been omitted. The honorifics 御 *mi-*, 坐 *-masu*, 賜 *-tamaFu*, and 奉 *-maturu* are often omitted, and one should compare these with places in which they have been included, and supply the appropriate reading accordingly.

There are also instances where the same word is written in one place in kana, and in another place in classical Chinese: in such instances, the word in classical Chinese is to be read in the same fashion as the word in kana. A case in point is "stood on the Heavenly Floating Bridge," which is written as 立二天浮橋一 (*amë nö uki-Fasi ni tata-si*),[21] and elsewhere as 於二天浮橋一多多志 (*amë nö uki-Fasi ni tatasi*).[22] <The note to the character 立, which indicates that it is to be read "*tatasi*" ('they stood'), 訓レ立云二多多志一 (立 *wo yömite tatasi tö iFu* 'in reading 立, say "tatasi"'),[23] illustrates the general principle that one is to read all examples of this type by following the reading of the passage that is written in kana.>

Other examples illustrate the principle whereby, when the same phrase is written both in the language of antiquity and in classical Chinese, one is to follow the reading for the passage which is written in the language of antiquity. The following are cases in point: the same phrase "defiant people" is found written both in classical Chinese, 不伏人 (*maturoFanu Fitö*),[24] and in the language of antiquity, 麻都漏波奴人 (*maturoFanu Fitö*).[25] In the note to 神世七代 (*kamï nö yö nana yö* "the Seven Generations of the Age of the Gods"),[26] 上二柱、獨神各云二一代一、次雙十神、各合二二神一云二一代一 (*Kamï nö Futa-basira nö Fitöri-gami Fa onö'onö Fitö yö tö iFu. Tugi ni naraberu tö-basira nö kamï Fa onö'onö Futa-basira nö kamï aFasete Fitö yö tö iFu*. 'The two single deities mentioned first are each called one generation. The ten deities which follow form pairs of two deities, and each pair is called a generation.');[27] the reference to the first two deities, 二柱 *Futa-basira* ('two deities'), is in the language of antiquity, while the references to the ten deities, 十神, and the pairs of deities,

二神, are in classical Chinese. One should follow the example which is written in the language of antiquity, and read 十神 as 十柱 *tö-basira* ('ten deities') and 二神 as 二柱 *Futa-basira* ('two deities'). In this fashion, when similar phrases in a given passage are written first in the language of antiquity and then in classical Chinese, one should read the phrases according to the principle set by the phrase that is written in the language of antiquity. All of the examples illustrate this principle. In other passages which give the numbers of deities, the counter for "deity" is written variously as 神 and as 柱: these also are to be read according to the example of antiquity. <In Books Two and Three, the numbers of imperial offspring are always indicated by writing "number" plus "柱 Fasira ('deities');" in light of this, when the numbers of deities are being related, as in 二柱(ノ)神 *Futa-basira nö kamï* ('two deities'), and 三柱(ノ)神 *mi-Fasira nö kamï* ('three deities'), the graph 柱 *Fasira* is sometimes omitted, with the phrase written as 二神(フタバシラノカミ) 三神(ミハシラノカミ) (*Futa-basira nö kamï, mi-Fasira nö kamï*). In such instances, one is to add the word *Fasira* when reading the character 神. One should follow the style of a given passage and read all examples in like fashion.>

There are also passages written completely in classical Chinese, in a style which is quite distant from that of the language of antiquity: one should read such passages by not relying upon the characters too heavily, but rather obtain an understanding of the meaning, and assign a reading in the language of antiquity which is appropriate to the tenor of the passage. The reading given for 顧眄之間, that of 此(ヲ) 云(二) 美屡摩沙可利爾(ミルマサカリニト)(一) (*köre wo miru ma-sakari ni tö iFu* 'this is to be read as "*miru ma-sakari ni*"'), in the first chapter on the Age of the Gods in the *Nihonshoki*,[28] is an example of this method. The reading of *itöFösi-gari-tamaFite* ('found it pitiful') which is assigned to 哀不忍聽 in the chapter on Emperor Sushun [r. 587-592],[29] also illustrates this method, although the reading itself is not given in a note. In the *Nihonshoki*, there are many readings which have been assigned in the language of antiquity, and, as noted in the Urabe commentary,[30] it is indeed true that many were assigned on the basis of readings in the *Kojiki*. Most of the archaic readings which do not depend upon the characters are taken from the words in the *Kojiki*; therefore, it is also the case that in seeking readings now for the *Kojiki*, many should be taken from the readings found in the *Nihonshoki*. This is because the language of antiquity, which is obscured in the *Kojiki* in those passages which are written exclusively in classical Chinese with no sections in kana, may quite unexpectedly be preserved in the readings for the *Nihonshoki*.

The proper mindset one should bring to the reading of the *Kojiki* is as I have discussed above. I shall now discuss those methods in more detail. Words are connected to other words by means of the *teniwoha*,[31] and it is by means of the *teniwoha* that we are able to create the subtle distinctions in meaning of the various syntagmatic relationships between words. The way in which the *teniwoha* are used constitutes an impressive system which allows for the proper connections between words; therefore, when attempting today to read the *Kojiki* in the language of antiquity, we must consider them carefully and determine them correctly. <Chinese does indeed have postpositional particles, but has nothing which corresponds to the *teniwoha*. The function of a particle is merely to assist other words; particles, unlike *teniwoha*, have no role in the creation of fine distinctions in meaning. Therefore, the meaning of

a sentence may be comprehended even if there are no postpositional particles. Since all of the chronicles of antiquity are written in Chinese, in reading them one must determine the *teniwoha* through intuition. In recent times, there are very few who have a clear understanding of the system of *teniwoha*, and for that reason there are always many errors. When one reads merely to grasp the meaning of a passage in Chinese, the meaning of the words assigned for the reading may not differ too markedly, but the arrangement of the *teniwoha* is likely to be quite different, and will not result in refined language *(miyabigoto)*>. To describe the various conventions in the system of *teniwoha* would require a lengthy treatment, and it would be difficult to completely account for them in a simple fashion here. In this matter, one may consult another work in which I have analyzed them in detail.[32)]

The distinctions between voiceless sounds and voiced sounds in kana are as I have described above. If we look at the use of voiceless sounds and voiced sounds in the *Kojiki*, the *Nihonshoki*, and the *Man'yôshû*, the *Kojiki* is especially correct in its representation of these distinctions; therefore, one should preserve these same distinctions between voiceless and voiced sounds when assigning a reading. It will not do for one to simply change the readings in a facile manner; the voiceless/voiced distinctions in many words have changed from antiquity to later ages, and it is therefore difficult to assign readings based on examples of words in the language of the present day. <In examples like 宮人 *miya-Fitö* ('courtier') and 里人 *sato-bitö* ('villager'), the 比 *Fi* of *miya-Fitö* is always written with the voiceless kana 比 *Fi* in the texts of antiquity, while the 比 *Fi* of *sato-bitö* is always written with the voiced kana 毘 *bi*. Therefore, for examples of this type, it is an error to assume that the initial

sound of the second member of a compound is automatically to be voiced. If the voiceless/voiced distinctions are not determined on the basis of the individual word, errors will be the result. The preference of many contemporary scholars of antiquity for voiced sounds, and their consequent voicing of many sounds which in fact should not be voiced in the assumption that this represents the language of antiquity is a mistake. One should assign a reading only after careful observation and comparison of the kana used in the texts of antiquity.>

With respect to the matter of rising and falling accent in the language of antiquity, the character 上 'rising' has been written in smaller size graphs and placed in the midst of things like the names of deities to indicate whether the sound is rising or falling, and this represents a borrowing of the concept of the "four tones" established for Chinese. There are a total of four tonal distinctions made for the sounds of Chinese: 平 ('level'), 上 ('rising'), 去 ('departing'), and 入 ('entering').[33] Our language also has the three accentual distinctions of "level," "rising," and "departing,"[34] if we are to borrow the terms from Chinese. <There is no "entering" accent: I will discuss the precise reasons for this elsewhere.>[35]

As Keichû [1640-1701] has stated, we can understand the meaning of these terms by looking at examples from, first of all, words of one syllable: *Fi* 'day' is level, *Fï* 'water pipe' is rising, *Fï* 'fire' is departing; *kë* 'hair' is level, *ke* 'to kick' is rising, *kë* 'sign' is departing; and, secondly, words of two syllables: *Fasi* 'bridge' is level, *Fasi* 'edge' is rising, *Fasi* 'chopsticks' is departing; *turu* 'string' is level, *turu* 'to fish' is rising, and *turu* 'crane' is departing. According to this theory, the "level" accent neither rises nor falls and is level, the "rising" accent rises, and the "departing" accent falls.

<In China, although they do not say "falling" (下), but rather "departing" (去), the tone is nonetheless one which falls, and the "four tones of the T'ang dynasty" which people speak of today are aberrations which depart from reality.> Keichû also notes that while *kamo* 'wild duck' has a level accent, in *Kamo-gawa* ('Kamo River'), it has a rising accent, and in *Kamo nö yasirö* ('Kamo Shrine'), it has a departing accent, i.e. the same word will undergo a change of accent in composition. When words are uttered in composition in this fashion, not only does the accent of the first word undergo a change, but also that of the latter member changes in like manner. The place name *Kamo* has a departing accent, but when we speak of *Simo-kamo* ('Lower Kamo'), the accent becomes level. Likewise, the bird *kamo* ('wild duck') has a level tone, but in *ma-gamo* ('mallard duck'), it has a rising accent. There are, in addition, differences in sound in all of the various provinces, so that even the same word will not be uttered in the exact same fashion from place to place: in such cases one should regard the forms of the capital and the home provinces as the correct forms, and view forms which differ from those as regional variants.

Now, in consideration of those places in the *Kojiki* where accent has been indicated, most are in Book One, with only a very few in Books Two and Three. Most of the examples in Book One are found in the names of deities, and this is most likely due to the fact that there were many mistakes in recitation, since deity names are not part of ordinary language. Accentual marks are not indicated when a graph is to be read with its original accent, rather, they are indicated only at the point where the accent of a word changes in composition. For example, in the name of the deity 豊(トヨ)雲(クモ)上野(ヌノ)神 (Töyö-kumo-nu-nö-kamï),[36] a rising accent is indicated after *kumo*, which in isolation has a level accent, to indicate that *kumo* in composition, *kumo-nu*, is to be read with a rising accent, and is not to be read mistakenly with the original level accent. The other examples are also to be interpreted in this fashion.

Although one would expect to find indications of a rising accent which changes into a level or departing accent, there are no indications of 平 ('level') or 去 ('departing'). To the question of why one should find only indications of 上 ('rising') accent, the answer may be that in most of the instances in which composition occasions a change in accent, the change is that of a level accent or a departing accent which changes to a rising accent. The change of a rising accent into a level or departing accent is extremely rare. Therefore, when the compilers were marking accent in the *Kojiki*, there may simply have been no instance where it was necessary to indicate a level or departing accent. The single instance of the indication of a 去 ('departing') accent occurs in the mention of the deity names 宇比地邇上神 (U-Fidi-ni-nö-kamï) and 須比地邇去神 (Su-Fidi-ni-nö-kamï);[37] here, in the two successive instances of the same word *Fidi-ni*, the accent of the first *ni* is rising, while the accent of the second *ni* is departing, and there is a sudden change in sound. <This " 邇 *ni*" is the *ni* which means 'earth,' and originally has a departing accent. In the first instance of compositon with *Fidi-ni*, it takes on a rising accent, therefore, this marking of the rising accent (上) is the same sort of marking that occurs in the other examples. One would not, however, expect to find the marking of the departing accent (去) in the second instance of *Fidi-ni*, since the original accent is the departing accent, yet it is so marked out of anticipation that one might be tempted to recite the second instance with a rising accent by analogy with the first example.>

In the many places where the deity name 山津見 (Yama-tu-mi) occurs as the second member in the name of a deity, accent is indicated in some cases, such as 大山$_{上}$津見 (OFo-yama-tu-mi)[38] and 奥山$_{上}$津見 (Oku-yama-tu-mi),[39] while in other cases, such as 淤縢山津見 (Odö-yama-tu-mi) and 闇山津見 (Kura-yama-tu-mi),[40] it is not. When accent is not indicated, one is to read *yama* with its original level tone. The examples 奥津嶋比賣命 (Oki-tu-sima-Fime-nö-mikötö) and 市寸嶋$_{上}$比賣命 (Itiki-sima-Fime-nö-mikötö)[41] are to be interpreted in like fashion. <If the compilers were to follow the example of 須比智邇 (Su-Fidi-ni), wherein they indicated the departing accent, then in these examples as well, when the original accent is maintained, this hould be indicated as "-山$_{平}$" and "-嶋$_{平}$." As for the matter of why they did not choose to do so, the former example occurs at the beginning of the text, where it is easy for one to make a mistake, while the latter examples occur in the midst of a list of deity names ending in 山津見 (-yama-tu-mi), some of which have accent indicated, and some of which do not. In the latter case, it should be easily understood that those in which accent is not indicated are to be read with the original accent. Furthermore, since the former example occurs as a model at the beginning of the text, it should be all the easier to understand examples such as 奥津嶋比賣 (Oki-tu-sima-Fime) and 山津見(-yama-tu-mi)>.

Most of the examples in which accent is indicated are similar to those discussed above. We have seen that in antiquity, people clearly indicated rising and falling of accent in the reading of the names of deities and so forth, and from this example, as well, one should understand that one is in all instances to treat language with the utmost rigor. How, indeed, can people of later generations take only the hollow principles of the Chinese spirit to be the essential truth, and treat the language with neglect, failing to realize that it is something which deserves special attention?

The so-called *zyosi* ('postpositions') are used in various ways in the *Kojiki*. In some cases, they are placed merely as supporting elements to classical Chinese, with no function at all in the language of antiquity, while in other cases, they are used as part of the language of antiquity, with no role to play in classical Chinese. There are still other instances in which they take the shape of classical Chinese, but correspond perfectly well to the language of antiquity. To constantly read all of these in the manner of the Chinese classics is to be in error much of the time; therefore, at this point I will list the types of postpositions, as well as some additional characters which appear frequently, and discuss how to read them.[42)]

〔之〕 This should be read as "能 *nö*" as is customarily the case. There are, however, cases in which one definitely should read it and cases in which one should definitely not read it at all. In general, when it follows inflected words (*hataraki-kotoba*), this is a convention of Chinese, so it is to be discarded and not read, as in 吾所生之子 (*a ga umeru* ○ *mi-ko* 'the child we have borne'),[43)] and 出向之時 (*ide-mukaFu* ○ *töki* 'when she came out to welcome him').[44)] <To read this sort of example as "能 *nö*" is not part of the language of the imperial country. People of later generations who assign a reading of "*nö*" in such places reflect the influence of habits acquired from reading the Chinese classics, and this is incorrect.> When it follows nouns, it should always be read, as in examples of the type 天之某 (*amë nö nani* 'X of the heavens'), 國之某 (*kuni nö nani* 'X of the earth'), or 淡路之穗之狹別 (AFadi-nö-Fo-nö-sa-wakë, child/island name):[45)] this postposition 能 *nö*, written with the graph 之, will certainly clarify the language of antiquity if read when it is meant to be read. Examples where those in later generations have erred in omitting "*nö*" from their reading should be corrected in accordance with the *Kojiki*. <There are many mistaken readings of the type "Kuni-tökö-tati" for the name 國之常立神 (Kuni-nö-tökö-tati-nö-kamï)>.[46] There is one other 之 which was customarily used in the classical Chinese written in Japan in the past: this 之 was always placed at the end of a phrase. This usage differs from the style of writing used by the Chinese, but there are many examples of it in the *Nihonshoki* and other texts as well; this type is definitely not to be read. The 之 in examples of the type 云々之 (○ *wo sikasika su* 'do such and such') is likewise not to be read.[47] There are also many places where 云 and 之 were mistakenly copied for one another: writing 詔云 for 詔之 (*nörasaku* 'announce-HONORIFIC-NOMINALIZER') is one such example.[48] As neither of these are to be found in the language of antiquity, they are not to be read.

〔於〕This character is to be read "邇 *ni*." It is used in phrases of the form 於某 (*nani ni* 'X LOCATIVE'), and there are many examples of this type in the texts of antiquity.[49]

〔者〕This is to be read as "波 *Fa*" as is ordinarily the case. In the example 於今者 (*ima ni* 'still'), only the reading of "伊麻 *ima*" is assigned, and one should not create a separate reading for the character 者.[50] Neither should one read the character 者 found in 者也 (*sö* 'EMPHATIC PARTICLE').[51]

〔而〕This is to be read as "弖 *te*" as is ordinarily the case. In the example 從八十神之教而 (*yaso-gamï nö wosiFesi mama ni site* 'did just as instructed by the eighty deities'), it is to be read as "志 *site*," in the sense of "to do" (爲而 *site*).[52] <It will not do to

read it as "*site*" in every instance, as the meaning will differ. The reading commonly assigned, however, to the above passage of "*wosiFe ni sitagaFite*" ('following the instructions') is not part of the language of antiquity.>

In examples of the type 隋二云々一而 (*sikasika no manima ni* 'X GENITIVE in accordance with'), 隋 is to be read as "麻爾麻爾 *manima ni*," and the character "而" is not to be read.[53] <The character 而 read as "*sitagaFite*" in the style of classical Chinese is added to the text. The character 而 always appears at the head of a phrase in classical Chinese, but in Japanese, it is always attached to the end of a phrase.> [54]

〔矣〕 This is used as the postposition 袁 *wo*. Examples such as 地矣阿多良斯登許曾 (*tökörö wo atarasi tö kösö* 'find the land wasteful') are also quite numerous in the *Man'yôshû*.[55] <Subsequently this usage disappears.> There are also cases where it functions merely as a particle in classical Chinese.[56]

〔乎〕 This is to be read as 夜 *ya*, 加 *ka*, 夜母 *yamö*, or 加母 *kamö*, depending upon the context.[57]

〔哉〕 The readings for this character are for the most part identical to the readings for the character 乎.[58] <The expression "加那 *kana*" is not found in the language of antiquity. Until the Nara Period [710-794], there was no postposition "*kana*." All such examples in the *Man'yôshû* are read as *kamö*, and the rare instances where such postpositions are written with 哉 are also to be read as *kamö*; the reading of *kana* is an error. There are notes in the *Nihonshoki* which give the reading of this character as 伽夜 *kaya* and 柯倿 *kane*.>[59]

〔也〕 This is used solely as a particle in classical Chinese. Most instances are placed in positions which would be suitable for 那理

nari. <Since this particle occurs in places where it would be appropriate to read it as "*nari*" even in the Chinese classics, "*nari*" has come to be the established reading for this character. Until the Nara Period [710-794], there was no fixed convention of using this character to write "*nari*." In the *Man'yôshû*, it is used only as the kana ヤ *ya*; to write "*nari*," only 有 (*nari*) and 在 (*nari*) are used, since *nari* is a result of the shortening of 爾阿理 *ni ari*.>

〔歟〕This is used in places which reflect uncertainty, as is ordinarily the case. It is also used as a particle with the same function as that of 焉 and other like particles.[60] Such examples are to be found in the *Nihonshoki* as well.

〔焉〕This is used solely as a particle in classical Chinese.[61]

〔故〕When it follows a word, this is to be read as 由恵 *yuwe* or 由恵爾 *yuwe ni*, as is customarily the case. <As the following examples demonstrate, this is a very archaic word: (1) in the song from the section in the palace at Karusima: 志波爾波,邇具漏岐由恵 (*siFani Fa niguroki yuwe* 'since the lower clay was dark'),[62] and (2) in the song from the chapter on Emperor Yuryaku [r. 456-479] in the *Nihonshoki*: 耶麼能謎能, 故思麼古喩衛爾 (*Yamanöbe nö Kosimako yuwe ni* 'on account of Kosimako of Yamanobe'.> [63]

At the head of a phrase, this character should be read as 迦禮 *kare*. Such examples are particularly numerous in the *Kojiki*, and most of these examples have nothing to do with the meaning of the character, but rather serve to introduce the following word, and are placed where one would expect to find 於是 *kökö ni* or some such expression.[64] With regard to *kare*, is it not perhaps a shortened form of *kakareba*?[65] *Kakareba* itself derives from *kaku areba* and is an expression which connects a preceding passage to the following passage. The objection that since the shortened form of *kakareba* should be *kareba*, why should *ba* have been omitted is easily refuted by the fact that there are many examples in the language of antiquity in which *ba* has been omitted yet which still retain the meaning of *ba*. <Many such examples are seen in the *Man'yôshû*, and I have discussed them elsewhere.[66] There are also examples found in *tyôka* ('long poem') where one would expect to find 奴禮婆(ヌレバ) (*-nureba*) and 都禮婆(ツレバ) (*- tureba*), yet what actually occurs are the abbreviated forms *-nure* and *-ture*; I will discuss these elsewhere.>

The question of why this character 故 should have been used to write the word *kare* may be answered by looking at other forms which contain the suffix *-ba*: forms such as 祁婆(ケバ) *-keba*, 泥婆(ネバ) *-neba*, 閇婆(ヘバ) *-Fëba*, and 禮婆(レバ) *-reba* in many cases correspond to the meaning of *yuwe* ('because').[67] <When the suffix *-ba* follows the fourth sound of the verbal conjugation,[68] its meaning often corresponds to that of *yuwe* (故): for example, the phrase "*yukeba narikeri*" ('it was because he goes') is equivalent to the phrase "*yuku yuwe narikeri*" ('it was because he goes'), and likewise, the phrase "*areba nari*" ('because it does exist') is equivalent to "*aru yuwe nari*" ('because it does exist').> By analogy, the meaning of *kakareba* ('since it is thus') corresponds to that of *kakaru yuwe* ('since it is thus'), and that is likely the reason why the character 故 was used to write this word. <Since the meaning of the postposition 加良爾(カラニ) (*kara ni* 'because') is close to that of *yuwe* ('because'), one might conclude that *kare* has the same function as *kara*, but that is not the case, and *kara* must be kept separate. The reading of *karu ga yuwe ni* ('therefore') which is assigned to the character 故 which appears at the head of a phrase in the Chinese classics should be regarded as a shortened form of *kakaru ga yuwe*

ni ('accordingly').[69] Or perhaps, given the reading of *sikau site* ('and') which is assigned to the character 而 appearing at the head of a phrase, *karu ga yuwe ni* is the result of the elision of *si* from *sikaru ga yuwe ni* ('therefore').>

〔爾〕This character is used quite frequently, and in most cases is to be read as 許々爾 *kökö ni.*[70] There are also places where it may be read as *kare*. It is the style of the *Kojiki* to place either 於是 *kökö ni*, 故 *kare*, or 爾 *kökö ni* as a conjunction connecting two phrases. In a comparison of the way each of the three is used, one will find that they have simply been chosen in accordance with the flavor of the context, and contain no fixed distinctions in meaning.[71] This is also true in those cases where they occur as the combined forms 故爾 *kare kökö ni* and 故於是 *kare kökö ni.* Most instances of the character 爾 occur in contexts which have the same force as passages with 於是 *kökö ni*, and while there are many instances of it in the combined form 故爾, there are no instances of a combined form 爾於是. One might, therefore, be tempted to conclude that all instances of this character are to be read as *kökö ni*, and none as *kare*. There are also isolated instances of it, however, in passages which have the same force as those which contain the character 故, and in such cases it is preferable to read it as *kare*, rather than *kökö ni*. In passages where the character is exceedingly numerous, some may simply be discarded and not read. <All three expressions 爾, 於是, and 故 have now become dialectal, and occur in the context where one would find 曾許傳 *sökö de* ('therefore'). If one were to read 爾 as *sönö*, then the meaning would correspond to that of *sökö*, and if one were to read 爾時 as *sönö töki* or *könö töki*, the meaning would also correspond. As *könö* and *kökö* are the same, if one reads 爾 as *kökö ni*, this will also correspond to the

meaning of the character. Furthermore, as *kökö* and *kaku* originate from the same form, and since *kare* is derived from *kaku areba*, the reading of *kare* as well corresponds naturally.>[72] The phrase 自レ爾 in Book One should be read either as "*söre yori*" ('after that') or "*köre yori*" ('after this'),[73] and the phrase 爾祟 should be read either as "*sönö tatari*" ('that curse') or "*könö tatari*" ('this curse').[74]

〔乃〕This is to be read as 須那波知 *sunaFati*.[75] Formerly, it was the practice to read this character and also 爾 in classical Chinese as "伊麻志 *imasi*." This was probably the result of a blending with the meaning of 汝 *imasi* ('you/one in front').[76] Yet, there are also the examples from the *Tosa nikki* [ca. 935]: "*imasi Fane to iFu tokoro ni kinu* ('Before long they arrived at a place called Hane')," [77] and "*imasi kamome-mure wite asobu tokoro ari* ('Before long there was a place where flocks of seagulls capered about')."[78] There are other instances which appear to have been placed only for classical Chinese: these are to be discarded and not read.

〔即〕This is used in the same fashion as the character 乃, and it is read in same way.[79]

〔爲〕以爲 is written to express 淤母本須 *omoFosu* and 淤母布 *omöFu*;[80] there are also one or two instances where 爲 is found by itself. It is also found in examples such as the following: 爲レ直二其禍一而 (*sönö maga wo naFosamu tö site* "in order to rectify these evils"),[81] and this is an example where the character 將 would be used in classical Chinese.[82] Examples of the type: 爲レ將レ出二幸上國一 (*uFa tu kuni ni idemasamu tö su* "about to journey to the upper lands"),[83] and 將二爲待攻一而 (*matisemëmu tö site* "intending to ambush")[84] are quite numerous. <The usage here differs from that employed in classical Chinese.>

〔將〕 This is used in the following way: 將レ罷 (*makara-mu* <'go-HUMBLE + PRESUMPTIVE suffix'> 'I will go').[85] It is also used in this fashion in the *Man'yôshû*, and all of the examples are written in the same way, as in 將レ見 (*mi-mu* 'will see') and 將レ聞 (*kika-mu* 'will hear'). There is also the example 將レ殺時 (*körösa-mu tö suru töki ni* "as they were about to kill him');[86] this is the same as the reading in classical Chinese.

〔欲〕 Most instances are used in the same fashion as 將, and are to be read simply as 牟 *-mu*, as in 欲レ爲二力競 (*tikara-kurabe se-mu* 'I desire to have a contest of our strength').[87] There is also the following reading in the chapter on Emperor Kinmei [r. 539-571] in the *Nihonshoki*: 爲レ欲二熟喫一 (*konasi-hama-mu tö su* 'they were crushing [sweet acorns] finely in order to eat [them]').[88]

There are also places where it is to be read as 淤母布 *omöFu*, as in the following example: 欲レ罷二妣國一 (*FaFa nö kuni ni makaramu tö omöFu* "I wish to go to the land of my mother").[89] Many of the examples in the *Nihonshoki* are read in this fashion. <Most of the examples in the *Nihonshoki* which could simply be read as 牟 *-mu* are in fact read as 淤母布 *omöFu* or 淤煩須 *obosu*: this reflects not a difference in meaning, but rather the necessity of conforming to the flavor of the passage.

In the example given above, 欲レ爲二力競一 (*tikara-kurabe se-mu* 'I desire to have a contest of our strength'),[90] if one assigns a reading of "*se-mu tö omöFu* ('I wish to do')" or "*se-ma-ku Forisu* ('I desire to do')," the meaning will be the same, yet such passages are not to be read in this fashion. To decide that since this character is always used to represent 本流 *Foru* ('to desire') or 本理須 *Forisu* ('to desire') in the *Man'yôshû* and other texts, it should always be read in this way in every other text is a mistake.

One must remember that there is no reading other than *-mu* which can be assigned for 欲 in the following examples of *senmyô* ('imperial proclamations') from the chronicles of Emperor Shômu [r. 724-749]: 欲レ奉レ造止思 (*tukuri-matura-mu to omoFu* 'we intended to create'),[91] and of Emperor Kônin [r. 770-781]: 御體欲レ養止奈母所念須 (*mi-mi yasinaFa-mu to namo omoFosu* 'desired to restore his health').[92] When the character 欲 is followed by 思 (*omöFu* 'to desire') or 所念 (*omoFosu* 'to desire-HONORIFIC), how can it possibly be read as "*omöFu*" or "*Forisu*?" In the Chinese classics, all examples are read as 本須 (*Fossu* 'to desire'), a contracted form of *Forisu.* Yet this reading is not appropriate for examples such as the following, said of *Fana* ('flowers'): 欲レ開 (*saka-mu to su* 'to be on the verge of blooming') and 欲レ落 (*tira-mu to su* 'to be on the verge of falling'). One should not use "*Forisu*" when speaking of inanimate things. Since the meaning here is that which is glossed in character dictionaries as 將スルレ然 (*sikara-mu to suru* 'to be about to do such and such'), one should read such examples as "*saka-mu to su*" and "*tira-mu to su.*" To conclude that all examples of 欲 in the ancient texts of Japan are to be read as "*Forisu*" shows that one is thinking merely of the note in character dictionaries which labels it as a word expressing 'expectation,' and is unaware of the passage which glosses the meaning as '*sikara-mu to suru*' ('to be about to do such and such').>

〔以〕 Examples of the type 以二云々一 (*unnun wo* 'such and such + *wo* <POSTPOSITION>') are for the most part to be read as 袁 *wo*. Examples which appear as 云々以 (*unnun-te* 'such and such + *te* <SUFFIX>') are mostly to be read as 弖 te. There are also, on occasion, places where it may be read as 余理弖 *yörite*. In addition, there are many places where it is read in the usual fashion [*möte*]. Of these, there should be those which derive from the language of antiquity, and those which are the result of the influence of reading in the style of classical Chinese. The use of 以 (*möte*) in phrases such as 是以 (*kökö wo möte* 'thereupon') may have originated in reading in the style of classical Chinese, yet even in this case it seems to have been idiomatic from very early on; the expression itself is quite old.[93] Many examples are to be found in the poems of the *Man'yô shû*, and it should be regarded as part of the language of antiquity.

The reading of 母ツ弖 (*motte*) is a corruption of a later age and is not worth consideration. The reading of 母弖 (*möte*) is actually an abbreviated form; the proper reading is 母知弖 (*mötite*). The following examples contain the reading of *möti*: (1) from a song in Book Two of the *Kojiki*, 岐許志母知袁勢 (*kikösi möti wose* "partake of it with pleasure"),[94] (2) from a song in Book Three of the *Kojiki*, 加微能美弖母知, 比久許登爾 (*kamï nö mi-te möti, Fiku kötö ni* 'to the zither played by the divine hands'),[95] and (3) from a poem in book twenty of the *Man'yô shû*, 麻蘇泥毛知, 奈美太乎能其比 (*ma-sode moti, namida wo nögöFi* 'she wipes her tears with her sleeves').[96] <If these examples were from a later age, they would be read "*mote*.">

The following passages contain the form *motite*: (1) from two poems in book three of the *Man'yôshû*, 我袖用手, 將隱乎 (*wa ga sode motite, kakusamu wo* 'I would have hidden [it] in my sleeves')[97] <it is written with the character 用, but the meaning is that of 以>, and 石卜以而 (*isi-ura motite* 'with divination by stones'),[98] and (2) from a poem in book eleven of the *Man'yôshû*, 何有依　以 (*ikanaramu yösi wo motite ka* 'with what sort of connection').[99] <Elsewhere in the *Man'yô shû*, examples containing

the characters 以, 持, and 用 which should be read as "*moti*" have generally been assigned the reading of "*mote*."> It is not an error, however, to assign the reading of "*mote*," as the following examples from books ten and fifteen of the *Man'yôshû* indicate: (1) 手折以而 (*ta-wori mote* 'break off with my hand and hold'),[100] and (2) 奈爾毛能母弖加, 伊能知都我麻之 (*nani mono mote ka, inöti tuga-masi* 'how could I continue my life').[101]

〔所〕 When the verb 生 *umu* 'to give birth' appears as 宇米流 *umë-ru* 'has borne,' or the verb 成 *naru* 'to become' appears as 那禮流 *nare-ru* 'has become,' the character 所 is added to write these forms, as in 所生 *umëru* and 所成 *nareru.*[102] All other instances of these forms are written in the same fashion. In the *Man'yôshû*, these forms are written by adding the character 有, as in 生有 *umëru* and 成有 *nareru*. <To assign a reading of "登許呂 *tökörö*" for the character 所 in such forms is a practice used in reading classical Chinese, and is not part of the language of antiquity.>[103] In the following example, the character 所 in the classical Chinese reading appears in the same place as in the examples like 所生 *umëru* discussed above: 不レ知レ所レ出 (*idemu tökörö wo sirazu* 'not knowing how to get out'),[104] yet the intended meaning of the passage is 不レ知二可レ出之處一 (*idu-bëki tökörö wo sirazu* 'not knowing how to get out'), so it should be read as "*tökörö*." In the following example from the section on the palace of Takatu in Book Three, the character 所 is also to be read as "*tökörö*," since the meaning is that of " 坐所 *masu tökörö* 'the place where [she] was')": 女鳥王之所レ坐 (*Me-döri-nö-miko nö masu tökörö* "the place where Me-döri-nö-miko was").[105]

〔耳〕 To read this character as 能美 *nömï*, as is customarily the case, simply because all instances of this character in the *Kojiki* have been placed according to the conventions of classical Chinese,[106] does not correspond to the language of antiquity. There are other ways in which it should be read. I will use one or two examples to illustrate this point: (1) the passage 欲レ奪二吾國一耳 should be read "吾國袁欲奪登爾許曾阿禮 (*a ga kuni wo ubaFamu tö ni kösö are* "he must wish to usurp my lands")."[107] (2) the passage 愛友故弔來耳 should be read "愛友那禮許曾弔來都禮 (*uruFasiki tömö nare kösö toburaFi-kiture* "I have come to mourn him because I am his beloved friend")" <here, *nare kösö* occurs in the sense of "*nareba kösö* ('because I am')">,[108] (3) the passage 起二邪心一之表耳 should be read "邪心袁起世流表爾許曾阿禮 (*asiki kökörö wo köseru sirusi ni kösö are* "is . . . an omen that . . . has devised some evil plans")."[109] and (4) the passage 是者無二異事一耳 should be read "是者異事無許曾 (*kö Fa kesiki kötö naku kösö* "there is nothing at all strange in this')."[110] In all of the above, the reading of 耳 as *kösö* (EMPHATIC POSTPOSITION) captures the meaning of the character 耳.

Now, one should realize that the following passage: 地矣阿多良斯登許曾, 我那勢之命 爲二加此一 (*tökörö wo atarasi tö kösö, a ga nase nö mikötö kaku siturame* "my brother must have done this because he thought it was wasteful to use the land thus")[111] will have exactly the same meaning if it is rephrased in the following way: 以レ地 爲二可 惜一故, 我那勢之命 爲二可此一 耳 (*tökörö wo atarasi tö omöFu ga yuwe ni, a ga nase nö mikötö kaku situru nömï* 'my brother has only done this because he found the land wasteful'). Why, then, are we not to read this character as *nömi*? To do so will not correspond to the language of antiquity, since in the language of our imperial country, *nömï* only occurs in mid-sentence, and is not used at the end of a sentence to close it. <The opinion

that closing a sentence with *nömï* does not run contrary to the language of antiquity is the mistaken notion of people of later generations whose eyes and ears are accustomed to nothing but the reading of the Chinese classics.>

Although there are examples which end with *nömï*, such as 多儴比等用能美 (*tada Fitöyo nömï* 'just one night only') from a song in the chapter on Emperor Ingyô [r. 412-453] in the *Nihonshoki*,[112] and 但一耳 (*tada Fitöri nömï* 'just one person alone') from book eleven in the *Man'yôshû*,[113] the *nömï* of such examples is a very weighty word. It occurs at the end of the phrases *tada Fitöyo nömï* ('just one night only') and *tada Fitöri nömï* ('just one person alone') in the sense of "not two nights," "not two persons," and as such, is different from the 耳 (EMPHATIC PARTICLE) of classical Chinese which is lightly tossed off. <The reason why the reading of "*nömï*" has been assigned to this character from antiquity is because this character in classical Chinese is called the "definitive" particle, and it occurs in the sense of "this matter is definitive—one need have no doubts at all about it." It is not, therefore, that the reading "*nömï*" is not suitable in classical Chinese, but rather that it is not part of the language of the imperial country to place "*nömï*" in such positions. One must use words constantly keeping in mind the fact that there are differences between our country and that country in the way words are used, and in the position they occupy, even when the meaning of the words is the same.>

〔亦〕There are places where this is read 麻多 *mata*, and places where it is read 母 *mö*.

〔且〕This is used in the same fashion as the character 又 *mata*. <In character dictionaries its meaning is listed as "又" (*mata*).> It is to be read 麻多 *mata*, and the inclination to read it as 加都 *katu* is mistaken. To give an example which will illustrate the distinction between *mata* and *katu*, the meaning of 且 in the following passage from the Chinese classics: 君子有レ酒,多且旨 *(kunsi sake ari, oFoku mata umasi* "the lord has wine, it is plentiful and good")[114] is that of "in addition to . . . is also." The character 且 in such examples should always be read "*mata*;" the reading of "*katu*" is not suitable. The same applies to the 且 which appears at the beginning of a clause. <One also finds the reading of 曾能宇閇 *sono uFe* 'moreover' assigned to the 且 which appears at the beginning of a clause in old books of the Chinese classics, and this is quite appropriate.>

The 且 which means "do X and also do Y" in examples such as: 我歌且謠 (*ware utaFi katu/mata utaFu* "I chant and sing")[115] may be read either as *mata* or *katu*. <Commentary to the ode states: 曲合レ樂曰レ歌,徒歌曰レ謠 'to sing a tune along with musical accompaniment is called 歌; to sing with voice alone is called 謠.'[116] This indicates that the meaning of 歌 and 謡 differ.>

The two incidences of 且 in the examples given above constitute a single word in classical Chinese, but when we read these texts in Japanese, we see that there is the following distinction: *mata* is the broader of the two, and may be used in either context, while *katu* means only "to do X, and also, at the same time, to do Y," and may thus only be used when the context suits this meaning. The meaning of *katu* can be determined by looking at the following example from a poem in the *Ise monogatari* [10th C.]: *katu uramitutu naFo zo koFisiki* ('I am bitter yet I also yearn to see you'),[117] here the meaning is that of '*uramesiku mo arinagara, mata koFisiku mo aru*' ('I am bitter yet I also yearn to see you'). <People in recent times are unaware of this distinction, and read all instances

of 且 as *katu*. The conviction that there is no difference even if one reads 且 as *katu* in places where it should be read *mata* is a result of people's mouths and ears having become accustomed to mistaken readings.>

The outcome of incorrect readings assigned to the character 且 in classical Chinese is that similar errors are made in the writing of our imperial country. I have explored the matter in some detail here because there are many who use *katu* in places where it should not be used. One should simply be aware that the character 且 in the *Kojiki* represents exactly the same thing that would be indicated had the character 又 *mata* been written instead. In addition, there are one or two places where it is to be read 麻豆 *madu*. <I shall discuss the details in their respective sections.>

〔及〕The character 及 which appears in the pattern "X 及 Y" is to be read 麻多 *mata*: the reading of 淤余毘 *oyobi* is used in the reading of classical Chinese, and is not suitable for the language of antiquity.[118] The following examples, in which the characters 及 and 亦 (*mata*) are used in exactly the same fashion, illustrate why 及 is to be read *mata*: (1) 天若日子之父天津國玉神及其妻子 (*Amë-nö-waka-Fiko ga titi Ama-tu-kuni-tama-nö-kamï mata sönö meko* 'Amë-nö-waka-Fiko's father, Ama-tu-kuni-tama-nö-kamï, and also his wife and children'),[119] and, shortly thereafter, (2) 天若日子之父亦其妻 (*Amë-nö-waka-Fiko ga titi mata sönö me* 'Amë-nö-waka-Fiko's father, and also his wife').[120]

The following examples, in which both 及 and 亦 occur in the same phrase, also indicate that they are used in exactly the same manner: (1) 八尺勾玉鏡及草那藝劍亦常世思金神 (*yasaka-nö-maga-tama kagami mata kusanagi nö turugi mata Tökö-yö-nö-o-möFi-kane-nö kamï* 'the *yasaka-magatama* beads, the mirror, and also the sword Kusanagi, as well as Tökö-yö-nö-omöFi-kane-nö-kamï'),[121] (2) 國造亦和氣及稻置 (*Kuni-nö-miyatuko mata Wakë mata Inaki* 'the Kuni-nö-Miyatuko, the Wakë, and also the Inaki').[122] <However, in considering why he did not repeat 亦 but instead used 及 for one of the instances, one might offer the following hypothesis. Since there was the inclination to read such passages as *oyobi* due to the early influence from reading in the style of classical Chinese, perhaps he felt the repetition of *mata* to be obstreperous, and therefore wrote down 及 for one of the instances with the intention of reading it as *oyobi*. Yet, if that were the case, then there would have to be some indication of the intent to read all such passages in this way, so this interpretation fails.>

For those who find the reading of *mata* to be completely unsatisfactory, one may read it as 登 *tö* or 波多 *Fata*, or each instance as 母 *mö*, in accordance with the context of the passage. There will be some instances which should be discarded and not read. At any rate, one should not read it as *oyobi*.

〔可〕For the most part, this is read in the customary fashion of 倍志 *bësi.*[123] There are also rare instances where it should be read otherwise, such as 可還 (*kaFeri-mase* "you must come back"),[124] where it is read as *-mase* (HONORIFIC-IMPERATIVE).

〔勿〕This is used in the meaning of "不" (NEGATION), and is to be read as "受 -*zu*." There are many examples of this in the *Nihonshoki* as well. <Although this particle, which is always glossed as the particle of prohibition, is used in contexts where it would be appropriate to read it as 那加禮 *nakare* ('do not'), it is not used in this fashion in the *Kojiki.*[125] All instances of this particle in the *Kojiki* are in places where one would find the character 不 ('NEGATIVE').>[126] The reading of "*sika-sika suru koto nasi*" ('no instance of doing X') may sound suitable, but the reading "*sika-sika sezu*" ('not doing X') is the correct one. <Furthermore, the use of the characters 非 ('not so')[127] and 不 ('NEGATIVE') are to be differentiated. Most of the instances of 非 being used when 不 should be used instead in the texts of antiquity are in examples of this type.>

〔雖〕 This should be read as 杼母 *dömö* or 登母 *tömö*. <In the Chinese classics, this character is read as 伊閇杼母 *iFedömö* ('even if') or 伊布登母 *iFudömö* ('even if'), and this is also found in the language of antiquity. Most of the examples in the language of antiquity occur in conjunction with *iFu*, and such examples are also found in the language of later ages. The difference in whether it co-occurs with *iFu* or occurs alone is akin to the difference in saying "*arazu to iu koto nasi*" ('there is no instance where it does not occur') where one should say "*arazaru koto nasi*" ('there is no instance where it does not occur').>

〔是〕 This is to be read as 許禮 *köre* or 許能 *könö*, as is the common practice. Or, alternatively, to say merely 許 *kö* for 許禮 *köre* is a feature of the language of antiquity. <This is the same sort of example as saying 曾 *sö* for 其 *söre*, and 和 *wa* for 吾 *ware*.> There are also many instances in which 許々 *kökö* is to be read instead of 許禮 *köre*. <This is the equivalent of saying 曾許 *sökö* for 其 *söre*.> There are also places which should be written as 於是 *kökö ni*, but are instead written with the single character 是 *kökö ni*. The character "是" in examples such as 天菩比神是可遣 *Amë-nö-Fo-Fi-nö-kamï köre yaru bësi* ('We should send Amë-nö-Fo-Fi-nö-kamï'),[128] and 八重言代主神是可白 *Ya-Fe-kötö-sirö-nusi-nö-kamï köre mawosu bësi* ("Ya-Fe-kötö-sirö-nusi-nö-kamï will say"),[129] resembles the usage of classical Chinese, but it is not quite the same. It is the language of antiquity, and should be read 許禮 köre. <That is to say, it differs from the sense in which it is used in classical Chinese.[130] In this case, one first introduces a name, and then follows it with something like "*sate könö kamï sikazika*" ('and then this deity . . .'). This is used in elaboration, as if one were to say "*Amë-nö-Fo-Fi-nö-kamï tö iFu kamï ari, könö kamï yaru bësi*" ('There is a deity named Amë-nö-Fo-Fi-nö-kamï. We should send this deity.'>

〔其〕This is to be read 曾能 *sönö* as is customarily the case. As it is used quite extensively, however, there also instances where it is to be discarded and not read. There are also places where it corresponds to the character 彼, and may be read either as 曾能 *sönö* or 加能 *kanö*, and places where it will be correct to read it as 許能 *könö*. There are also instances where this character is used for 曾禮 *söre* to indicate something which has been discussed above, as in the following example: 如魚鱗所造之宮室、其綿津見神之宮者也 (*sakana nö iroko nö götö tukureru miya, söre wata-tu-mi-nö-kamï nö miya nari* "a palace made as if with the scales of fish. This is the palace of Wata-tu-mi-nö-kamï").[131] One also finds examples of the same sort in the *monogatari* texts of mid-antiquity, where there are many places which introduce a personal name or the like, and follow it with "*sore sikazika*" ('that/he etc.'). This use of *söre* should therefore be regarded as part of the language of antiquity.

〔相〕This should be read 阿比 *aFi*, as is the customary practice. There are a great many instances of this character, and some of these should be discarded and not read.

〔竟〕This should be read 袁波理弖 *woFarite*, or 袁閇弖 *woFete*, or 波弖々 *Fatete*, and so forth. There are also places where these readings will cause difficulty, and in such cases, it is to be discarded and not read.

〔訖〕 This is used in exactly the same fashion as the character 竟, and the reading is also the same.

〔至〕 For the most part, this is to be read simply as 麻傳 *made*; places where it is to be read as 伊多流麻傳 *itaru made* are extremely rare. In the following example, the meaning is that of 至レ到 *itaru made* ('until reaching'): 八拳須至二于心前一 *ya-tuka Figë muna-saki ni itaru made* ("until his beard eight hands long extended down over his chest").[132] <This is because the meaning here is that of "until becoming the age at which his beard had reached down to his chest," and the "*itaru*" here is the *itaru* ('extending, reaching') of the "beard reaching down to his chest." The "*made*" is the *made* ('until') of "until becoming the age." In this instance, the reading of *itaru made* differs from the ordinary simple reading of *made*.>

〔到〕 As is customary, there are instances where this is to be read 伊多流 *itaru*, but there are also instances where it is to be read as 由久 *yuku* or 伊傳麻須 *idemasu* and the like.[133]

〔臨〕 This character is used for the most part as a particle in classical Chinese, and to read it as 能叙牟 *nozomu* as is customarily the case is not part of the language of antiquity. It should be given a reading which is appropriate to the context in which it is found, as in the following examples: the passage 臨二産時一 should be given the reading 産時爾那理弖 (*ko umu töki ni narite* "when they bear young"),[134] and the passage 懷妊臨産 should be given the reading 壞妊阿禮麻佐牟登須 (*Faramaseru mi-ko aremasamu tö su* "<the child which she> was carrying was about to be born").[135]

〔各〕There are places where it is suitable to read this as 淤々能々 *onö'onö* or 淤能母淤能母 *onömö'onömö* as is customarily the case. There are also places where it should be read as 阿比 *aFi*, 美那 *mïna*, or 迦多美邇 *katami ni*, depending upon the context.[136)]

〔諸〕When this character appears at the end of a word or phrase, it represents the language of antiquity, and is to be read 毛々呂々 *mörömörö*, as in the following examples: 天神諸 (*ama tu kamï mörömörö* "the heavenly deities, all"),[137)] 八百萬神諸 (*yaFoyörödu nö kamï mörömörö* "all the eight-hundred myriad deities"),[138)] and 御子達 諸 (*mi-ko-tati mörömörö* 'his children, all').[139)]

When it appears at the head of a word, as in such examples as 諸人, 諸国, and 諸神, there will be some expressions which are part of the language of antiquity, and others which are classical Chinese. Since the expression 毛呂比登 (*möröFitö* 'all of the people') is found in the *Man'yôshû*, 諸人 *(möröFitö)* is part of the language of antiquity. Expressions such as 諸国 appear to be classical Chinese: in the *Nihonshoki* and other texts they are given readings like 久爾具爾 (*kuniguni* 'countries'), and such examples in the *Kojiki* should be read in this fashion. The expression 諸神 should be read as 迦微多知 (*kamï-tati* 'deities') or, by analogy with the example of *kuniguni* ('countries'), as 迦微賀微 *kamïgamï* ('deities'). < The reading of "毛呂加微 *mörökamï*" is in all likelihood erroneous.>[140)] In all instances, the reading of "毛呂某" (*mörö-nani* 'all X' will be suitable in some cases and unsuitable in others. The reading of "毛呂毛呂能某" (*mörömörö nö nani* 'all X'), on the other hand, may be applied to any example.

〔於是〕This is to be read 許々爾 (*kökö ni*). <This corresponds to the phrase 曾許傳 *sökö de* which is used in places of emphasis in the present-day rural vernacular.> In Book One, there are passages where one should say " 在二于此處一" (*kökö ni ari* 'is here'), but which are instead written as 於是有 (*kökö ni ari*).[141] These differ from the rest of the examples, and are to be found here and there throughout the *Kojiki*.

〔是以〕This is read 許々袁母弖 (*kökö wo mote*).[142] This phrase does not sound as if it were originally part of the language of the imperial country, and probably has its origins in placement as a device for reading the Chinese classics. Nonetheless, it does sound like something from remote antiquity, and its usage is quite old. The reading of 許々袁 (*kökö wo*), rather than that of 許禮袁 (*köre wo*), is the one that is suitable for the language of antiquity. <In antiquity, it was more common to say 曾許 (*sökö*) than 曾禮 (*söre*), and to say 許々 (*kökö*) rather than 許禮 (*köre*). In the *Man'yôshû*, where one would expect to find 曾禮由惠爾 (*söre yue ni*), one finds 曾許由惠爾 (*sökö yue ni*): this is the same sort of thing as saying 許々毛閇婆 (*kökö moFeba*) where one would expect to find 許禮袁思閇婆 (*köre wo omöFeba*). In reading the Chinese classics today, the reading that we give for 是以 of 許々袁母弖 (*koko wo motte*) is a rare remnant from the *kun* readings of antiquity. There are many other such examples where a form that is not attested in pre-Nara Japanese texts is preserved in the readings assigned to the Chinese classics, and one must exhaust all possibilities when searching for readings.>

〔故爾〕This is to be read 迦禮許々爾 (*kare kökö ni*).[143] 故 (*kare*) is an expression which is used lightly.

〔即爾〕The character 爾 is to be discarded and not read.[144]

〔爾即〕Here, as well, the character 爾 is not to be read.[145]

〔云爾〕There is just one instance of this in Book Two, at the end of an utterance, and it is to be read simply as 伊布 (*iFu* 'said').[146] The character 爾 is to be discarded and not read.

〔如此〕This is read as 迦久 (*kaku*). The expression 迦久能碁登 (*kaku nö götö* "thus") is also part of the language of antiquity, and appears in a song of the Emperor of Asakura Palace [Yûryaku, r. 456-479].[147] In general, however, it is to be read only as 迦久 (*kaku*).

〔然而〕This should be read 斯加志弖 (*sikasite*). <The practice of reading this in the Chinese classics as 斯加宇志弖 (*sikausite*), with the sound 宇 (*u*) added for euphony (*onbin*) is part of rustic language.> It may also be read as 佐弖 (*sate*). There are examples of 然而毛 (*satemo*) in the *Man'yôshû*; it is quite common to shorten 斯加 (*sika*) to 佐 (*sa*). <Along these lines, 佐弖 (*sate*) is actually 斯加弖 (*sikate*), which gives one the feeling that something is missing, but such is not the case. The form 佐弖 (*sate*) is the shortened form of 斯加阿理弖 (*sika arite*): 阿 (*a*) is elided to form 斯加理弖 (*sikarite*), and the further elision of 理 (*ri*) yields 佐弖 (*sate*), with each stage of elision independently motivated. One may well ask whether one might then read this as 斯加理弖 (*sikarite*), but there are no examples with this reading to be found.>

〔然後〕This is to be read either as 斯加志氏能知 (*sikasite nöti*) or 佐弖能知 (*sate nöti*).[148]

〔以爲〕This is to be read 淤母布 (*omö Fu*) or 淤母本須 (*omoFosu*). <The forms 淤煩須 (*obosu*) for 淤母本須 (*omoFosu*) and 淤煩由 (*oboyu*) for 淤母本由 (*omoFoyu*) are corrupted forms

created through sound euphony (*onbin*), and should not be assigned as readings in the *Kojiki* and other early texts. >

〔所謂〕 This is to be read 伊波由流 (*iFayuru*), as it is the same sort of expression as 所有 (*arayuru*). <There are those who think that this is a reading that is used for the Chinese classics, but such is not the case; it is part of the language of antiquity prior to the Nara period [710-794]. The expression 伊波由流 (*iFayuru*) is in fact the same as 伊波流々 (*iFaruru*), and the expression 阿良由流 (*ara-yuru*) the same as 阿良流々 (*araruru*). There are many instances in the *Man'yôshû* and other texts of the substitution of 良流 (*-yuru*) for 流々 (*-ruru*), and therefore this is an expression from great antiquity. It is to be used both following an item, as in "某といはゆる" (*nani to iFayuru* '"X" is said'), and "いはゆる某" (*iFayuru nani* 'so-called X'). Although the latter usage is a bit less certain, one can assume that people were accustomed to this usage from antiquity, since it is found in the *monogatari* texts of mid-antiquity.>

〔所由〕 This is to be read 由恵 (*yuwe*).

〔所以〕 This is to be read 由恵 (*yuwe*).

〔者也〕 In most instances, this is found in a place where one should read it as 那理 (*nari*), which is the same reading one would give were the character "者" not used. There are also rare instances where it has been used in the meaning of "神也" (*kamï nari* 'deity + Copula'), and in such instances, the reading of 迦微那理 (*kamï nari* 'deity + Copula') should be assigned.[149)]

〔故於是〕 This is to be read in the same fashion as 故爾, 迦禮許々爾 (*kare kökö ni*).

〔故是以〕 This is to be read 迦禮許々袁母弖 (*kare kökö wo möte*).[150)] It occurs in the Chapters on Emperor Tenmu [r. 672-

686] in the *Nihonshoki*,[151] and there are many instances of it in the imperial proclamations of the *Shoku Nihongi* as well. It is, therefore, likely to be an old expression.

〔何由以〕This is to be read as 那叙 (*nazö*), 那杼 (*nadö*), 伊加傳 (*ikade*), or 伊加爾志弖 (*ika ni site*), depending upon the context. The same is true for 何由, 何故, 何以, and others of this sort: to read them simply according to each character is not part of the natural style of our language.[152]

〔詔之〕〔告之〕〔白之〕<The character 之 in each of these is written with "云" in the Nobuyoshi manuscript. All other manuscripts, however, have "之," so we will retain it for the present.>〔告言〕〔白言〕〔問曰〕〔答曰〕〔答詔〕〔答告〕〔答言〕〔答白〕〔誨告〕〔誨白〕〔議云〕〔議白〕To read all of these, as is the common practice, strictly according to the characters, will not conform with the style of the language of antiquity. One should read 詔之, 告之, and the like in accordance with such examples found in the *senmyô* ('imperial edicts') of the *Shoku Nihongi* [797] as 詔賜都良久 (*nöritamaFituraku* 'issued an imperial edict/said-HONORIFIC'),[153] and 詔豆良久 (*nöritamaFituraku* 'issued an imperial edict/said-HONORIFIC').[154] 白之, 白言, and the like are to be read in accordance with 白都良久 (*mawosituraku* 'said-HUMBLE') in Book One of the *Kojiki*.[155] 議云, 議白, and the like are to be read in accordance with 謀家良久 (*Fakarikeraku* 'plotted') in the *senmyô*.[156] <都良久 *-turaku* is 都流 *-turu*, and 家良久 *-keraku* is 祁流 *-keru*.>[157]

For the most part, the others should be read in accordance with the examples above: 問曰 should be read 斗比祁良久 (*toFikeraku* 'asked'),[158] 答曰 should be read 許多閇祁良久 (*kötaFëkeraku* 'answered'),[159] 答詔 should be read 許多閇多麻比都良久 (*kötaFë-tamaFituraku* 'answered-HONORIFIC'),[160] 誨告 should be read 袁志閇多麻比都良久 (*wosiFëtamaFituraku* 'taught-HONORIFIC'),[161] and so forth. In places where it is troublesome to read them with 都良久 (*-turaku*) and 祁良久 (*-keraku*), one may read 詔之 and the like as 能理多麻波久 (*nöritamaFaku* 'issued an imperial edict/said-HONORIFIC'), and 白言 and the like as 麻袁佐久 (*mawosaku* 'said').[162]

There are many instances where it will be troublesome to read the character 答 with its ordinary reading of 許多閇 (*kötaFë* 'answer'); in such instances, 答詔 should be read 能理多麻波久 (*nöri-tamaFaku* 'issued an imperial edict/said-HONORIFIC'), 答白 should be read 麻袁佐久 (*mawosaku* 'said-HUMBLE'), and so forth.[163] In the texts of antiquity, the character 告 is used to represent the word 能流 (*nöru* 'issue a proclamation/say'), and since it is used in the same meaning as the character 詔 in the *Kojiki*, the reading should also be the same as that of 詔.[164]

In regard to the matter of assigning abbreviated readings to the second member in all of the expressions above, 詔之 is to be read as 云々登詔多麻布 (*sikasika tö nöritamaFu* 'X QUOTATIVE issue an imperial edict/say-HONORIFIC'), 問曰 is to be read as 云々登問 (*sikasika tö toFu* 'X QUOTATIVE ask'), and so forth, depending upon the force of the passage.

In reading passages of the sort where one finds 詔 云々 (*nö-ritamaFaku sikasika* 'said-HONORIFIC X'), 曰云々 (*iFaku sikasika* 'said X'), 白 云々(*mawosaku sikasika* 'said-HUMBLE X'), and the like, one must follow the practice of antiquity whereby one first assigns a reading of 詔 (*noritamaFaku* 'issued an imperial edict/said-HONORIFIC'), 曰 (*iFaku* 'said'), and 白 (*mawosaku* 'said-HUMBLE'), and then, at the end of the quotation〔云々〕, adds the expressions 登能理多麻布 (*tö nöritamaFu* 'QUOTATIVE issued an imperial edict/said HONORIFIC'), 登伊幣理 (*tö iFeri* 'QUOTATIVE said'), and 登麻袁須 (*tö mawosu* 'QUOTATIVE said-HUMBLE').[165] The texts of antiquity were all written in classical Chinese, and do not, therefore, contain these expressions, but such expressions are found in all works where the language of antiquity has been written down in unadulterated form. In the *Kojiki*, one finds such examples as the following: 詔 云,豊葦原之水穗國者,云々有祁理 告 而 (*nöritamaFaku, Töyö-asi-Fara-nö-midu-Fo-nö-kuni Fa . . . arikeri tö nöritamaFite* 'he said: "Töyö-asi-Fara-nö-midu-Fo-nö kuni is . . . ," thus saying'),[166] and 詔 云,此地者云 々 甚吉 地 詔 而 (*nöritamaFaku, kökö Fa . . . ito yöki tökörö tö nöritamaFite* 'he said: "This . . . is a very fine place," thus saying').[167] <One must remember that all other examples are to be assigned readings which correspond to these examples.>

Further examples which exhibit this same sort of quotative pattern are numerous; the following are representative: (1) in the "Laudatory Ritual to the Kami Offered by the Local Chieftain of Izumo":"乃 大穴持命乃申給久, 云々 申天 (*sunaFati oFonamoti no mikoto no mawositamaFaku sikasika to mawosite* 'Then Oho-namoti-no-mikoto said: "X" QUOTATIVE, thus saying'),[168] (2) in the *norito* "Ritual to Dispel a Malevolent Kami:" 諸神等皆量 申久,天穗日之命乎遣而,平氣武止申支 (*kamitati mina Fakari mawosaku Ame-no-Fo-Fi-no-mikoto wa tukaFasite kotomukemu to mawosiki* 'The deities all deliberated and said: "We will send Ame-no-Fo-Fi-no-mikoto to subdue them," QUOTATIVE, thus saying'),[169] (3) in the *senmyô* of the *Shoku Nihongi*: 云天在良久,云々云利 (*iFite araku . . . to iFeri* 'as is stated . . . QUOTATIVE is stated'),[170]

(4) 謀家良久, 云々等謀家利 (*Fakarikeraku . . . t o Fakarikeri* 'they plotted . . . QUOTATIVE they plotted'),[171] (5) 是東人波常爾云久, 云々止云天 (*kono adumabito Fa tune ni iFaku . . . t o iFi-te* 'The Aduma-bito always say . . . QUOTATIVE they say'),[172] (6) in songs as well, in the *Man'yôshû*, Book 9: 吾妹兒爾, 告而語久, 云々登, 言家禮婆 (*wagimoko ni nörite kataraku . . . tö iFikereba* 'He said to his wife . . . QUOTATIVE, and since he said'),[173] (7) in Book 13: 里人之, 吾丹告樂, 云々登, 人曾告鶴 (*satobitö nö are ni tuguraku . . . tö Fitö zö tugeturu* 'The villagers told me . . . QUOTATIVE, the people did tell me'),[174] and (8) in Book 17: 乎登賣良我, 伊米爾都具良久, 云々等曾, 伊米爾都氣都流 (*wotömera ga imë ni tuguraku . . . tö zö imë ni tugeturu* 'a girl told me in a dream . . . QUOTATIVE so indeed she did tell me in a dream').[175]

This sort of pattern is found not only in the language of antiquity, but also in the texts of mid-antiquity. <In the *Kokinshû* [ca. 905]: 親王の云けらく, 狩して天川原に至る, といふ心をよみて, 盃はさせと云ければ (*Miko no iFikeraku, kari site ama no kawara ni itaru, to iFu kokoro wo yomite, sakaduki Fa sase to iFikereba* 'The Prince said: "Offer the sake cup with a poem on the theme of reaching the riverbed of heaven after hunting," QUOTATIVE as he said');[176] in the *Tosa nikki* [ca. 935]: かぢとりの云やう, 黒き鳥のもとに, 白き波をよすとぞ云 (*kaditori no iFu yoo, kuroki tori no moto ni sirokinami wo yosu to zo iFu* 'As the oarsman said: "Beneath the black birds, white waves approach," QUOTATIVE he said');[177] and in *Genji monogatari* [ca. 1010], in the Tamakazura chapter: 此男どもを召取て, かたらふことは, おもふさまになりなば, 同じ心に, いきほひをかはすべきこと, などかたらふに (*kono wotoko-domo wo yobitorite, kataraFu koto Fa, omoFu sama ni narinaba, onazi kokoro ni, ikiFoFi wo kaFasu beki koto,*

nadi kataraFu ni 'He summoned the sons to him and what he said was: "If things turn out as I wish, then, in the same spirit, I will share some of my power with you," as he spoke').[178] There are many such examples.> The readings for these expressions are to be assigned in parallel fashion as indicated above.

<Even when writing today, we do not always deviate from this convention. Nonetheless, in the minds of people today, placing a word for the second time at the end of a sentence when one has already used it at the beginning is simply a troublesome and inferior repetition of words. People seem to prefer to omit the second instance at the end, and simply close the sentence with "*to*" (QUOTATIVE). This is due to the cleverness of the readings of Chinese writing in recent times, and is a mistake. One will find that readings like トイヘリ (*to iFeri* 'QUOTATIVE [he] said') have consistently been assigned in the *kunten* (Japanese reading) manuscripts of the Chinese classics. In fact, there are just one or two examples which end in *to* alone, such as the following from the *Kokinshû* [ca. 905]: (1) 此歌は, 或る人の云く， 柿本人まろがなりと (*Kono uta Fa, aru Fito no iFaku, Kakinomoto no Fitomaro ga nari to* 'This poem, some say, is a poem of Kakinomoto no Hitomaro QUOTATIVE'),[179] and (2) ならのみかどの御歌なりと(*Nara no mikado no oFomu-uta nari to* '[Some say that this is] a poem of the Nara Emperor QUOTATIVE').[180] These are examples which occur in notes to the left of the poems, and since no words follow them, they are not so displeasing to the ear. If one simply terminates such examples with "*to*" when words follow, however, the result will be that both the preceding and subsequent portions will be in discord. I have treated this in exhaustive detail because the people of today,

with their clever minds, are in error with regard to these expressions.>

Notes

1) Here Motoori is paraphrasing, rather than quoting from directly, one section of Yasumaro's preface to the *Kojiki* (*Kojiki*, NST 1:14).

2) *Kojiki*, NST 1:18, lines 1-2.

3) *Kojiki*, NST 1:24, line 7.

4) See note 34 below.

5) This discussion can be found in Motoori's *Kogo shinan*, MNZ 14:645-657.

6) The capital was moved to the province of AFumi (Ômi) after the death of Empress Saimei (r. 655-661) in 661 by Crown Prince Tenji (Emperor Tenji, r. 668-671), and the court was called the Siga-no-OFotu-no-miya. During the reign of Emperor Tenmu (r. 672-686), the capital was in Asuka, and the court was called the Asuka-KiyomiFara-no-miya.

7) For text in translation and discussion, see Felicia Gressit Bock, trans., *Engi-Shiki: Procedures of the Engi Era*, Books VI-X (Tokyo: Sophia University, 1972), 84-88.

8) Motoori subsequently wrote a commentary on this *norito* titled *Oho-harai no kotoba kôshaku* (1795), MNZ 7:75-163.

9) For text in translation and discussion, see Bock, trans., *Engi-Shiki: Procedures of the Engi Era*, Books VI-X, 102-105. Motoori subsequently also wrote a commentary on this *norito* titled *Izumo no kuni-miyatsuko kamuyo-goto kôshaku* (1792), MNZ 7:15-74.

10) Motoori termed the language of the pre-Nara and the Nara periods *huru-koto*, that of the Heian period and the refined language of poetry in subsequent periods *miyabigoto*, and the colloquial language of later periods *satobi-goto* (Nakada Norio and Tsukishima Hiroshi, "Kokugo-shi," in Kokugo-gakkai, eds., *Kokugogaku daijiten* <Tôkyôdô, 1980>, 402). Nakada and Tsukishima argue that although Motoori recognized a division of language based on historical time periods, his division did not reflect a scientific observation

of language as undergoing change over time, since he had the proclivity to view the language of antiquity as representing the pure, "correct" form of Japanese. Other Edo period nativists such as Kamo no Mabuchi (1697-1769) in his *Goi* (1769) distinguished three types of language in general: *miyabigoto*, the language of antiquity and the "correct" language in use at the time; *tsunekoto*, language in everyday use which was without errors, but not refined; *satobigoto*, language marked by regional accent and provincial expressions (Nagayama Isamu, "Zokugo," in Kokugogakkai, eds., *Kokugogaku jiten* <Tôkyôdô, 1955>, 604).

11) See note 10 above.

12) See note 5 above.

13) In Ôno Susumu's estimation, it is inaccurate to state that people read the Chinese classics by assigning Japanese readings to them. In looking at Japanese readings assigned to Buddhist sutras from the beginning of the Heian period (794-1185), one finds that the Chinese reading is the reading which has been assigned to the characters in a great many instances, rather than the Japanese reading. Ôno notes that this is something which has come to light as the result of great strides made by post-war scholarship on *kanbun-kundoku* (reading a Chinese text as Japanese) (*Kojiki-den*, MNZ 9:523, supplementary note "page 35, line 12").

14) *Kojiki*, NST 1:18, line 1, and elsewhere. This reference is to the first instance of this phrase, which is found in the first sentence in the text.

15) *Kojiki*, NST 1:38, line 12. Aoki et al. note that heretofore, the same phrase has been written simply as 所成神名. Here, we find that 坐 (*-mas-*) has been added to the text as an honorific. These appended words (*yomisoe go*) function as guides to the reading, and are to be applied to all similar constructions throughout the text (*Kojiki*, NST 1:38, footnote 7). This is the same principle being articulated by Motoori in this section.

16) *Kojiki*, NST 1:46, line 2, and elsewhere. Aoki et al. note that this is the first time for the word 名 (*na* 'name') to appear with the honorific prefix 御 (*mi-*) (*Kojiki*, NST 1:46, footnote 3). Some of the manuscripts lack this prefix.

[17] This is the same example cited in note 15 above (*Kojiki*, NST 1:38, line 12).

[18] *Kojiki*, NST 1:40, line 8.

[19] *Kojiki*, NST 1:96, lines 9-10. Aoki et al. read 拝 ('worship') as *worö-gamu*, rather than *ituku*, due to the fact that what immediately follows this clause is *ituki-mature* ('worship-HUMBLE-IMPERATIVE'), written in *on* phonograms, and it would be an exception to the general practice of writing in the *Kojiki* to have the same word appear in the same passage written in phonograms in one instance, and with a logogram in the other. The meaning of *ituku* is 'to observe purification in reverence to the power of the gods or the emperor', while the meaning of *worögamu* is 'to bow in gratitude' (*Kojiki*, NST 1:514, supplementary note "拝"). Philippi, *Kojiki*, 140.

[20] *Kojiki*, NST 1:148, line 11. The reading assigned by Aoki et al. to this passage differs slightly: *wa ga maFe wo matura-simëba*, and lacks the honorific prefix 御 (*mi-*), as it does not appear in the Shinpukuji-bon manuscript (*Kojiki*, NST 1:148, footnote 4). Philpi, *Kojiki*, 201.

[21] *Kojiki*, NST 1:20, line 6; Philippi, *Kojiki*, 49.

[22] *Kojiki*, NST 1:80, line 15; Philippi, *Kojiki*, 120.

[23] *Kojiki*, NST 1:20, line 6. Philippi does not translate the *kuntyû* ('notes on readings').

[24] *Kojiki*, NST 1:128, line 4; Philippi, *Kojiki*, 177.

[25] *Kojiki*, NST 1:180, line 5; Philippi, *Kojiki*, 205, translated as "disobedient people."

[26] *Kojiki*, NST 1:20, lines 2-3. Aoki et al. omit *nö*. Philippi, *Kojiki*, 48.

[27] *Kojiki*, NST 1:20, line 4. Aoki et al. read *Futa-Fasira* rather than *Futa-basira*, *onömö'onömö* rather than *onö'onö*, and *tö-Fasira* rather than *tö-basira*. Philippi's translation appears on page 48.

[28] *Nihonshoki*, Vol. 1, NKBT 67:89, lines 7-8.

[29] *Nihonshoki*, Vol. 2, NKBT 68:167, line 7. Sakamoto et al. read *itö Fösi-gari-tamaFu*.

[30] The *Shaku Nihongi*, mid-Kamkura period (1185-1333), compiled by Urabe Kanekata (13th century). This commentary represents the culmination

of research done on the *Nihonshoki* by the Urabe family, known for the study of Shinto in the Kamakura period (Maeda Tomiyoshi, "*Shaku Nihongi*," in Satô Kiyoji, ed. *Kokugogaku kenkyû jiten* <Meiji shoin, 1977>, 636-637).

31) See chapter 7, note 73 above.

32) In the *Teniwoha himokagami*, 1771, Motoori outlined the relations between postpositions and verbal inflections (*kakari-musubi*) (MNZ 5:1-4), and in *Kotoba no tama no wo*, 1785, he elaborated on these relations and illustrated with examples (MNZ 5:5-318).

33) The *Qièyùn* (601) distinguishes four tonal categories for Middle Chinese: 平 (*píng* 'level'), 上 (*shang* 'rising'), 去 (*qù* 'departing'), and 入 (*rù* 'entering'). Karlgren viewed the names of these tonal categories as descriptive terms, and assigned the following values: "*píng*, 'level and non-abrupt', *shǎng* 'rising and non-abrupt', *qù* '(probably) falling and non-abrupt', *rù,* 'abrupt—that is, ending in a stop'" (Bernhard Karlgren, *Etudes sur la phonologie chinoise. Archives d'études orientales*, vol. 15 <in 4 parts>, <Leiden: E. J. Brill; Uppsala: K. W. Appelberg, 1915-26>, as discussed in Jerry Norman, *Chinese* <Cambridge: Cambridge University Press, 1988>, 52). Norman faults Karlgren's assignment of tonal values on two points: (1) the terms may not have been strictly descriptive, but were also chosen to exemplify their respective categories, (2) such assignment is deceptive, because it cannot be verified by reconstruction of the values from Modern Chinese dialects, since present-day techniques do not allow abstraction from the wide variety of values found for each of these tonal categories in the Modern Chinese dialects (Norman, Ibid., 52-53). See E. G. Pulleyblank for a detailed discussion of the history of terms used to describe tone in Chinese, and the historical development of tone in Chinese ("The Nature of the Middle Chinese Tones and Their Development to Early Mandarin," *Journal of Chinese Linguistics* 6 <1975>:173-203).

34) Motoori's analysis, which he borrows from Keichû, is regarded simply as a hypothesis by modern scholars, such as Ôno:

> The accentual system of the Nara period (710-794) is still not entirely clear, but with regard to the 平, 上, 去 accentual system, it has been

determined that 平 was a low, level tone, 上 was a high, level tone, and 去 was a tone which rose from level to high. Recently, in the research of Komatsu Hideo it has become clear that both a light level tone and a heavy level tone played a role in accent, and that the accentual system of the Heian period (794-1185) is more complex than previously determined. Accordingly, there are many points in Norinaga's system which should be reconsidered. Various theories have been proposed in regard to the interpretation of the values of the accentual markers of 上 and 去 in the *Kojiki*, but as yet none have convincingly resolved the issue (MNZ 9:523-524, supplementary note "page 37, line 16").

Aoki et al. give a list of recent references containing theories proposed to account for the values of these accentual markers *(Kojiki*, NST 1:488-489, supplementary *kundoku* note "上").

35) The discussion appears in *Kanji san'on kô* (1785) (MNZ 5:419). See J. R. McEwan ("Motoori's View of Phonetics and Linguistics in his *Mojigoe no kanazukai* and *Kanji san on kô*," *Asia Major* 1 <1949>: 109-118) for a synopsis of Motoori's analysis of the tonal systems of Chinese and Japanese (especially pp. 113-115).

36) *Kojiki*, NST Vol. 1:18, line 9. Aoki et al. here read Töyö-kumo-no-nö-kamï, the " 野" 'field' of his name ("abundant clouds field deity," Philippi, *Kojiki*, 615) having been mistakenly read by Motoori as "*nu*". See chapter 7, note 100 for a discussion of this issue.

37) Both examples appear in *Kojiki*, NST 1:18, line 11.

38) *Kojiki*, NST 1:26, line 13.

39) *Kojiki*, NST 1:32, line 5.

40) Both examples appear in *Kojiki*, NST 1:32, lines 4, 5.

41) Both examples appear in *Kojiki*, NST 1:46, line 3.

42) Ôno discusses the problems inherent in reconstructing a method of *kun*-reading for the early Nara period (710-794), and cautions that the readings Motoori proposes below may not necessarily be those which were used in

that period (*Kojiki-den*, MNZ 9:522-523, supplementary note "page 31, line 2"). The problems have to do with the fact that the only Japanese prose of this period is to be found in the *senmyô* of the *Shoku Nihongi* (797) and the *norito* in Book Eight of the *Engi shiki* (927), and these texts tend to follow a set format which is lacking in variation. In addition, their quantity is small. Therefore, while Motoori closely studied these texts and relied on them to determine his readings, they may have been too specialized to supply a model for all of the variety of text in the *Kojiki*. The *Man'yôshû* (759) and other anthologies of poetry are a good source for determining the readings of individual lexical items, but as poetry, they differ in structure from the prose sections of the *Kojiki*.

Ôno suggests that one method of determining the suitability of readings assigned by Motoori would be to compare them with the *kun* readings written down on Buddhist sutras from the early Heian period (794-1185). The caution one must observe in this respect has to do with the fact that while, on the one hand, the style of writing in some parts of the *Kojiki* is said to have been based on the style of Chinese translations of Buddhist sutras, the *Kojiki* itself differs greatly from Buddhist sutras, so they may not provide a totally valid model. In addition, there is a hundred-year gap between these Buddhist texts and the *Kojiki*, and due consideration must be given to any changes which might have taken place.

Ôno uses the work of Kobayashi Yoshinori ("*Kojiki* no kundoku to kanbun-kundoku-shi," *Jôdai bungaku* 35 <Oct. 1974>:14-34; Ôno cites a paper by the same title appearing in Tôyô Daigaku, *Jôdai bungaku kenkyûkai kaihô*, No. 14) to make a comparison of the *kun* readings in the *Kojiki* and the *kun* readings in the early Heian Buddhist sutras. Specifically, Ôno takes data from six representative *kanbun-kundoku* texts of the early Heian period for a comparison of readings assigned to postpositions. He found that the *Kojiki-den* and the *kanbun-kundoku* texts are in agreement on the readings assigned for the following twenty-eight characters: 之 *nö*; 於 *ni*; 者 *Fa*; 而 *te*; 矣 auxiliary character; 乎 *ya*, *ka*; 哉 *ya*, *ka*; 也 auxiliary character; 焉 postposition; 故 *kare*; 乃 *sunaFati*; 即 *sunaFati*; 爲 *-mu tö su*; 將 *-mu*; 欲 *-mu*, *omöFu*, *obosu*; 以 *-te*, *mötite*; 亦 *mata*, *mö*; 且 *mata*; 及 *mata*, *tö*; 可

bësi; 勿 *-zu*; 非 *-zu*; 雖 *tömö, dömö*; 是 *köre, könö*; 其 *söre, sönö*; 彼 *sönö*; 於是 *kökö ni*; 是 *kökö wo möte*. Therefore, the places where the *Kojiki-den* and the *kanbun-kundoku* materials are in agreement on the readings assigned to postpositions are extremely numerous. As examples of places where they differ in the assignment of *kun* readings, Ôno lists the following: *Kojiki-den* reads 哉 as *kamö*, while the early Heian materials read it as *kana* (善哉 *yoi kana*); *Kojiki-den* reads 耳 as *ni kösö are*, but in the early Heian materials it corresponds to *raku nomi* (ラク耳 *raku nomi*); *Kojiki-den* reads 然而 as *sikasite* or *sate*, while the early Heian materials assign the reading of *sikaredomo*, etc.

43) *Kojiki*, NST 1:22, line 8. Aoki et al. do not read "*mi-*" (HONORIFIC). Philippi's translation appears on page 52. In classical Chinese, 之 is a structural particle linking a modifier to a head. I am indebted to Liu Le Ning for the description of the functions of these grammatical markers in classical Chinese.

44) *Kojiki*, NST 1:32, line 12. Aoki et al. read this passage as *idemukaFuru töki*. Philippi's translation appears on page 61.

45) *Kojiki*, NST 1:22, line 14.

46) *Kojiki*, NST 1:18, line 9.

47) One such example may be 故、明レ将レ打二其土雲一之歌曰、(*kare, sönö Tutigumo wo utamu tö suru kötö wo akaseru uta ni iFaku* "The song which was a signal for smiting the Tuti-gumo was . . ." (*Kojiki*, NST 1:124, 126, lines 17, 1; Philippi, *Kojiki*, 174), where the "之" following *Tutigumo*, marked by "*wo*" and the direct object of *utamu to suru*, is not read.

48) Takagi and Tomiyama indicate that several manuscripts have 詔云 for 詔之 in one such example (*Kojiki sôsakuin,* Vol. 1: *Honbun hen*, 14), which appears as 詔之 in Aoki et al. (*Kojiki*, NST 1:22, line 10).

49) One example appears in line 1 of the *Kojiki*: 於二高天原一成 (*Takama-nö-Fara ni narimaseru* "there came ing [*sic*] into existence in Takama-nö-para" (*Kojiki*, NST 1:18; Philippi, *Kojiki*, 47). The primary function of the preposition 於 in classical Chinese was to indicate location.

[50] *Kojiki*, NST 1:62, line 11; Philippi's translation appears on p. 95. One of the uses of the particle 者 in classical Chinese was as a structural marker in sentences expressing a judgment, taking the form of NP_1者NP_2也.

[51] One such example occurs in the explanatory line to a song: 此者嘲咲者也 (*Kö Fa azawaraFu sö* "This is to laugh to scorn") (*Kojiki*, NST 1:124, line 12; Philippi, *Kojiki*, 173). Aoki et al. explain that the reading of *sö* for 者也 was given by analogy with the preceding explanatory line, which has parallel structure, but is written in *on* phonograms: "此者 . . . 曾" (*Kojiki*, NST 1:124, footnote 10). See also note 149, this chapter.

[52] *Kojiki*, NST 1:60, line 13. Aoki et al. read the passage as: *yaso kamï nö wosiFe ni sitagaFite*, thereby differing with Motoori's reading for this character in this passage. Philippi's translation appears on p. 93.

[53] One such example is: 随二詔命一而 (*mikötönöri nö manima ni* "in accordance with these words") (*Kojiki*, NST 1:64, line 14; Philippi, *Kojiki*, 98).

[54] The character 而 has several different functions in classical Chinese, but the one referred to here is that of a link between two sentences, sometimes with no particular meaning, which occurs sentence-initially.

[55] *Kojiki*, NST 1:48, 50, lines 15, 1; Philippi's translation appears on p. 79.

[56] See note 58 below. 矣 is a mood particle in classical Chinese expressing certainty.

[57] Aoki et al., citing the work of Onoda Mitsuo, note that there are 31 instances of the particle 乎 in the *Kojiki*, all of them from the *Kuji* material, and all in passages of conversation. The particle occurs both sentence-finally, and after a clause or phrase, in questions or in exclamations. In questions, the reading of *ya* or nothing is assigned, while in exclamations, the reading of *kamö* is assigned (*Kojiki*, NST 1:511-512, supplementary *kun* reading note "乎"). 乎 in classical Chinese is an all-purpose question marker.

[58] Citing the work of Onoda Mitsuo, Aoki et al. note that there are 5 instances of the particle 哉, all from the *Kuji* material, and all found in conversation. This particle also occurs both sentence-finally, and after a clause or phrase. In questions or expressions of uncertainty, the reading of *ya* is

assigned, while in the one exclamation, the reading of *kamö* is assigned (Ibid.). In classical Chinese, 哉 is used as an interjection to express strong feeling, or as a marker of a rhetorical question.

The other sentence-final particles 歟, 耶, 矣, 焉, and 耳 are from the *Kuji* material and are found mostly in conversation; 者也 and 是也 are also found in the *Kuji* material. 也, on the other hand, is found in material from both the *Kuji* and the *Teiki*. According to Ishizuka Tatsumaro (1764-1823), the use of these sentence-final particles, with the exception of sections from the *Teiki* material, corresponds to their usage in classical Chinese (Ibid.).

[59)] Ôno notes that while one manuscript does contain 柯佞 (*kane*), others have 柯倭 (*kawa*), which is more likely to be correct, as there are no other examples of the use of 佞 as a phonogram, and no other instances of *kane* in the Nara period (710-794) literature, while there was an interjection *wa* at this time. *Kawa* corresponds to the *kane* found in later Japanese (*Kojiki-den*, MNZ 9:524, supplementary note "page 40, line 5").

[60)] According to Aoki et al., 歟, which they render as *ka*, occurs as an exclamation of questioning oneself, in passages of conversation (*Kojiki*, NST 1:160, footnote 8). The following is an example: 愛レ兄歟 (*iröye zö utukusiki ka* 'Is it my brother who is dearer to me?' (*Kojiki*, NST 1:160, line 7. Philippi's translation appears on page 214). In classical Chinese, 歟 is an all-purpose question marker.

[61)] An interrogative word in classical Chinese, 焉 appears not to have been given a *kun* reading by Aoki et al. when it appears at the end of a phrase (Kobayashi Yoshinori, "*Kojiki* on-kun hyô: jô," *Bungaku* 47:8 <1979>: 56-84, especially 74); examples appear on pages 14, 36, 54, 160, 180 (*Kojiki*, NST 1). In the preface, at the head of a phrase, it is rendered as *kökö ni* "hereupon" (*Kojiki*, NST 1:14, line 15; Philippi, *Kojiki*, 43). See also note 58 above.

[62)] *Kojiki*, NST 1:210, lines 9-10; Philippi's translation appears on p. 278.

[63)] *Nihonshoki*, Vol. 1, NKBT 67:489, line 8; Aston's translation has "for the sake of" (*Nihongi*, Vol. 1:360), but Sakamoto et al. note that *yuwe ni* indicates "cause" (*gen'in*) (*Nihonshoki*, Vol. 1, NKBT 67:488-489, headnote 10).

64) Aoki et al., however, relate the two senses in which 故 is used to the meaning of the character, which is used when one links what precedes with what follows. This occurs in two senses: (1) 故 links the preceding and following clauses as cause and effect (Modern Japanese *yue ni*, *dakara* 'therefore'), and (2) 故 links by indicating only the temporal sequence of preceding and subsequent event (Modern Japanese *sosite* 'and then', *kôsite* 'in this fashion' (*Kojiki*, NST 1:306, supplementary note 4). In classical Chinese, 故 functions as either a causal link or link of unspecified relation.

65) Ôno rejects the idea that *kare* derives from *kaku areba*, or from *kareba*. He states that *kare* derives from *ka are* (彼有レ), wherein *ka* corresponds to the *kô* ('thus') of Modern Japanese, and *are* is the realis (*izenkei*) of *ari* ('exists'). In Old Japanese, the realis form used by itself could indicate "fixed conditions" (*kitei zyôken*), so the entire expression *ka are* had the meaning of *kô aru kara* 'because of this'. The contracted form *kare*, with the meaning of *kô da kara* 'because it is thus', was therefore used as a *kun* reading for 故 (*Kojiki-den*, MNZ 9:524, supplementary note "page 40, line 13").

66) This issue is discussed in Motoori's *Kotoba no tama no o* (1785) (MNZ 5:283).

67) The forms are the realis form (*izenkei*) of the verb, plus the conjunctive particle *ba*.

68) "Fourth sound" indicates the realis form (*izenkei*).

69) According to Ôno, *karu ga yuwe ni* derives from *ka aru ga yuwe ni*, and not *kakaru ga yuwe ni* (*Kojiki-den*, MNZ,9:524, supplementary note "page 41, line 1").

70) Aoki et al., summarizing previous research on the use of this character in the *Kojiki* by Onoda Mitsuo, Kojima Noriyuki, and Yamada Yoshio, read this as *sikasite*. There are 254 examples of 爾 used independently, and previous research has argued that 爾 and 於是 (*kökö ni*) need to be differentiated in the readings assigned to them because they differ in function. 於是 occurs at the beginning of a passage which represents a new development of facts

from the preceding section, while 爾 occurs within a passage headed by 於是, and represents the development of the narrative within the same context. It does not represent the continuation of the same subject, but rather, in most instances, the passage of time, so a *kun* reading based on the deictic stem of *so-* ('medial', 'known to both parties') or *si-* ('medial') is appropriate. See Aoki at al. for further details on the evidence whereby the reading of *sikasite* is obtained (*Kojiki*, NST 1:490-491, supplementary *kun* reading note "尓").

71) There are many passages, however, which correspond to the semantic discourse functions described in note 70 above. For example, all three may be found in the same narrative passage (*Kojiki*, NST 1:20): 於是 *kökö ni* "at this time" (line 4; Philippi, *Kojiki*, 49, line 1) heading a passage in which 故 *kare* "thereupon" (line 6; Philippi, *Kojiki*, 49, line 6) subsequently appears, and 於是 *kökö ni* "at this time" (line 9; Philippi, *Kojiki*, 50, line 3) preceding the appearance of 爾 *sikasite* "then" (line 11; Philippi, *Kojiki*, 50, line 9).

72) Ôno rejects this derivation. See note 65 above.

73) Two instances are found in Book One: *söre yori* "after that" (*Kojiki*, NST 1:78, line 2; Philippi, *Kojiki*, 116) and *söre yori* "from that time" (*Kojiki*, NST 1:112, line 1; Philippi, *Kojiki*, 155). 爾 has several functions in classical Chinese, one of which is proximate deictic pronoun 'this'.

74) Aoki et al. read *sönö tatari* "the curse" (*Kojiki*, NST 1:166, line 7; Philippi, *Kojiki*, 220).

75) Aoki et al. agree with the reading of *sunaFati*, and provide an outline of the ways in which it is used, illustrated by examples (*Kojiki*, NST 1:496-497, supplementary kun reading note " 乃").

76) One of the functions of both 爾 and 乃 in classical Chinese was to mark the second person pronoun.

77) The item in question, *imasi*, is the adverb 今し 'before long' (Hasegawa Masaharu, Imanishi Yûichirô, Itô Hiroshi and Yoshioka Hiroshi, eds., *Tosa nikki, Kagerô nikki, Murasaki Shikibu nikki, Sarashina nikki;* Shin Nihon koten bungaku taikei 24 <Iwanami, 1989>, 12, line 10).

78) Ibid., 25, line 11.

79) See Aoki et al. for a discussion of the ways in which it is used (*Kojiki*, NST 1:497, supplementary *kun* reading note "乃").

80) According to Aoki et al., early Heian *kanbun-kunten* texts (classical Chinese texts with markings for reading in Japanese) indicate the reading of *omöFu* for 以爲 (*Kojiki*, NST 1:491, supplementary *kun* reading note "以爲"). In classical Chinese, 以爲 means 'to consider . . . as'.

81) *Kojiki*, NST 1:38, line 14; Philippi, *Kojiki*, 69. In classical Chinese, 爲 in this example is a preposition meaning 'for'.

82) In classical Chinese, one of the uses of 將 is as an adverb meaning 'soon', which, in combination with a verb, serves as a future tense indicating action in the future, or will or desire.

83) *Kojiki*, NST 1:110. Aoki et al. read *sitamaFu* rather than *su*. Philippi, *Kojiki*, 154.

84) *Kojiki*, NST 1:122, line 13; Philippi, *Kojiki*, 171.

85) *Kojiki*, NST 1:42, line 13; Philippi's translation appears on page 74. Kobayashi Yoshinori analyzes the representation of *-mu* and other PRESUMPTIVE (*suiryô*) suffixes in the *Kojiki*, and finds 18 instances in which 將 is used to represent *-mu*, all of which occur in conversation or interior monologues. 13 of the examples occur in the sense of speaker's intention or desire for his own action, 3 occur in the sense of requesting the action of another, and 2 occur in the sense of predicting the future ("*Kojiki* ni okeru suiryô hyôgen to sono hyôki to no kankei," in Satô Shigeru kyôju taikan kinen ronbun-shû kankô-kai, *eds., Satô Shigeru kyôju taikan kinen: Ronshû kokugogaku* <Ôfûsha, 1980)>, 157-176). For the function of 將 in classical Chinese, see note 82 above.

86) *Kojiki*, NST 1:90, line 15; Philippi, *Kojiki*, 133. Kobayashi Yoshinori finds 41 examples of 將 or 將 plus 爲 which are to be read *-mu tö su*, 35 of which occur in narrative, and 6 of which occur in conversation (Ibid., 166).

87) *Kojiki*, NST 1:90, lines 11-12. Aoki et al. read 為むト欲ふ (*se-mu tö omöFu*). Philippi's translation appears on page 132. Kobayashi Yoshinori finds 39 examples of 欲, all of which are used in the sense of a person's intention or desire; the range of meaning of 欲, while overlapping with one

of the senses of *-mu,* is therefore much narrower than that of *-mu,* and he argues that *omöFu* 'to desire' or *omoFosu* 'to desire-HON' is the appropriate reading for 欲. Given the principle of differentiating the readings of characters having similar meanings, 將 will thus be read as *-mu/-mu tö su*, and 欲 as *omöFu* or *omoFosu.* This is in fact what one finds in the *kunten* materials of the early Heian period (794-1185) (Ibid., 166-167). In classical Chinese, 欲 is used in the sense of 'want' or 'will' following animate subjects only. 將, with a similar function, can be used with inanimate subjects as well.

88) *Nihonshoki*, Vol. 2, NKBT 68:93, line 2. Sakamoto et al. read 熟し喫むと為欲ふ (*konasi-hama-mu tö omöFu*). Aston's translation appears in *Nihongi*, Vol. 2:58-59.

89) *Kojiki*, NST 1:42, line 9; Philippi, *Kojiki*, 73.

90) See note 87 above.

91) This passage appears in a proclamation from the reign of Empress Kô-ken (r. 749-758) (Kaneko Takeo, *Shoku Nihongi senmyô kô* <Takashina shoten, 1989, reprint of 1941 edition>, 179, lines 1-2). I was unable to find a like passage from the reign of Emperor Shômu (r. 724-749) as indicated by Motoori.

92) Kaneko, *Shoku Nihongi senmyô kô*, No. 59, p. 423, line 4.

93) Aoki et al. read 是以 as *kökö wo mötite* (one example is *Kojiki*, NST 1:36, line 12).

94) *Kojiki*, NST 1:214, line 4; Philippi, *Kojiki*, 283.

95) *Kojiki*, NST 1:274, line 9; Philippi's translation appears on p. 357.

96) *Man'yôshû,* Vol. 4, NKBT 7:434, poem 4398.

97) *Man'yôshû,* Vol. 1, NKBT 4:156, poem 269.

98) Ibid., 200, poem 420.

99) *Man'yôshû,* Vol. 3, NKBT 6:168, poem 2396.

100) Ibid., 68, poem 1891. The text lacks the character 而 (*-te*), and the passage is read as *ta-wori moti.*

101) *Man'yôshû,* Vol. 4, NKBT 7:98, poem 3733.

102) Motoori is refering to verbs of the fourth conjugation (*yodan*) which combine with the suffix *-ri* (CONTINUATIVE/PERFECTIVE) in their realis (*izenkei*) or imperative (*meireikei*) forms.

[103] In classical Chinese, 所 serves as an affix which nominalizes a verb phrase, and expresses the consequences of the action of the verb.

[104] *Kojiki*, NST 1:66, line 7. Aoki et al. read the passage as *iduru wo siranu*, and note that 所 is used here as a particle, in the sense of 'way to get out'. They also note that the *kun* reading of "*tökörö*" is expressed with either of the two characters 地 or 処, both meaning 'place' (Ibid., footnote 7). Philippi's translation appears on page 99.

[105] *Kojiki*, NST 1:240, line 4. Aoki et al. read the passage as *Me-döri-nö-oFokimi nö imasi ni*, noting once again that the character 所 represents a particle, and that the characters 地 and 処 are used to represent the word *tökö-rö* in the sense of 'place' (Ibid., footnote 3). Philippi, *Kojiki*, 317.

[106] In classical Chinese, 耳 is a sentence-final particle meaning 'just' or 'only', or serving to mark the end of a passage of speech.

[107] *Kojiki*, NST 1:42, line 15. Aoki et al. read 耳 as *ni kösö*, and note that it appears in conversation (Ibid., footnote 13). Their reading of the passage is: *wa ga kuni wo ubawamu tö omöFu ni kösö*. In a general discussion of 耳, they note that there are 12 instances of it in the *Kojiki*, 4 of which occur in conjunction with 唯 (*tadasi* 'only'). For those 8 which occur independently, the reading adopted by Motoori, *ni kösö*, is assigned, due to the fact that such usage corresponds to the way *kösö* is used as a sentence-final emphatic postposition in Old Japanese. In the early Heian *kunten* materials, however, it is treated as an "*okizi*" ('character to be discarded and not read') (Ibid., 502, supplementary *kun* reading "耳"). Of the 4 examples which occur in the form 唯 . . . 耳, one is assigned the reading of *nömï nari*, while the rest are assigned the reading of *ni kösö* (Ibid., 494, supplementary *kun* reading note "唯"). Philippi, *Kojiki*, 74.

[108] *Kojiki*, NST 1:86, line 13. Aoki et al. read the passage as *utukusiki tömö ni aru yuwe ni toburaFi-kituru ni kösö*. Philippi, *Kojiki*, 127.

[109] *Kojiki*, NST 1:152, line 16. Aoki et al. read the passage as *kitanaki kökörö okösesi sirusi tö suru ni kösö*. Philippi, *Kojiki*, 206.

[110] *Kojiki*, NST 1:242, lines 9-10; Philippi, *Kojiki*, 319.

[111] *Kojiki*, NST 1:48, 50, lines 15-16, 1. Aoki et al. read *siture* rather than *siturамë*. Philippi, *Kojiki*, 79.

112) *Nihonshoki*, Vol. 1, NKBT 67:443, line 14. Aston's translation appears on page 321 (*Nihongi*, Vol. 1).

113) *Man'yôshû*, Vol. 3, NKBT 6:234, poem 2751.

114) Poem number 170, "Yü li" (Bernard Karlgren, ed., *The Book of Odes: Chinese Text, Transcription, and Translation* <Stockholm: The Museum of Far Eastern Antiquities, 1974>, 115. I am indebted to Cynthia Chennault for locating this reference.

115) Poem number 109, "Yüan yu t'ao" (Karlgren, *The Book of Odes*, 70).

116) The commentary further states that "standing alone, 歌 does not necessarily imply playing, as well as singing" (James Legge, trans., *The Chinese Classics*, Vol. 4: *The She King* <Oxford: Henry Frowde, 1871; Hong Kong: Hong Kong University Press, 1960, second edition>, 167. I am indebted to Cynthia Chennault for locating this reference.

117) Katagiri Yôichi, Fukui Teisuke, Takahashi Shôji, and Shimizu Yoshiko, eds., *Taketori monogatari, Ise monogatari, Yamato monogatari, Heichû monogatari;* Nihon koten bungaku zenshû 8 (Shôgakkan, 1972), 154, episode 22.

118) Aoki et al. agree that the reading of *oyobi* is a later usage, which began in the mid-Heian period. In classical Chinese, 及 is a conjunction of coordination. The early Heian *kunten* materials read 及 with the postposition *tö* when two nouns are conjoined, i.e. N_1 *tö* N_2 *tö* (*Kojiki*, NST 1:520, supplementary *kun* reading note "及"). 34 of the 35 examples of 及 used as a conjunction in the *Kojiki* link two nouns, and the single remaining example links two clauses. As a clause link, the reading of *mata* is assigned. Aoki et al. notice the following pattern in the conjoining of nouns: when two nouns are conjoined, only 及 is used; when three or more nouns are conjoined, the pattern of 及 plus 与 or 及 plus 亦 is used, and the reading of N_1 *tö* N_2 *tö* N_3 *tö* should be assigned (Ibid., 504, supplementary *kun* reading note "切鬚及手足爪"). They therefore disagree with the readings Motoori assigns below.

119) *Kojiki*, NST 1:86, line 4. Aoki et al. read 及 as *tö . . . tö*, i.e. ". . . ト其ノ妻子及 (. . . *tö sönö meko tö*)." Philippi's translation appears on p. 126.

[120] *Kojiki*, NST 1:86, line 9. Aoki et al. read 亦 as *tö . . . tö*, i.e. ". . . ト其ノ妻亦 (. . . *tö sönö me tö*)." They also read *nö* rather than *ga* for the GENITIVE POSTPOSITION. Philippi's translation appears on p. 127.

[121] *Kojiki*, NST 1:96, line 8. Aoki et al. read ". . . 及. . . 亦" as . . . *tö* . . . *tö* . . . *t ö*." Philippi's translation appears on p. 139.

[122] *Kojiki*, NST 1:172, line 17. Aoki et al. read ". . . 亦. . . 及" as ". . . *tö* . . . *tö* . . . *t ö*." Philippi's translation appears on page 229.

[123] Kobayashi Yoshinori finds that 38 of the 39 instances of 可 in the *Kojiki* are to be read *bësi* ("*Kojiki* ni okeru suiryô hyôgen to sono hyôki to no kankei," 172). The remaining example appears to have been assigned the reading of *yösi* (Kobayashi, "*Kojiki* on-kun hyô: jô," 65). In classical Chinese, 可 is an adverb denoting possibility or ability.

[124] *Kojiki*, NST 1:32, line 13. Aoki et al. read this instance of 可 as *bësi* (*kaFeru bësi*). Philippi, *Kojiki*, 61.

[125] Aoki et al. note that desiderative sentences introduced with *negaFu* ('to implore') in the early Heian *kunten* materials end with a verb followed by the presumptive suffix *-mu*; accordingly, 勿 in this position, following a sentence-final verb in a passage introduced by *negaFu*, is assigned the reading of *-zi* ('NEGATIVE PRESUMPTIVE') (*Kojiki*, NST 1:112, footnote 10). Of the 8 examples of 勿 in the *Kojiki*, 2 are assigned the reading of *-zi* (p. 92, line 4; p. 112, line 12), 5 are assigned the reading of *-zu* (p. 152, line 13; p. 174, lines 6 and 8; p. 208, line 6; p. 230, line 6), and one is assigned the reading of *naku* (p. 166, line 4) (Ibid.). See also Kobayashi for discussion of 勿 representing the negative presumptive suffix *-zi* ("*Kojiki* ni okeru suiryô hyôgen to sono hyôki to no kankei," 171-172).

[126] Kobayashi assigns the character 不 the readings of *-zi* ('NEGATIVE PRESUMPTIVE') or *-zu* ('NEGATIVE') when following a verb (Ibid., 62).

[127] Kobayashi assigns the character 非 the readings of *arazu* ('not so'), *arazi* ('cannot be so'), or *-zu ari* ('NEGATIVE') (Ibid., 83).

[128] *Kojiki*, NST 1:82, line 7; Philippi's translation appears on p. 121.

[129] *Kojiki*, NST 1:90, lines 2-3; Philippi, *Kojiki*, 130.

[130] In classical Chinese, 是 is a deictic pronoun which can modify a noun or occur independently. It also functions as a particle whose purpose is

simply to mark a noun which has deviated from the ususal word order.

[131] *Kojiki,* NST 1:106, lines 4-5. Aoki et al. read "*iroko*" for 魚鱗, and "*sö*" for 者也. Philippi, *Kojiki,* 150.

[132] *Kojiki*, NST 1:42, line 5. Aoki et al. read "*kökörö-saki*" for 心前. There is an extended discussion of this particular item in Kobayashi Yoshinori, "The *Kun* Readings of the *Kojiki*," *Acta Asiatica* 46 (1984): 62-84. Philippi, *Kojiki*, 72.

[133] Kobayashi assigns the reading of *itaru*, or, in composition with 'come' (到来), the reading of *kitaru* to note geographical arrival ("*Kojiki* on-kun hyô: jô," 64).

[134] *Kojiki*, NST 1: 112, line 7. Aoki et al. agree that *nozomu* is not a suitable reading for 臨, as there are no confirmed instances of *nozomu* in Old Japanese, save for such examples of a reading of *nozumu* assigned to a *senmyô* in the *Nihonkôki* (840), likely due to the influence of classical Chinese. They note that there are 10 examples of 臨 in the *Kojiki*, and in each instance, the reading of *mukaFu*, which is attested for Old Japanese, is appropriate. They also note that the reading *mukaFu* is listed under this character in the Kanchi'inbon manuscript of the *Ruijumyôgishô* (Kamakura period, 1185-1333) (supplementary *kun* reading note "臨," 503-504). They read this passage as *umu töki ni mukaFëba*. Philippi, *Kojiki*, 156.

[135] *Kojiki*, NST 1:198, line 14. Aoki et al. read the passage as *Faramimaseru ga umu töki ni mukaFu*. Philippi, *Kojiki*, 264.

[136] Kobayashi assigns the reading of *onömö'onömö* for all instances ("*Kojiki* on-kun hyô: jô," 65).

[137] *Kojiki*, NST 1:20, line 4; Philippi, *Kojiki*, 49.

[138] *Kojiki*, NST 1:52, line 11; Philippi, *Kojiki*, 85.

[139] *Kojiki*, NST 1:190, line 1. Aoki et al. read this passage as *mi-ko-tati tö, mörömörö*. Philippi's translation appears on page 250.

[140] Aoki et al. give the readings of *mörö-kamï* and *mörö-kamï-tati* for 諸神, in two instances, respectively (*Kojiki*, NST 1:84, lines 2, 13), while Takagi and Tomiyama read *mörömörö nö kamï-tati* in each instance (*Kojiki*

sôsakuin, Vol. 1: *Honbun-hen*, 88). Kobayashi lists only the readings of *mörö*, *mörömörö*, and *mörömörö nö* for 諸 ("*Kojiki* on-kun hyô: jô," 80).

141) *Kojiki*, NST 1:94, line 16. Philippi's translation appears on p. 138. The expression in question, 於是, occurs adverbially at the beginning of a sentence in the meaning of 'then', or 'at this time', while the example discussed by Motoori occurs at the end of a sentence before *ari* as a locative ('here').

142) As seen in note 93 above, Aoki et al. read 是以 ('this is the reason,' 'hereupon') as *kökö wo mötite*.

143) Aoki et al. read 故爾 as *kare sikasite* (e.g. *Kojiki*, NST 1:66, line 13). See note 70 above for a discussion of the reading of 爾.

144) None of the listings in Takagi and Tomiyama contain this combination (即爾) (*Kojiki sôsakuin,* Vol. 1: *Sakuin hen* <Heibonsha, 1974>. Liu Le Ning suggests that it may be an error for 既而, with which it is homophonous (personal communication).

145) Aoki et al. read 爾即 as *sikasite*, *sunaFati* (e.g. *Kojiki*, NST 1:184, line 2).

146) Aoki et al. read 云ㇾ爾 as *sika iFu* 'in this fashion, he spoke' (*Kojiki*, NST 1:224). Philippi's translation appears on p. 294. Kobayashi lists the following *kun* readings for 爾 in addition to *sikasite*: *sikasu*, *sika*, *sikari*, *sönö*, *söre* ("*Kojiki* on-kun hyô: jô," 68). In classical Chinese, 云爾 is used to quote someone's words in disparagement.

147) *Kojiki*, NST 1:274, line 17. The example appears in *on* phonograms. Philippi, *Kojiki*, 358. Aoki et al. agree that it is to be read *kaku* (e.g. page 128, line 3).

148) Aoki et al. read 然後 as *sikasite nöti ni*, noting that both the readings *sikasite nöti ni* and *sikakusite nöti ni* are found in the early Heian *kunten* materials (*Kojiki*, NST 1:492, supplementary *kun* reading note "然後").

149) Aoki et al. read all instances of 者也 as sentence-final particle *sö*, by analogy with the *on* phonograms in the commentary to a song in Book Two (*Kojiki*, NST 1:32, footnote 1). See note 51 above, and Aoki et al. for a discussion of the function of this particle (Ibid., 521). Thus, the example 神者也 is read *kamï sö* (*Kojiki*, NST 1:32). In classical Chinese, 者也 is used

when one is stating facts with certainty.

[150] Aoki et al. read 故是以 as *kare, kökö wo mötite* (e.g. *Kojiki*, NST 1:58, line 4).

[151] *Nihonshoki*, Vol. 2, NKBT 68:405, line 10; Aston's translation: "for this reason, therefore" (*Nihongi*, Vol. 2:318).

[152] Contrary to Motoori, Aoki et al. read such examples according to the characters: 何故以 is read *nani nö yuwe ni ka* (*Kojiki*, NST 1:52, lines 10-11); 何由 is read *nani nö yuwe ni* (Ibid., 150, line 11) or *nani nö yuwe ni ka* (Ibid., 218, line 1); 何故 is read *nani nö yuwe ni ka* (Ibid., 44, line 6); and 何以 is read *nani wo mötite* (Ibid., 44, line 11).

[153] Kaneko, *Shoku Nihongi senmyô kô*, No. 5, p. 86, line 4. The form itself, *nöri-tamaFi-tur-aku* 'speak-HONORIFIC-PERFECTIVE-NOMINALIZER' is an Old Japanese form created through the "so-called *-ku* mode of expression (*-ku gohô*)" wherein the nominalizing suffix **aku* is added to the attributive form (*rentaikei*) of the verb, and the final vowel of the attributive form is elided (Ôno et al., *Kogo jiten*, 10-11). Ôno et al. define the meaning of **aku* as 'matter' (*koto*) or 'place' (*tokoro*), and locate its origin in the root *aku* found in the Old Japanese verb *akugaru* 'to stray away from where one should be', which is a composition of *aku* 'place' plus *karu* 'to leave'. See also Martin for a discussion of this form (*The Japanese Language Through Time*, 805).

[154] Kaneko, *Shoku Nihongi senmyô kô*, No. 7, p. 112, line 9.

[155] *Kojiki*, NST 1:44, line 8. Kobayashi Yoshinori discusses forms of quotation in Old Japanese, and notes that with the exception of quotations of *darani* (Sanskrit *dhâraṇî* 'mystic incantations'), the quotations of verbal utterances in the early Heian *kunten* materials consistently take the pattern of introducing the quote with a verb in the *-ku* mode of expression (see note 153 above), and closing the quote with the particle *tö* followed by the same verb form minus the *-ku* mode of expression ("*Kojiki* kundoku ni tsuite," 668-669). Accordingly, in the passage in question, the quoted utterance is introduced by *mawosituraku*, and closed by *tö mawositu*. Aoki et al. consistently follow this pattern in assigning readings to the expressions Motoori is addressing in this section. The expressions discussed thus far are assigned the

following readings: 詔之 and 告之 are assigned the readings of *nörasaku . . . tö nörasu* (*Kojiki*, NST 1: 84, line 2) or *nörasaku . . . tö nörasite* if in mid-sentence (Ibid., 84, line 12); likewise, 白之 and 白言 are assigned the reading of *mawosaku . . . tö mawosu* (Ibid., 82, line 6; 52, line 16). Deviation from this pattern occurs when there is a series of quotations being presented in the same passage coupled with anaphora and relative clauses (Ibid., 52, lines 11-12).

Kobayashi notes that the patterns used to introduce songs in the *Kojiki* differ from the duplication pattern described above, and share several features in common with the patterns used to quote *darani* in the early Heian *kunten* materials ("*Kojiki* kundoku ni tsuite," 668).

[156)] Kaneko, *Shoku Nihongi senmyô kô*, No. 30, p. 268, line 1. Aoki et al. read 議云 and 議白 as two verbs: 議云 is *Fakarite iFaku . . . tö iFite* (*Kojiki*, NST 1:22, line 8) or *Fakarite nörasaku . . . tö nörasite* (Ibid., 116, line 3), while 議白之 is *Fakarite mawosaku . . . tö mawosu* (Ibid., 82, line 6).

[157)] *-Turaku* is *-turu* ('PERFECTIVE', in attributive form), plus **aku*, i.e. *-turu* in the *-ku* mode of expression (see note 153 above), with the meaning of "*sita koto*" ('what he did') (Ôno, *Kojiki-den*, MNZ 9:524, supplementary note "page 47, line 14"). Likewise, *-keraku* is *-keru* ('EVIDENTIAL/OBJECTIVE', in attributive form, plus **aku*, with the meaning of "*sita to iu koto*" ('what he is said to have done') (Ibid.).

[158)] Aoki et al. read 問日 as *toFite iFaku . . . tö iFu* (*Kojiki*, NST 1:108, line 13).

[159)] As mentioned in note 155 above, the quotation of songs follows patterns that differ from the form of quotation of verbal utterances. Three patterns are found: (1) a clause containing an anaphoric element follows the song, such as 加此歌而 (*kaku utaFitamaFite* "thus singing") (*Kojiki*, NST, 1:212, line 11; Philippi, *Kojiki*, 281), (2) an explanation of the song follows its recitation, such as 此歌者 . . . 歌者也 (*könö uta Fa . . . uta sö* 'this song is the song . . .') (*Kojiki*, NST 1:214, line 5; Philippi's translation appears on p. 283), and (3) no anaphoric element or explanation follows (Kobayashi, "*Kojiki* kundoku ni tsuite," 668). Accordingly, Aoki et al. do not assign readings according to the duplicate *-ku* mode of expression described above (note 153) when the verb in question introduces a song. 答日 is given the reading *kötaFëte nörasaku* when introducing a song (*Kojiki*, NST 1:130, lines 6-7), but when verbal utterances are quoted, it is given the reading *kötaFëte iFaku . . . tö iFu* (Ibid., 150, line 11).

160) Aoki et al. read 答詔 as *kötaFëte nörasaku . . . tö nörasu* (*Kojiki*, NST 1:56, line 5).

161) Aoki et al. read 誨告 as *wosiFë-nörasisiku . . . tö nörasiki* (*Kojiki*, NST 1:62, line 7).

162) It is up to the reader to make a choice between past and non-past, or imperfective and perfective, since expression of tense/aspect, while represented in sections composed in *on* phonogram notation, is virtually unrepresented elsewhere (Kobayashi, "*Kojiki* kundoku ni tsuite," 669). Kobayashi finds that in the sections composed in *on* phonograms which describe events from the past, the suffix *-ki* ('EVIDENTIAL/SUBJECTIVE') is fairly numerous, and is found at the onset of a narrative, while the suffixes *-tu* ('PERFECTIVE') and *-zu* ('NEGATIVE') also occur, but only in the middle sections of the narrative. The suffix *-keri* ('EVIDENTIAL/OBJECTIVE'), on the other hand, occurs only four times, and in each case, in conversation (Ibid., 670-674). For this reason, and also because *-keri* is hardly used in the *kun* reading of Chinese Buddhist texts, whose purpose is also to narrate and explain events of the past, Aoki et al. made the decision not to read *-keri* into the text as a verbal suffix (Ibid., 675).

163) Aoki et al. appear to have read all instances of 答 as *kötaFu* (Kobayashi, "*Kojiki* on-kun hyô: jô," 77).

164) Aoki et al. appear to have read 告 as *nöru* ('to say') or *tugu* ('to announce') (Ibid., 65), and 詔 as *nörasu* ('to say/HONORIFIC') or *nöru* ('to say') (Ibid., 80).

165) In regard to this point, Ôno cites a paper by Kobayashi Yoshinori ("*Kojiki* no kundoku to kanbun-kundoku shi," paper presented at the Jôdai bungaku gakkai, Spring Meeting, 1974, Mihara City) which notes that while this reduplicative pattern of quotation is quite common in the early Heian

kunten materials, it is by no means universal; occasionally the end of a quote is framed merely by *tö* ('QUOTATIVE'), or contains no marker at all, as in inserted notes, when the quotation itself comes at the end of a passage, when several utterances continue in succession, or when preceded by an element forming the head of a clause (Ôno, *Kojiki-den*, MNZ 9:524, supplementary note "page 48, line 2"). By and large, however, Aoki et al. have followed the reduplicative pattern of quotation. See notes 155 and 159 above.

166) The only example with this structure is slightly different, with the quotation enclosed by 詔之 . . . 告而 (*nörasaku . . . tö nörasite*), and the quotation itself beginning and ending with "*Töyö-asi-Fara-nö-ti-iFo-aki-nö-midu-Fo-nö-kuni Fa . . . ari nari.*" *Kojiki*, NST 1:82,84); Philippi's translation appears on p. 120.

167) *Kojiki*, NST 1:98, lines 8-9. Philippi, *Kojiki*, 141.

168) *Kojiki, Norito*, NKBT 1:454, lines 6-7. Bock's translation appears in Bock, Felicia Gressit, *Engi-Siki: Procedures of the Engi Era,* Books VI-X (Tokyo: Sophia University, 1972), 103.

169) *Kojiki, Norito*, NKBT 1:448, lines 3-4. Bock's translation appears in *Engi-Shiki: Procedures of the Engi Era,* Books VI-X, 100.

170) Kaneko, *Shoku Nihongi senmyô kô*, No. 34, p. 285, lines 1-2.

171) Ibid., no. 30, p. 268, lines 1-2.

172) Ibid., no. 45, p. 351, lines 5-6.

173) *Man'yôshû*, Vol. 2, NKBT 5:384, poem 1740.

174) *Man'yôshû*, Vol. 3, NKBT 6:378, poem 3303.

175) *Man'yôshû*, Vol. 4, NKBT 7:238, 240, poem 4011.

176) Kojima Noriyuki and Arai Eizô, eds., *Kokin wakashû;* Shin Nihon koten bungaku taikei 5 (Iwanami, 1989), 136, preface to poem 418.

177) Hasegawa et al., eds., *Tosa nikki, Kagerô nikki, Murasaki Shikibu nikki, Sarashina nikki;* Shin Nihon koten bungaku taikei 24, p. 18, lines 9-10.

178) Abe Akio, Akiyama Ken, and Imai Gen'e, eds., *Genji monogatari*, Vol. 3; Nihon koten bungaku zenshû 14 (Shôgakukan, 1972), 88, lines 8-9.

[179] Kojima Noriyuki and Arai Eizô, eds., *Kokin wakashû*, Shin Nihon koten bungaku taikei 5, 76, afterword to poem 211.

[180] Ibid., 79, afterword to poem 222.

9

Naobi no mitama
(The Spirit of Rectification)

<What follows is a discussion of the Way>

The Imperial Country [Japan] is the land of the birth of the awesome goddess Ama-terasu-ô-mi-kami, ancestor of the gods (*kamu mi-oya*).[1)]

> Of the reasons why Japan is superior to all countries, this is the most salient. There is no country that does not receive the sacred blessings of this august deity.

When the goddess took the heavenly symbols into her august hands,

> these are the three divine treasures which are transmitted from generation to generation,

she mandated that this country would be ruled by her descendants for many thousands of long autumns,

> and it was thereby established that the throne of the heavenly successor should remain steadfast along with heaven and earth.

It was established that as far as the trailing clouds, and as far as the toad wanders,[2)] this land would be ruled by her imperial descendants. There were no gods causing harm to humans, nor people who were not obedient.

How frightening to think that, in the course of generations, some servant might defy the emperor. Yet, in the course of generations, when some vile servant did chance to oppose the emperor, he caused his power to be radiant and destroyed him in an instant, just as in the events of antiquity in the Age of the Gods (神代).

Until the last reign of ten million generations, the emperor will be the child of the gods.

The emperors throughout the ages will be the children of the goddess Amaterasu, and that is why they are called the Child of the Heavenly Deity (*Ama-tu kami ni mi-ko*) or the Child of the Sun (*Hi no mi-ko*).

The emperor makes the will of the heavenly gods to be his own:

in every act, he does not stand resolute in his own will, but rather conducts affairs and rules in accordance with the events of antiquity in the Age of the Gods. On those occasions when he has doubt, he will ask the will of the heavenly deities by means of divination.

He makes no distinction between the Age of the Gods and the present:

it is not merely the imperial descendant who conducts himself in this fashion, but everyone, from the Imperial Chieftains and the Deity Chieftains to the servants at court, has valued the clans and ranks. The descendants of many generations have continued the work of their households, and, not deviating from the ways of their ancestors, have served the emperor just as in the Age of the Gods, as if they were all part of the same generation.

Since our country is ruled peacefully as a safe and divine land, one should carefully consider the words in the chapter on Emperor Kôtoku [r. 645-654] in the *Nihonshoki*: *Kamunagara* means "to follow the Way of the Gods, or again to possess in oneself the Way of the Gods."[3] "To follow the Way of the Gods" means that in the act of ruling under heaven, one simply acts in accordance with what has been in existence since the Age of the Gods, without adding a bit of one's own cleverness. When one rules magnanimously as in the Age of the Gods, the Way of the Gods will work spontaneously, and one will have no need to seek elsewhere; this is what "to possess in oneself the Way of the Gods" means. Therefore, to speak of "the Manifest God who rules the Great Eight Island Land,"[4] means that the rule of the emperors of each generation is none other than the rule of the gods. The term "*kamunagara*," found in the poems of the *Man'yôshû*, has reference to the very same thing.[5] The Koreans were exactly right when they spoke of Japan as "*kami-guni*" ('the land of the gods').[6]

In the world of antiquity, there was no invoking (*kotoage*) of the Way.[7]

This is why it is stated in the language of antiquity that "Our land of the Reed Plains, abundant in ears of rice, is a divine land which does not utter *kotoage*."[8]

This is simply because there was merely a "way" which led one somewhere.

> The term *miti* (美知 'way') is a combination of the word *ti* (路 'road'), which is to be seen in the words *yamadi* ('mountain path') and *nodi* ('path through a field'), and the honorific prefix *mi* (御).[9] This is apparent from the way it is written in the *Kojiki* as 味御路 (*umasi miti* 'a good way'),[10] and the meaning was simply that of a "way" which leads to something. In light of this fact, there simply was no "Way" in the age of antiquity.

To refer to the idea that there must be an underlying principle to all things, and the myriad of teachings as "this or that Way" is the custom of foreign countries.

> Since foreign countries are not the countries of the goddess Amaterasu, they have no determined ruler. Deities like flies in summer have taken sway, and due to their violence, people's hearts are impure and their customs in disarray. Even a vile servant may become ruler in an instant, having seized the country. Those at the top concentrate on not being overpowered by those below, while those below plot to seize power, looking for a weak moment on the part of those above. Each regards the other with hostility, and such countries have been difficult to pacify since antiquity.
>
> A person in such countries who, with power and deep wisdom, having won the devotion of a people and taken over their country, exerts great measures to ensure that he will not be overthrown, rules the country for some time and becomes a model for future generations is called a "sage" in China. In a world in disorder, many great leaders in battle who have become practiced in the act of war will naturally appear; in like fashion, such clever persons have also appeared, and are the

result of generations pondering over and over again how to best stabilize a country whose customs are in disorder and which is difficult to pacify. It is a mistake, however, to believe that these sages, like deities, are superior and possessed of miraculous powers.

What these sages constructed and determined is indeed called the Way. In China, therefore, the Way consists of nothing but these two essential factors: how to seize the country of a people, and how not to have that power taken away. In devising plans to take away the country of a people, a sage will stretch his mind to the limit and suffer physical hardships. Provided he is doing only what is good, he will endear himself to the people, and thus indeed appear to be a virtuous person. Likewise, the nature of the Way which he has constructed and set in place may appear to be wonderful and superbly sufficient in all respects, yet the sage himself will have, in the first instance, betrayed the Way by destroying the ruler and seizing the country. Therefore, it is all falsehood. In truth, these are not good men, but rather very wicked men indeed.

Perhaps it was because it was a Way originally designed with impure intentions, with the purpose of deceiving people, that people of later ages carried on as if they respected it on the surface, but in reality, there was not a single person who endeavored to preserve it. It was of no use at all to the country, and only its name spread far and wide. Before long, it ceased to be practiced, and the Way of the sages became nothing more than the mumbling voices of generations of Confucianists criticizing the people in vain. Therefore, it is a grave error for the adherents of Confucius to adhere only to the Six

Classics,[11] and to proclaim loudly that China is the country which is possessed of the proper Way. The creation of a Way to rectify the situation is an act which implies that, originally, the Way was not proper. To nonetheless think and speak of it as something lofty is indeed foolish. Even so, there may have been some in later ages who followed this Way faithfully, but one will be hard pressed to find even a single such person if one looks at the histories of successive generations.

Now, what is the nature of their Way? They created various grandiose terms such as humanity, righteousness, propriety, deference, filial piety, brotherly respect, loyalty, and faithfulness to strictly instruct and control people. The Confucianists complained that the laws of later ages contradicted the Way of the ancient kings, yet, surely, the Way of the ancient kings was none other than the law of antiquity. They even created the *Yijing*, and spoke as if they were giving great consideration to things, thereby convinced that they had exhaustively determined the principles of heaven and earth. Yet this, too, was simply a stratagem to draw and pacify the people.

The principles of heaven and earth are entirely the work of the gods, and wondrously miraculous and awesome. These deeds are difficult to fathom within the limits of human intelligence, so how could one be able to discern them clearly and understand them? It is very foolish to interpret and value everything the sages say as the ultimate in reason.

People of later generations take the deeds of the sages as their model, and try to figure out everything with their own individual intelligence; this is the habit in China. Those who wish to pursue study of Japan should constantly be aware of this, and by no means let themselves be deceived by the theories of the Chinese. In China attention is paid to every detail and everything is debated and defined, with the result that people's minds deteriorate and have only the pretense of erudition. In fact, they only complicate the situation, so that the country becomes all the more difficult to rule. Thus, the Way of the sages was created in order to rule the land, but it may also become the seed which throws the country into disorder. It is better to deal with all matters simply and, should any gaps persist, be satisfied nonetheless.

For this reason, despite the fact that in the antiquity of our imperial country there were no such noisome teachings, there was no rebellion down to the lowest subjects, the realm under the heavens was ruled peacefully, and the imperial throne was transmitted for a long time. Therefore, to speak of it in the terms of that foreign country, this is the incomparable, superior, great Way. In truth, because there was the Way, there was no word for the Way; there was no concept of the Way, yet the Way existed. Think of the difference between arguing vehemently about all the details, and not doing so at all. The phrase "*kotoage sezu*" ('does not utter *kotoage*') means not to make noisome assertions as is done in foreign countries.[12)]

Just as a person who is superior in all respects does not speak of it, while an unimpressive person of no accomplishment speaks excessively and boasts of every trivial thing, so, too, do countries like China, whose Way is deficient, engage in extensive academic disputes about the Way. The Confucianists do not understand this, and belittle our imperial country as having no Way.[13)] That the Confucianists do not understand this is to be expected in minds that view China as venerable in all things. Even scholars in Japan do not understand this, and envy China with its so-called Way, and their arguing against one another, some saying that in Japan, also, the Way exists,[14] and others, that it does not, is like a monkey looking at a human being and laughing because he has no fur. The human being, ashamed, announces that he, too, has fur, and argues the point by indicating his tiny hairs. Is this not the action of a fool who does not understand that it is quite all right to have no fur?

At a later time, after books had come to Japan, and people had begun to read and study them, it reached the point where people learned the customs of China, and employed them along with the native customs in all areas. It was at this time that the term "Way of the Gods" (*kami no miti*) was created in order to distinguish the venerable customs of antiquity in Japan. So that people would not confuse it with the various Ways of China, the term "Gods" (*kami*) was used, in addition to borrowing the term "Way" (*miti*) and using it here as well.[15]

I will explain in detail the reasons for speaking in terms of the "Way of the Gods" below.

As the ages passed, the learning and study of Chinese customs became even more predominant, and it eventually reached the point where even the act of governing below the heavens was entirely based on the Chinese model.

By the time of the reigns of Emperor Kôtoku [r. 645-654] and Emperor Tenji [r. 668-671], all government institutions had become Chinese. The result was that the customs of antiquity were used only in Shinto rituals (*kamuwaza*), and this is why, in later ages, most of the indigenous customs have survived only in Shinto ritual.

Even the hearts of the people drifted to the Chinese spirit.

That people do not take the will of the emperor as their own, but instead follow their own impertinent whims, is due to the contagion of the Chinese spirit.

Noisy disorder began to arise in our imperial country, which until that time had been tranquil and peaceful. In subsequent years, events similar to those in foreign countries began to occur.

Putting aside the extremely felicitous way of our great country, people considered the cleverly troublesome conduct and spirit of that foreign country favorably. As they imitated the customs of China, the hearts and conduct of the people, which had been straight and pure, became dirtied and crooked, and it became difficult to govern without the severe Way of that foreign country. Having viewed the state of affairs in these later years, those who are prone to conclude that it would be difficult to rule the country without the Way of the sages simply do not realize that the reason the country has become difficult to govern lies in that very same Way of the sages. They should recall that in the august age of antiquity, the country was very well governed without the borrowing of that Way.

All things that exist in heaven and earth are subsumed by the will of the gods.

All things in this world, such as the changing of the seasons, the precipitation of rain and snow, and all manner of events good and evil in the life of an individual or the nation are the work of the gods.

There are good as well as evil among the gods, and good and evil in their works as well, making it difficult to measure them with conventional principles of reason. Yet the people of this world, both the wise and the foolish, are totally deceived by the theories in the Ways of foreign countries, and do not understand this. This is something which those who study our imperial country should know from looking at the texts of antiquity; how can it be that even they are unable to discern it?

In foreign countries, good and evil are attributed to *karma* in the Way of the Buddha, and, in the Ways of China, to acts of Heaven, which are termed the Mandate of Heaven. All of these are mistaken. As the theories in the Way of the Buddha have been well understood by scholars at large, I will not discuss them here. Even wise people, however, are deceived by the Chinese theory of the Mandate of Heaven, and no one has realized that it is false. I shall therefore discuss it here and attempt to cause them to realize this falsity.

The Mandate of Heaven is a pretext contrived by the sages in ancient China to avoid blame for their crime of destroying their ruler and seizing the country. In truth, since heaven and earth have no will, neither should they have a Mandate. If, indeed, heaven did have a mind and was possessed of reason as well, so that it could give the country to good people who would govern well, then by all means a sage should have appeared at the end of the Zhou dynasty [1122-256 B.C.].[16] How is it that it did not happen? I cannot agree with those who would argue that later ages did not produce any sages because the Way had already been established by the Duke of Zhou and Confucius. Such arguments would be more convincing if, after Confucius, the Way had been carried out throughout the land and the country ruled well. What did happen was that the Way was abandoned, its teachings became empty, and the country fell into even more disorder. What sort of perverse heart of Heaven was it that viewed things as sufficient at that time, produced no sage, did not reflect upon the disaster in the country, and, finally, gave the country to a rough person like Emperor Shi of Qin [r. 221-210 B.C.], causing the people to suffer?[17)] This I would indeed like to know.

Although some may argue that since the Mandate of Heaven was not granted to rulers such as Emperor Shi, they could not last for long, how could there be any principle which would allow such an evil person to hold power even for a short time?

Furthermore, if there is a Mandate of Heaven for the ruler who governs the country, should there not also be a sign indicating good and evil for all of the people below? By this principle, the good should thrive for a long time, and the evil quickly encounter misfortune. Such is not the case, for otherwise, how could it be that both now and in the past there are many good people who are unlucky, and many evil people who are fortunate? If it truly were the work of heaven, such a perverted state of affairs would not exist.

In later years, as people became more sagacious, they ceased to accept the seizing of the country as the Mandate of Heaven, and seizure took the form of abdication of the throne. Although this practice is criticized, the sages of antiquity did not really differ from this. What sort of delusion is it to believe that the kings of later times did not receive the Mandate of Heaven, yet the Mandate of Heaven of the people in antiquity was true? It is laughable to say that there had been a Mandate of Heaven in antiquity but not in later times.

Certain people claim that Shun seized the country of Yao, and that Yu in turn seized the country of Shun;[18)] this may well be the case. In a later period, Wang Mang and Cao Cao appeared to succeed through abdication, when in fact they seized power.[19)] This may have been true for Shun and Yu as well. In antiquity, people were naive, and if they were told that abdication had occurred, they accepted it as the truth. People all throughout the country seem to have been deceived. At the time of Wang Mang and Cao Cao, however, people had become clever and were not deceived; thus their acts appeared to be evil ones. Figures such as these would have been revered as sages in antiquity.

The violence of the will of the Maga-tu-bi-no-kami produces acts of extreme sadness about which nothing can be done.[20)]

The causing of terrible injury in this world and all other such events simply do not conform to just principles. The many instances of wickedness are all attributable to the will of these gods. When they are extremely violent, there are times when even the great power of Amaterasu and Taka-ki-no-kami[21)] cannot restrain them, so there is absolutely nothing that can be done within the realm of human power. Such things as the good meeting misfortune and the bad meeting good fortune, indeed most things which run counter to everyday principles, are all the result of the acts of these gods. In foreign countries, people have no correct transmission from the Age of the Gods, and are therefore unaware of this. The result is that they construct the theory of the Mandate of Heaven, and try to determine every single thing on the basis of this principle of reason, which is extremely foolish.

Amaterasu, however, resides in the Plain of High Heaven, and her magnificent light, never dimmed by clouds, illuminates this world. The heavenly signs have been transmitted undamaged, and the realm under heaven is ruled by her grandchild as was commanded.

In foreign countries, there is no predetermined ruler, so ordinary people suddenly become kings, and kings suddenly become ordinary people, or fall to ruin in death; such has been the custom since antiquity. Those who scheme to seize the country but are unable to do so are called rebels, and are disdained and despised, while those who succeed are called sages and are revered and venerated. The so-called sages are thus merely those who have succeeded in a rebellious act.

Our sacred emperors do not stand in equal rank with the kings of such lowly countries. They are part of the imperial lineage granted to them by the ancestral deities who gave birth to this august country. From the beginning of heaven and earth, the realm under heaven was preordained as their land to rule.

As there is no decree on the part of the august deities that one must not submit to the emperor if he is evil, one cannot stand aside and judge whether the emperor is good or bad. As long as heaven and earth exist, and as long as the sun and moon shed their light, no matter how many generations pass, our lord will remain steadfast. For this reason, in the ancient texts the emperor of that age is called a god. Since he is indeed a god, people refrain from having arguments having to do with good and evil, and revere and obey him completely. This is the true Way.

In the disorder of the middle ages, however, there were those who went against the Way by being hostile to the court and troubling the emperor. Men such as Hôjô Yoshitoki, Hôjô Yasutoki, and Ashikaga Takauji were vile rebels who brazenly ignored the benevolence of the heaven-illuminating august Sun Deity.[22)] The will of the Maga-tu-bi-no-kami is a mysterious thing: the people of the world trembled and submitted to them, so that they flourished for some time to the end of their descendants.

There are rogues in the world who know that the heaven-illuminating august Sun Deity who shines on this world is by all means to be venerated, yet do not know that the emperor is by all means to be revered. This is because they are confused by the spirit of Chinese writing, and view the muddled customs of that country as clever. They do not understand the correct Way of our imperial country, do not believe that the heavenly Sun Deity illuminating the world at this moment is Amaterasu, and have forgotten that the present emperor is her descendant.

With regard to the High Seat of the Heavenly Sun Lineage,

The reason why the imperial lineage is called the Sun Lineage (*hi-tugi*) is because the emperor makes the will of the Sun Deity (*Hi-no-kami*) his own, and continues her work. And the throne is called the High Seat (*taka-mi-kura*) not merely because it is lofty, but because it is the throne of the Sun Deity

(*Hi-no-kami*). Here one should recall the words from the language of antiquity which are associated with the term "Sun" (*hi*): *taka-hikaru* ('high-shining'), *taka-hi* ('high sun'), and *hi-daka* ('sun-high').[23] As the emperors succeed to the Seat of the Sun Deity and occupy that Seat, there is no doubt that they are of equal status to the Sun Deity. Who among those who receive the august goodness of the heavenly Sun Deity would not revere, honor, and serve the emperor?

This High Seat remains steadfast for eternity along with heaven and earth, and is proof that this Way is mysterious and wondrous, superior to all the various Ways of foreign countries, and true, lofty, and venerable.

In China, people speak of a Way, but there is no Way. Therefore, what was originally confusion gave rise to more and more disorder and disruption, and the country was finally taken over by the people of a neighboring country. Although the Chinese despised them as barbarians and did not even consider them to be human beings, because they seized the country with great force people had no choice but to call their leader "Son of Heaven" and hold him in awe. Is this not a deplorable state of affairs?

Despite this, the Confucianists still seem to consider China to be a good country. Not only is there no fixed lineage for the king, for the most part there are no fixed stations for the noble and the common. Up until the Zhou dynasty [1122-256 B.C.], such distinctions seem to have been in existence in conformity with a type of "feudal system," but when the line of the king changed, the classes below also changed in their turn, so in fact there were no distinctions. Since the Qin dynasty [221-210 B.C.], this Way has progressively ceased to function, and in the ensuing disorder people do not view it as shameful when a woman of lowly station suddenly rises to the position of queen through the favor of a ruler, or the daughter of a king is joined with a man of no station at all. The example of one who was until yesterday a humble mountain woodcutter suddenly rising to be a high-ranking official of the government today indicates that there is no distinguishing between those of high and low station. This is no different from the state of affairs among the birds and the beasts.

"Well then, what is the Way?" one asks. It is not the Way which arises spontaneously in heaven and earth.

One must be well aware of this, and not mistakenly assume that it is the same thing as the ideas of Lao-zi and Zhuang-zi of China.

Neither is this a Way that has been devised by human beings; rather, it is derived from the august spirit of the wondrous God Taka-mi-musubi.

All events and things in this world have come into existence through the spirit of this great God. [24)]

The ancestral Gods Izanagi and Izanami initiated this Way.[25)]

All events and things in this world have their origins in these two Gods.

It is the Way which the Amaterasu received, preserves, and transmits. For this reason, it is called the Way of the Gods.

The term "Way of the Gods" first appears in the Chapter on Emperor Yômei [r. 585-587] in the *Nihonshoki*,[26)] but the passage speaks only of his ritual worship of the Gods. The first time that the Way of the imperial country is spoken of precisely in its broader sense is in the Chapter on Emperor Kôtoku [r. 645-654] where it states: "The phrase *kamunagara* means to follow the Way of the Gods, or again to possess in oneself the Way of the Gods."[27) In this broader sense, the intent is not to indicate a special type of behavior for the Way. Therefore, the reference simply to ritual worshiping of the Gods, as in the first passage above, ultimately indicates the same Way.

Some, however, point to the passage in the Chinese classics which states that: "The sage frames his doctrine by the Way of the Gods,"[28) and try to say that this is the same "Way." This is a confusion caused by false understanding of the heart of things. First of all, that which is indicated by the term "Gods" was originally different in Japan and China. In China, as it seems to indicate the unfathomable mysteries of Heaven and Earth, and yin and yang, it is merely an empty principle of logic, and the thing itself certainly does not exist. The Gods of the imperial country are the progenitors of the emperor who rules under the heavens in reality today, and are not the same sort of phenomenon as an empty principle of logic. In short, the Way of the Gods in the Chinese classics means a Way which is unfathomably mysterious, while the Way of the Gods in the imperial country is the Way which the ancestral Gods initiated and preserve, and in this sense, they are very different indeed.

The meaning of this Way can be quite well understood even now by studying the *Kojiki* and other texts of antiquity. Yet the minds of generations of scholars have all been bewitched by the Maga-tu-bi-no-kami, and are captivated by the Chinese classics. What they think and say is all in the spirit of China or of Buddhism, and they simply cannot understand the spirit of the true Way.

Since there was no discussion (*kotoage*) about the Way in antiquity, there are no illustrative concepts or terms to be seen in the texts of antiquity. Prince Toneri and subsequent scholars could not apprehend the meaning of the Way.[29] Their minds were instilled with nothing but the theories in Chinese writing which are put forth in such academic and tedious fashion, and they became convinced that these represented the natural principles of heaven and earth. Although it was not their intention to become entangled by such theories, they inadvertently became enmeshed, and seemed to drift in that direction alone. Their belief that the Way of a foreign country could be instrumental to the true Way indicates that their minds had been captivated by that foreign Way.

Most of the theories of China, beginning with yin and yang, and *qian* and *kun*,[30] were originally constructed as hypotheses by the sages using their own wisdom. Initially they sound profoundly logical, but if one will position oneself outside the theory and take a good look, one will find that they do not consist of much at all and are quite flimsy. It is deplorable that the people of this world, both at present and in ancient times, are fenced in with this delusion, and cannot extricate themselves.

The teachings of this great country are just as they have been transmitted from the Age of the Gods. As they remain untouched by any bit of human cleverness, they sound quite shallow indeed, but in reality they are bottomless and filled with profound, magnificent principles which human intelligence is unable to measure. If one is not able to understand this, it is because one has become fenced in by the delusion of Chinese writing. Until one is able to extricate oneself from this, even if one were to devote oneself to hundreds and thousands of years of study, it would be a vain effort providing no sign at all to aid in understanding the Way.

Since ancient books, however, have all been recorded in Chinese, one should have a general knowledge of that country. One should also study the Chinese classics, if time permits, in order to learn about such things as the writing system. Provided one's Japanese spirit is fixed and unshakable, there can be no harm in doing this.

Various teachings regarding the Way of the Gods appeared which prescribed that one should conduct certain rituals on an individual basis. These are all idiosyncratic constructs of recent years which were developed out of envy of the teaching of the various Ways in China.

Elaborate esoteric teachings which were transmitted secretly to a select group of people were created in later ages; all are false. It is best that all good things circulate widely in the world. To appropriate something for oneself, and hide it away not letting others know of it at all is extremely mean-spirited.

It is unthinkable that the lowly should try to convert the Way wherein the Emperor rules the realm below heaven into something which is theirs alone.

When those below simply follow the wishes of those above in all respects, then this corresponds to the Way. Even if there are other acts which may be done according to the Way of the

Gods, will it not become a private act performed in disobedience to one's superiors if one decides to teach, study, and carry them out on one's own?

People came to life through the august spirit of the Musubi-no-kami,[31)] and thus they naturally know and perform well those acts which they should be expected to perform.

All living things in this world, even lowly birds and insects, instinctively know well and perform those acts which they must each perform, and this all comes about through the august spirit of the Musubi-no-kami. Human beings are born into this world as especially gifted beings, and, in correspondence with these gifts, know what they are supposed to know, and do what they are supposed to do. Why compel people to obey something further than this?

If one claims that people cannot know or do anything without being taught, then this means that they are inferior to birds and insects. Acts of humanity, righteousness, propriety, deference, filial piety, brotherly respect, loyalty and faithfulness should be innate to human beings, and people should know these and behave accordingly, without being taught explicitly.

The Way of the sages was created to enforce rule over a country that was originally difficult to govern, and since it is a type of coercion which goes beyond what people are naturally equipped to do, and seeks to instruct in a severe manner, it does not correspond to the true Way. While people elaborated upon it in speech, there were very few throughout the ages who actually put it into practice. It is a mistake to believe that that Way is the true Principle of Heaven.

Now, I do not understand why they despise people who reject their Way, and make reference to human desire. From where and for what reason does human desire arise? Since it must have arisen from some corresponding principle, is not human desire itself part of the Principle of Heaven?[32)]

Furthermore, even in that country, rules such as that which prohibited marriage between persons of the same clan, even though a hundred generations may have passed, had not been in place from antiquity, rather, they date from the Zhou dynasty. The reason for this strict forbiddance was that the customs in the country were evil, and there were many instances of illicit relations between parent and child, and brother and sister. Because it was difficult to govern without such distinctions, does not the strictness of the prohibition itself reflect the humiliation of the country? In all instances, severity of the law is a result of there being numerous violations.

These conventions were established as rules, but they did not constitute the true Way. Since they did not correspond to human emotion, there were very few indeed who followed them. In later times, their numbers were even fewer; even in the Zhou dynasty, there were many lords who violated these prohibitions, so one can imagine the situation in later generations. There were even cases of immoral acts with sisters.

The followers of Confucius, however, have forgotten that people have been unable to abide by these rules since ancient times, and they take up these worthless rules as something important. In order to disparage our imperial country, they often call attention to the fact that siblings had sexual relations here in antiquity, and decry this as the behavior of birds and beasts. Scholars in Japan also view this with distaste, and regard it as a national disgrace. They try to gloss over the matter, and the reason why they have as yet been unable to reach a conclusion about it is because they are under the delusion that the cleverness of the sages represents the ultimate in logic, and they defer to this. If one were not in awe of the sages, what would be the harm in not being in agreement with them?

In ancient Japan, it was only liaisons between siblings of the same mother that were avoided. The practice of marriage between a half-sister and a half-brother with the same father but different mothers began with the emperor, and became quite common. There was no prohibition against it even after the capital moved to Kyoto. There was, however, a proper distinction between nobles and commoners, and there naturally arose no disorder. This is the correct, true Way established by our ancestral Gods.

In later generations, however, in the spirit of observing the rules of China, half-siblings of different mothers were termed brother and sister, and it was determined that they should not marry one another. In the present day, therefore, committing this type of union is thought to be improper. Antiquity had its own laws, however, and one should not debate the matter taking the rules of a foreign country as the normative practice.

In the age of antiquity, everyone down to the lowest subjects made the will of the Emperor his own.

Each served according to the will of the Emperor, and there was not a bit of self-interest.

All revered the Emperor, and cloaking themselves in his august protection, venerated the ancestral Gods.

The Emperor worships and governs the country before his august ancestral Gods. So, too, all of the people, from the Imperial Chieftains, the Deity Chieftains, and the court officials down to the common subjects, each venerates his ancestral Gods. Just as the Emperor prays to the Heavenly Gods and the Earthly Gods for the benefit of the court and the land, so, too, the subjects pray to the good Gods if they seek good fortune, and pacify the evil Gods if they wish to ward off misfortune. If they should sin or become impure, they pray and cleanse themselves. These are all actions of the human heart, which must of necessity be done.

The school of thought which suggests that it is enough to follow the true Way in one's heart alone[33)] may well be true of the teachings of the Buddha or the ideas of Confucianism, but it is entirely contrary to the Way of the Gods. In foreign countries, they value principles before all else, even when it comes to worship, and discuss and debate them. There are also instances where they claim false idolatry in worship, and ban it. All of it is false human cleverness.

The Gods differ in essence from the Buddha and others. There are not only good Gods, but evil Gods as well, and their hearts and deeds are correspondingly good and evil. This is why it is common in the world that people who do evil deeds prosper, and people who do good deeds suffer. The Gods are not to be measured according to whether or not they are in accordance with principles. One must simply stand in awe of their wrath, and accord them the utmost respect.

When worshiping the Gods, there is an appropriate mental attitude, and one should perform acts which are likely to please the Gods. First of all, one must abstain from and purify everything, so that there are no defilements. Then, one presents the Gods in abundance offerings which are as pleasing as possible, or, one venerates them by entertaining them with playing the koto or the flute, and singing and dancing. These rituals can all be traced back to the Age of the Gods, and are the Way of antiquity. The notion that worship is simply a matter of how one feels in one's heart, and has nothing to do with offerings or conduct is a mistaken notion of the Chinese spirit.

In the veneration of the Gods, maintaining the ritual purity of fire is of foremost importance. This is apparent from the section which deals with the land of the dead in the book on the Age of the Gods.[34] One must never allow fire to become defiled, and should guard against it not only in religious ritual, but at all other times as well. If fire becomes impure, the Maga-tu-bi-no-kami seize the opportunity to wreak havoc, and all kinds of disasters occur in the world.[35] Therefore, contamination of fire should be avoided at all times for the sake of the people and the world at large.

In the present day, however, this prohibition is observed at best only in rituals for the Gods or places they inhabit. That it is not observed elsewhere is the result of the widespread dispersion of the superficially clever Chinese spirit, which views it foolish to think in terms of the pollution of fire. How is it that even those scholars through the ages who have interpreted and explained the texts about the Gods make an issue of nothing but principles of Chinese logic, and hardly touch upon the doctrine of the avoidance of pollution?

All that is necessary is that people go through life doing those deeds which are befitting their station, and live peacefully and contentedly.

What other form of teaching beyond this could one want? To be sure, children were taught about the nature of things, craftsmen were taught the methods of making things, and artists were taught the various arts in antiquity as well. Upon superficial inspection, the teachings of Buddhism and Confucianism do not seem to differ from these sorts of instruction, but if one looks at the matter carefully, it will be found that they are not the same.

Still, one may ask, surely there must be special instructions to receive and deeds to carry out under the rubric of this Way?

In this context, someone once asked me whether the Way was the same as that of Lao-zi and Zhuang-zi of China. I answered that both Lao-zi and Zhuang-zi disliked the sophistries of the adherents of Confucius and valued that which is natural, and in that sense, there is some similarity. They were, however, born in an impure land which is not the land of the Gods. As they were accustomed to hearing nothing but the theories of generations of sages, their concept of what was "natural" was simply that which the sages considered to be "natural." Furthermore, they did not know that everything arises from the will of the Gods, and results from their deeds. Thus, their teaching was in essence quite different.

If one is at all costs determined to seek the Way, one should purify oneself of the tainted spirit of Chinese writings, and, with the pure

Japanese spirit, study the ancient texts diligently. Once one has done this, one will automatically realize that there is no Way which a person must learn and carry out. To know this is in itself to carry out the Way of the Gods. To discuss matters so explicitly as I have done departs from the substance of the Way, but I could not remain silent as I watched the workings of the Maga-tu-bi-no-kami. I wanted to receive the spirit of Kamu-naobi-no-kami and Ô-naobi-no-kami and rectify this misfortune.[36)]

> All that I have written above comes not from my own mind, but derives from the ancient texts. Those who scrutinize the matter shall have no doubt.

I write this on the 9th day of the 10th month in the 8th year of Meiwa [1771], and, with utmost respect, hereby conclude it.

Ise Province, Iitaka-gun
The Emperor's subject
Taira no Asomi Norinaga

Notes

[1)] There is a German translation of "Naobi no Mitama" (The Spirit of Rectification) by Hans Stolte ("Motoori Norinaga: Naobi no mitama," *Monumenta Nipponica* II:1 <1939>, 193-211), as well as a recent English translation by Sey Nishimura ("The Way of the Gods: Motoori Norinaga's *Naobi no Mitama*," *Monumenta Nipponica* 46:1 <1991>, 21-41). As it forms the closing section of Book One of *Kojiki-den*, however, and provides the foundation for the ideology Motoori applied to interpreting the *Kojiki*, I wished to provide my own translation and include it here. In addition to the above two translations, I also benefited from an unpublished translation by H. D. Harootunian ("Naobi no Mitama <The Spirit of Renovation>," ms, University of Chicago).

[2] Two phrases from poem number 800 in the *Man'yôshû*: *amakumo nö mukabusu kiwami* (Motoori substitutes *kagiri* for *kiwami* here)/ *taniguku nö sa-wataru kiwami* (*Man'yôshû*, Vol. 2, NKBT 5:60). The "as far as the toad wanders" (*taniguku nö sa-wataru kiwami*) phrase also appears in poem 971 of the *Man'yôshû* (Ibid., 156) and in two *norito*, "The Toshigoe Festival" (*Kojiki, Norito*, NKBT 1:390) and "The Tsukinami Festival" (Ibid., 412). In his commentary on the narrative of the deity Sukuna-biko-na, in which a toad suggests a source of information, Motoori remarks that this is not without reason, given the fact that it was common knowledge that toads had the power to do miraculous acts, a belief that is also seen in the Chinese classics (*Kojiki-den*, MNZ 10:5).

[3] Aston, *Nihongi*, Vol. 2:226; *Nihonshoki*, Vol. 2, NKBT 68:301, line 10. The passage is: 惟神 惟神者,謂レ随二神道一。亦謂三自有二神道一也。

[4] The phrase appears in the *norito* "Laudatory Ritual to the Kami Offered by the Local Chieftain of Izumo" (*Kojiki, Norito*, NKBT 1:452). Reference to the emperor as a "Manifest God" (明津神 *akitu kami*) also appears in poem 1050 of the *Man'yôshû* (*Man'yôshû*, Vol. 2, NKBT 5:188).

[5] *Kamunagara* (神在随) is an adverb meaning 'according to the will of the Gods' (*shin'i no mama ni*). It is found at the beginning of poem 3253 in the *Man'yôshû*: *AsiFara nö miduFo nö kuni Fa kamunagara kötöagë senu kuni* "The Rice-abounding Land of Reed Plains/ Is a land where things fall out/ As will the gods, without lifted words of men" (*Man'yôshû*, Vol. 3, NKBT 6:350; Nippon Gakujutsu Shinkôkai, trans., *The Manyôshû* <New York: Columbia University Press, 1965>, 59). It also appears in poems 38, 39, 199, 4040, 4094, and 4257 of the *Man'yôshû*.

[6] Aston, *Nihongi*, Vol. 1:230: "[The king of Silla] said: I have heard that in the east is a divine country named Nippon;" *Nihonshoki*, Vol. 1, NKBT 67:339.

[7] Although *kötöagë* has been defined simply as "uttering words" (*Nihonshoki*, Vol. 1, NKBT 67:95, headnote 18), or "assertion of one's will" (*Kojiki, Norito*, NKBT 1:218, headnote 10), Konishi Jin'ichi views it as a ritualistic use of language in a particular situation, and characterizes it as

"spell" (*A History of Japanese Literature*, Vol. 1: *The Archaic and Ancient Ages* <Princeton: Princeton University Press, 1984>, 100-105). One utters a desired outcome in the hope that the spiritual forces inherent in language (*kötödama*) will bring about the desired result. Carelessly uttered *kötöagë*, however, can bring about disaster, as in the case of Yamato Takeru's encounter with the mountain deity (Philippi, *Kojiki*, 246). In his commentary on this passage, Motoori defines *kötöagë* as "to raise the issue of how things ought to be, and discuss it" (*koto no sama aru beki sama o, sikasika to agete iitatsuru o, kotoage to iu nari*) (*Kojiki-den*, MNZ 11:266). See also Roy Andrew Miller for a discussion of *kötöagë* and the four *Man'yôshû* poems in which it is mentioned (nos. 942, 3250, 3253, 4124) ("The Spirit of the Japanese Language," *Journal of Japanese Studies* 3:2 <1977>:251-298).

8) Poem 3253 of the *Man'yôshû*. See note 5 above.

9) Motoori has *nudi*, due to theory at the time assigning a reading of *nu* to the *on* phongram 野. See chapter 7, note 100 above for discussion of this issue.

Ôno Susumu's theory on the formation of the word *miti* is that *mi-*, an honorific prefix attached to deities' possessions, was attached to *ti* 'road' out of the belief that the thoroughfares traversed by humans were possessed by *kami* or by lords (Ôno et al., *Kogo jiten* <Iwanami, 1974>, 1223).

10) *Kojiki*, NST 1:106, line 4. Philippi, *Kojiki*, 150: "a very good tideway."

11) The *Book of Odes* (詩經 *Shijing*), *Book of History* (書經 *Shujing*), *Book of Rites* (禮記 *Liji*), *Book of Changes* (易經 *Yijing*), *Book of Music* (樂記 *Yueji*), and *Spring and Autumn Annals* (春秋 *Chunqiu*). The *Book of Music* text is lost, and was replaced in the Six Classics cannon with the *Rites of Zhou* (周禮 *Zhouli*) in the Sung dynasty (960-1279).

12) See notes 5 and 7 above.

13) See Maruyama Masao for a discussion of the concept of "Way" in the dialogue between Tokugawa nativists and Confucianists (Maruyama Masao, *Studies in the Intellectual History of Tokugawa Japan*, trans. Mikiso Hane <Tokyo: University of Tokyo Press, 1974>, 143-154). In particular, the

Tokugawa Confucianist Ogyû Sorai (1666-1728) "denied the independent existence of Shinto" due to "his belief in the universal validity of the Way of the Sages" (Maruyama, Ibid., 98). In his *Taiheisaku*, Ogyû states that "there is no such thing as Shinto, but these spirits and demons must be worshipped" (quoted in Maruyama, Ibid., 99). Ogyû's disciple, Dazai Shundai (1680-1747), also rejected the notion of Shinto, calling it "the Way of the Sorcerers" in his *Bendôsho* (quoted in Maruyama, Ibid., 152).

[14] Some scholars, such as Fujiwara Seika (1561-1619) and his disciple Hayashi Razan (1583-1657), sought to unify or see no differentiation between Confucianism and Shinto, while others, such as Yamasaki Ansai (1618-1682), incorporated concepts of Chinese philosophy in the development of new schools of Shintoism (Maruyama, Ibid., 151).

[15] On the history of the Chinese word for "Way," Fung Yu-lan provides the following: "the word *tao* 道, one of the most important terms in Chinese philosophy, has a primary meaning of 'road' or 'way'. Beginning with this primary meaning, it assumed already in ancient times a metaphorical significance, as the 'Way of man,' that is, human morality, conduct or truth. During this time, its meaning was always restricted to human affairs, whereas when we come to the *Lao-tzu*, we find the word *tao* being given a metaphysical meaning" (*A History of Chinese Philosophy*, Vol. 1: *The Period of the Philosophers* <Princeton: Princeton University Press, 1952>, 177).

[16] The latter part of the Zhou dynasty was a period of political instability called the Warring States period (403-221 B.C.), during which seven major states ceased to submit to the dominion of the house of Zhou, and carried on intermittent warfare. The Zhou were overthrown by the Qin in 256 B.C., but the country was not unified politically again until 221 B.C.

[17] Qin Shi Huang Di, China's First Emperor, is admired for such major achievements as centralization of administration, and standardization of weights and measures, but is also notorious for his "excesses," the burning of books and the execution of literati.

[18] The three legendary human emperors, who followed the first semi-divine emperors of China. According to legend, Yao and Shun had each

abdicated and given the throne over to their prime ministers. The *Han shu* describes the process as follows: "When Emperor Yao abdicated, he said to his successor: 'Ah, Shun! The Heaven-appointed succession now rests in you.' Shun used the same words in transmitting his mandate to Yü" (Pan Piao, *Han shu*, 100 A:8a; *Wen hsüan*, 52, in Wm. Theodore de Bary, Wing-tsit Chan, and Burton Watson, comps., *Sources of Chinese Tradition*, Vol. 1 <New York: Columbia University Press, 1960>, 177). Yu is credited with founding China's first dynasty, the Xia. These legendary abdications were used as precedents by Wang Mang (45 B.C.-A.D. 23) and Cao Pei when they sought to wrest power from the Han (Carl Leban, "Managing Heaven's Mandate: Coded Communication in the Accession of Ts'ao P'ei, A.D. 220," in David T. Roy and Tsuen-hsuin Tsien, eds., *Ancient China: Studies in Early Civilization* <Hong Kong: The Chinese University Press, 1978>, 315-339, especially p. 330). See also note 19 below.

[19)] Wang Mang (45 B.C.-A.D. 23), appointed Imperial Regent for the Imperial Heir Apparent infant Prince Liu Ying in A.D. 6, overthrew the Former Han dynasty in A.D. 9, creating a new dynasty, the Xin. In this case, abdication came in the form of a document sealed in a bronze casket, wherein the founder of the Han dynasty, Gao Zu, requested that the Han dynasty abdicate according to the will of Heaven, and transfer the Mandate to Wang Mang (Rudi Thomsen, *Ambition and Confucianism: A Biography of Wang Mang* <Aarhus: Aarhus University Press, 1988>, 100-101). The Mandate of Heaven was originally a Zhou concept, and was not evoked in the establishment of either the Qin or the Former Han dynasties (Leban, "Managing Heaven's Mandate," 316). In the Han dynasty, as Confucianism came to be the dominant ideology, the concept was revitalized and elaborated upon, principally by Dong Zhong-shu (179-104 B.C.) (Ibid., 318-319). It was this new Mandate of Heaven, which included portents and omens signaling the vitiation of the ruling house, and the suitability of a potential leader to form a new house, that enabled transfer of power to take place in the form of abdication.

In the midst of the breakdown of Han authority and warlord rivalry, Cao Cao (155-220) captured the Han sovereign in 196, and in the name of defender of the Han, succeeded in unifying northern China. His eldest son Cao Pei (186-226) came to power with the death of his father in 220, and founded a new dynasty, the Wei, after receiving the abdication of the "Proffering" Han Sovereign (Ibid., 321).

[20] Two deities, Yaso-maga-tu-bi-nö-kamï and OFo-maga-tu-bi-nö-kamï, who come into existence from the pollution incurred by Izanagi in his visit to Yomi. The word *maga* means either 'crooked', or 'misfortune'; the raging spirits of these two deities were believed to cause disaster to occur (*Kojiki, Norito*, NKBT 1:412, headnote 13). Immediately after the birth of these two deities, three deities are born to "rectify" the evil: Kamu-naFobi-nö-kamï, OFo-naFobi-nö-kamï, and Idu-nö-me-nö-kamï (Philippi, *Kojiki*, 69). In the *norito* "Festival of the August Gates," both sets of deities are mentioned: "that there be no encounter nor speaking together with those known as heavenly, evil-working *kami* [*ame no maga-tu-Fi to iFu kami*];" "If there be any misdeed or accident, let it be rectified to the eye and to the ear by the deities Kamunaobi and Oonaobi" (Bock, *Engi-Shiki*, Books VI-X, 83-84; *Kojiki, Norito*, NKBT 1:420).

[21] Another name for Taka-mi-musubi-nö-kamï, one of the three deities who are the first to come into existence at "the beginning of heaven and earth" (Philippi, *Kojiki*, 47). Philippi notes that he is the only one of the three to "play an active role" in subsequent events (Ibid., 397). The role he does play in those events seems to be that of co-ruler, along with the Amaterasu, of Takama-nö-Fara ('Plain of High Heaven') (Ibid., 121, footnote 6).

[22] Abdicated Emperor Go-Toba (1180-1239, r. 1183-98) sought to restore power to the Imperial House and threaten the Kamakura Shogunate by creating an alliance between certain monasteries and chieftains in Western Japan beginning in 1219. Matters came to a head in 1221 when he refused to consult with the Kamakura Shogunate, headed by Hôjô Yoshitoki (1163-1224), on a matter of succession, and word of his plot was leaked to Kamakura. On June 6, the Court declared Hôjô Yoshitoki an outlaw, and Shogunate forces were sent to attack Go-Toba's forces under the leadership of Hôjô Yoshitoki's son, Hôjô Yasutoki (1183-1242). The Kamakura forces were victorious, and

the whole episode is referred to as the Jôkyû Disturbance. Go-Toba was then banished by the Kamakura Shogunate (George Sansom, *A History of Japan to 1334* <Stanford: Stanford University Press, 1958>, 377-382).

Ashikaga Takauji (1305-1358) also confronted imperial troops in battle in another attempt at restoration of the throne, that of the Kenmu Restoration initiated by Emperor Go-Daigo (r. 1318-1339). Ashikaga Takauji initially allied himself with Emperor Go-Daigo, and turned against Kamakura Shogunate troops in Kyoto in 1333. Dissatisfied with his position within the restoration government, however, he broke allegiance with Go-Daigo in 1335, and defeated imperial troops at the Battle of Minato River in 1336. He then went on to form the Muromachi Shogunate, and appointed a new emperor, Emperor Kômyô (r. 1337-1348), to establish a rival Northern Court in opposition to the Southern Court of Go-Daigo.

[23)] *Taka-Fikaru* ('shining brilliantly on high') is a pillow word used to modify *Fi* ('sun'), and occurs 5 times in the *Kojiki*, all of them in song: 4 are addressed to a prince or emperor, termed *Fi nö mi-ko* ('descendant of the Sun Deity') (Philippi, *Kojiki*, 245, 321, 364, 365); 1 is uttered by Emperor Yûryaku in praise of the court, *taka-Fikaru Fi nö miya-Fitö* ("the high-shining Sun-palace courtiers") (*Kojiki*, NST 1:280; Philippi, *Kojiki*, 366).

Taka-Fi ('sun which shines on high') is a noun, which occurs with the verb *sirasinu* ('rules') to express the death of an emperor or imperial prince, in the sense of 'gone to the Plain of High Heaven as a god, to rule over heaven' as in *Man'yôshû* 202: *wago-oFokimi Fa takaFi sirasinu* ("our Lord is gone to rule the high heavens") (*Man'yôshû*, Vol. 1, NKBT 4:113; Ian Hideo Levy, *The Ten Thousand Leaves* <Princeton: Princeton University Press, 1981>, 131).

The characters 日高 occur as an element in the names of a related group of male deities in the *Kojiki*, such as 天津日高日子番能迩々藝能命, which Aoki et al. read as *Fiko* ('heavenly lad'), with 高 as an *on* phonogram (Ama-tu-Fiko-Fiko-Fo-nö-ninigi-nö-mikötö, *Kojiki*, NST 1:100), but Takagi Ichinosuke and Tomiyama Tamizo read as *Fi-daka* ('sun-high') (Ama-tu-Fidaka-Fiko-Fo-nö-ninigi-nö-mikötö, *Kojiki sosakuin*, Vol. 1: *Honbun hen* <Heibonsha, 1974>, 108).

[24] Motoori viewed this deity, along with his female counterpart, Kamu-musubi-nö-kamï, as representing the "mysterious divine force which gave rise to all things" (*Kojiki-den*, MNZ 9:129). His reading of the meaning of *musubi* (産巣日) is 産靈 (*musubi* 'generative spirit'). See also note 21 above.

[25] The last pair of deities to come into existence at the very beginning of the *Kojiki*, in the "Seven Generations of the Age of the Gods" (Philippi, *Kojiki*, 48). At the command of the heavenly deities, Izanagi and Izanami stand on the Heavenly Floating Bridge and create the island of Onogoro with the jeweled spear. They then descend to this island, and proceed to bear land and deities together until Izanami is burned in the birth of the fire god, dies, and enters the land of Yomi. One of the deities they bear is Amaterasu, the Sun Goddess, ancestor of Japan's imperial line. Philippi is of the opinion that Japan's indigenous mythology must have begun with these two deities, and that the other material found at the beginning of the *Kojiki*, in the Seven Generations of the Age of the Gods, was material simply tacked on in the manner of the Chinese classics to provide some context in the official record for the emergence of these two deities (*Kojiki*, 397, Additional Note 1). He bases his reasoning on Tsuda Sôkichi (*Nihon koten no kenkyû*, 2 Vols. <Iwanami, 1948-50>, Vol. 1, 325-41).

[26] 天皇信㆓佛法㆒尊㆓神道㆒ (*Nihonshoki*, Vol. 2, NKBT 68:155, line 5); "The Emperor believed in the Law of the Buddha and revered the Way of the Gods" (Aston, *Nihongi*, Vol. 2:106).

[27] For text and reference, see note 3 above.

[28] Aston, *Nihongi*, Vol. 2:106, quoting from the *Yijing*. The passage in question contains two instances of 神道: 觀天之神道而四時不 。聖人以神道設教。而天下服 。(Honda Wataru, trans., *Eki;* Chûgoku koten sen 1 <Asahi shinbunsha, 1966>, 161); "He affords them a view of the divine way of heaven, and the four seasons do not deviate from their rule. Thus the holy man uses the divine way to give instruction, and the whole world submits to him" (Richard Wilhelm, trans., *The I Ching or Book of Changes, The Richard Wilhelm Translation rendered into English by Cary F. Baynes* <Princeton: Princeton University Press, 1967>, 486).

29) The *Nihonshoki* was presented to Empress Genmei in 720 under the name of Prince Toneri (676-735), son of Emperor Tenmu. The *Shoku Nihongi* states that Prince Toneri received the command to compile the *Nihonshoki*, but he is not believed to have played an active role in the compilation (Sakamoto Taro, *The Six National Histories of Japan*, translated by John S. Brownlee <Vancouver: UBC Press, 1991>, 35-37). See chapter 2 above for Motoori's views on the use of the Chinese classics as models for compilation of the *Nihonshoki.*

30) See chapter 2, note 10.

31) See notes 20 and 24 above.

32) The spontaneous acts of man derive from Heavenly Principle (天理 *tian li*), which is a "natural tendency or force," but the acts of man which derive from secondary, selfish motivation are termed "human desire" (人欲 *ren yu*). "Human desire" obscures Heavenly Principle, and man should try to rid himself of "human desire" (Fung Yu-lan, *A History of Chinese Philosophy*, Vol. II, translated by Derk Bodde <Princeton: Princeton University Press, 1953>, 506, 560).

33) Stolte and Nishimura remark in their respective translations that this phrase is to be found a poem attributed to Sugawara Michizane (845-903) (Stolte, "Motoori Norinaga: Naobi no mitama," 208-209, footnote 39; Nishmura, "The Way of the Gods: Motoori Norinaga's *Naobi no Mitama*," 39, footnote 53). Kodaka Toshio notes that the *Chômei shiki monogatari* quotes the poem attributing it to the deity of Kitano Shrine, i.e. Sugawara Michizane, and that the poem also appears in the Nô text *Hanjo* by Zeami. He concludes, therefore, in his notes to Ishida Baigan's (1685-1744) *Tohimondô* (1739), in which it also appears, that the poem must have been widely known as a poem of the deity of Kitano Shrine (Ienaga Saburô et al., eds., *Kinsei shisôka bunshû;* NKBT 97 <Iwanami, 1966>, 400, headnote 10).

The poem itself reads: *kokoro dani/ makoto no miti ni/ kanahinaba/ inorazutotemo/ kami ya mamoran* 'If simply in one's heart/ one will follow the true Way/ even if one should not pray/ the gods will protect one' (Ibid, 400).

[34] Philippi, *Kojiki*, 61-67. Izanami, having given birth to the fire god, passes away and goes to the land of Yömï. She is unable to return with Izanagi, who has come to fetch her, because she has "eaten at the hearth of Yömï" (Ibid., 61). Philippi discusses Motoori's commentary on this passage, which states that Izanami was unable to return "because she had eaten food cooked with the impure fire of Yömi" (Ibid., 401, Additional Note 7). In Motoori's view, there are two types of fire, pure and impure, and people must be on guard lest they allow fire to become impure (*Kojiki-den*, MNZ 9:241).

[35] Motoori in fact attributes all misfortune to the pollution of fire, which allows the Maga-tu-bi-no-kami to wreak havoc (Ibid.).

[36] See note 20 above. The said passage, in which they are introduced, is the only place that these two deities appear in the *Kojiki*. Motoori defines *naobi* (直毘) as "the divine spirit which rectifies misfortune (*maga*)" (*Kojiki-den*, MNZ 9:274).

References

Unless otherwise noted, the place of publication is Tokyo.

Abe Akio, Akiyama Ken, and Imai Gen'e, eds. *Genji monogatari*, Vol. 3. Nihon koten bungaku zenshû, Vol. 14. Shôgakukan. 1972.

Aoki Kazuo, Ishimoda Shô, Kobayashi Yoshinori, and Saeki Arikiyo, eds. *Kojiki*. Nihon shisô taikei, Vol. 1. Iwanami shoten. 1982.

Aston, W. G., trans. *Nihongi: Chronicles of Japan from the Earliest Times to A.D. 697*, 2 vols. in 1. Rutland, Vermont: Charles E. Tuttle. 1972.

Beddell, George Dudley. "Kokugaku Grammatical Theory." Ph.D. diss., Massachusetts Institute of Technology. 1968.

Blacker, Carmen. "Divination." In Kodansha Encyclopedia of Japan, Vol. 2, 121.

Bock, Felicia Gressit, trans. *Engi-Shiki: Procedures of the Engi Era, Books I-V*. Tokyo: Sophia University. 1970.

____, trans. *Engi-Shiki: Procedures of the Engi Era, Books VI-X*. Tokyo: Sophia University. 1972.

Brownlee, John S. "The Jeweled Comb-Box: Motoori Norinaga's *Tamakushige*." *Monumenta Nipponica* 43:1 (Spring 1988), 35-44.

Chamberlain, Basil Hall, trans. *The Kojiki: Records of Ancient Matters*. Rutland, Vermont: Charles E. Tuttle. 1981 reprinting of 1882 edition.

Chan, Wing-tsit. *A Sourcebook in Chinese Philosophy*. Princeton: Princeton University Press. 1963.

Chang, Kwang-chih. *The Archaeology of Ancient China*. New Haven: Yale University Press. 1986, 4th ed.

de Bary, Wm. Theodore, Wing-tsit Chan, and Burton Watson, comps. *Sources of Chinese Tradition*, Vol. 1. New York: Columbia University Press. 1960.

Fukuda Ryôsuke. "Jindai moji." In Kokugogakkai, eds. *Kokugogaku daijiten*, 531-532.

Fung, Yu-lan. *A History of Chinese Philosophy*, Vols.1 and 2. Trans. by Derk Bodde. Princeton: Princeton University Press. Vol. 1 1952, 2nd ed. in English; Vol. 2 1953.

Furuta Tôsaku and Tsukishima Hiroshi. *Kokugogaku shi.* Tôkyô Daigaku shuppansha. 1972.

Habein, Yaeko Sato. *The History of the Japanese Written Language*. Tokyo: University of Tokyo Press. 1984.

Hachiya Kiyohito. "*Wajikai.*" In Satô Kiyoji, ed. *Kokugogaku kenkyû jiten*, 693.

Harootunian, H. D. *Things Seen and Unseen: Discourse and Ideology in Tokugawa Nativism.* Chicago: University of Chicago Press. 1988.

____, trans. "Naobi no mitama (The Spirit of Renovation)." University of Chicago, ms photocopy.

Hasegawa Masaharu, Imanishi Yûichirô, Itô Hiroshi, and Yoshioka Hiroshi, eds. *Tosa nikki, Kagerô nikki, Murasaki Shikibu nikki, Sarashina nikki.* Shin Nihon koten bungaku taikei, Vol. 24. Iwanami shoten. 1989.

Hasegawa Michiko. *Karagokoro: Nihon seishin no gyakusetsu.* Chûô kôronsha. 1986.

Hashimoto Shinkichi. "Kodai kokugo no *e* no kana ni tsuite" (1942). In *Moji oyobi kanazukai no kenkyû.* Iwanami shoten. 1949, 192-225.

Hayashi Chikafumi. "Nihon no kanji-on." In *Nihon no kanji.* Nihongo no sekai, Vol. 4, edited by Nakada Norio. Chûô kôronsha. 1982, 297-400.

Hayashi Ôki. "Kogo." In Kokugogakkai, eds. *Kokugogaku daijiten*, 423.

Hayashi Rokurô, ed. *Shoku Nihongi*, Vol. 1. Gendai shichôsha. 1985.

Hisamatsu Sen'ichi. *Keichû.* Yoshikawa kôbunkan. 1963.

____, trans. "*Kojiki-den: Sôron.*" In *Motoori Nori-naga shû.* Koten Nihon bungaku zenshû, Vol. 34. Chikuma shobô. 1960, 81-96.

Honda Wataru, trans. *Eki.* Chûgoku koten sen, Vol. 1. Asahi shinbunsha. 1966.

Hôsei'in shozô, Reproduction; intro. by Kojima Noriyuki. *Kojiki: Kokuhô Shinpukuji-bon.* Ôfûsha. 1978.

The I Ching or Book of Changes: The Richard Wilhelm Translation rendered into English by Cary F. Baynes. Princeton: Princeton University Press. 1967, 3rd ed.

Ikeda Tadashi. *Classical Japanese Grammar Illustrated with Texts.* Tôhô gakkai. 1975.

Inoue Minoru. *Kamo no Mabuchi no gakumon.* Yagi shoten. 1944.

Inoue Seinosuke. "Teniwoha." In Kokugogakkai, eds. *Kokugogaku daijiten*, 617- 619.

Jôdai-go jiten henshû i'inkai, eds. *Jidai betsu kogo daijiten*: Jôdai-hen. Sanseidô. 1967.

Kada no Azamamaro. 1728. *S ôgakkôkei*. In Taira Shigemichi and Abe Akio, eds. *Kinsei Shintôron: Zenki kokugaku*. Nihon shisô taikei, Vol. 39. Iwanami shoten. 1972, 329-337.

Kamo no Mabuchi. *Kamo no Mabuchi zenshû*, ed. by Hisamatsu Sen'ichi. Zoku gunshoruijû kanseikai. 1978.

Kaneko Takeo. *Shoku Nihongi senmyô kô*. Koka shoten. 1989, reissue of original 1941 Hakuteisha edition.

Karlgren, Bernard, ed. *The Book of Odes: Chinese Text, Transcription, and Translation*. Stockholm: The Museum of Far Eastern Antiquities. 1974.

Katagiri Yôichi, Fukui Teisuka, Takahashi Shôji, and Shimizu Yoshiko, eds. *Taketori monogatari, Ise monogatari, Yamato monogatari, Heichû monogatari*. Nihon koten bungaku zenshû, Vol. 8. Shôgakukan. 1972.

Katô Shûichi. *A History of Japanese Literature*, Vol. 2: *The Years of Isolation*. London: The Macmillan Press and Paul Norbury Publications, Ltd. 1983.

Keichû. *Keichû zenshû*, ed. by Hisamastu Sen'ichi. Iawanami shoten. 1972.

Kobayashi Hideo. *Motoori Norinaga*. Shinchôsha. 1977.

Kobayashi Yoshinori. "*Kojiki* no kudoku to kanbun-kundoku-shi." *Jôdai bungaku* 35 (October 1974), 14-34.

____. "*Kojiki* on-kun hyô: jô." *Bungaku* 47:8 (August 1979), 56-84.

____. "*Kojiki* on-kun hyô: ge." *Bungaku* 47:11 (November 1979), 69-86.

____. "*Kojiki* ni okeru suiryô hyôgen to sono hyôki to no kankei." In Satô Shigeru Kyôju taikan ki'nen ronbun-shû kankô-kai, eds. *Satô Shigeru Kyôju taikan ki'nen: Ronshû kokugogaku*. Ôfûsha. 1980, 157-176.

____. "*Kojiki* kundoku ni tsuite." In Aoki Kazuo et al., eds. *Kojiki*, 649-692.

____. "The *Kun* Readings of the *Kojiki*." *Acta Asiatica* 46 (1984), 62-84.

Kodaka Toshio, ed. *Tohimondô*. In Ienaga Saburo et al., eds. *Kinsei shisôka bunshû*. Nihon koten bungaku takei, Vol. 97. Iwanami shoten. 1966.

Kodansha Encyclopedia of Japan, 9 Vols. Tokyo: Kodansha. 1983.

Kojima Noriyuki. "Kaisetsu, Part 1: Shomyô, seiritsu, shiryô." In Sakamoto Tarô et al., eds. *Nihonshoki*, Vol. 1, 3-23.

___ and Arai Eizo, eds. *Kokin wakashû*. Shin Nihon koten bungaku taikei, Vol. 5. Iwanami shoten. 1989.

Kokugogakkai, eds. *Kokugogaku daijiten*. Tôkyôdô shuppan. 1980.

___, eds. *Kokugogaku jiten*. Tôkyôdô shuppan. 1955.

Konishi Jin'ichi. *A History of Japanese Literature*, Vol. 1: *The Archaic and Ancient Ages*. Trans. by Aileen Gatten and Nicholas Teele; ed. by Earl Miner. Princeton: Princeton University Press. 1984.

Koyasu Nobukuni. "Kokugaku," in *Kodansha Encyclopedia of Japan*. Vol. 4, 257-259.

___. *Motoori Norinaga*. Iwanami shoten. 1992.

Kurano Kenji. "Norinaga no *Kojiki* kun-hô no hihan." *Kojiki nenpô* 2 (January 1955), 1-15.

___ and Takeda Yukichi, eds. *Kojiki, Norito*. Nihon koten bungaku takei, Vol. 1. Iwanami shoten. 1958, 1979 printing.

Kuroita Katsumi. "Hanrei." In Kuroita Katsumi and Kokushi taikei henshû-kai, eds. *Kojiki, Sendai kuji hongi, Shintô gobusho*. Kokushi taikei, Vol. 7, 1-8.

___ and Kokushi taikei henshû-kai, eds. *Kojiki, Sendai kuji hongi, Shintô gobusho*. Kokushi taikei, Vol. 7. Yoshikawa kôbunkan. 1966.

Lange, Roland E. *The Phonology of Eighth-Century Japanese: A Reconstruction Based on Written Records*. Tokyo: Sophia University. 1973.

Leban, Carl. "Managing Heaven's Mandate: Coded Communication in the Accession of Ts'ao P'ei, A.D. 220." In Roy, David T. and Tsuen-hsuin Tsien, eds. *Ancient China: Studies in Early Civilization*. Hong Kong: The Chinese University Press. 1978, 315-339.

Legge, James, trans. *The Chinese Classics*, Vol. 4: *The She King or The Book of Poetry*. Hong Kong: Hong Kong University Press. 1960, second edition; original edition: Oxford: Henry Frowde. 1871.

Levy, Ian Hideo, trans. *The Ten Thousand Leaves: A Translation of the Man'yoshu, Japan's Premier Anthology of Classical Poetry*, Vol. 1. Princeton: Princeton University Press. 1981.

Liu, James J. Y. *Chinese Theories of Literature*. Chicago: University of Chicago Press. 1975.

Mabuchi Kazuo. *Kokugo on'in ron*. Kasama shoin. 1971.

Maeda Tomiyoshi. "Keizyû." In Kokugogakkai, eds. *Kokugogaku daijiten*, 266- 267.

___. "*Shaku Nihongi*." In Satô Kiyoji, ed. *Kokugogaku kenkyû jiten*. Meiji shoin. 1977, 636-637.

Martin, Samuel E. *The Japanese Language Through Time*. New Haven: Yale University Press. 1987.

Maruyama Masao. *Studies in the Intellectual History of Tokugawa Japan*. Trans. by Mikiso Hane. Tokyo: University of Tokyo Press. 1974.

Matsumoto Shigeru. *Motoori Norinaga, 1730-1801*. Cambridge: Harvard University Press. 1970.

Matsumura Hiroji and Ishikawa Tôru, eds. *Sagoromo monogatari*, 2 Vols. Nihon koten zensho. Asahi shinbunsha. Vol. 1, 1965; Vol. 2, 1967.

Mayuzumi Hiromichi. "Kigen." In *Kodansha Encyclopedia of Japan*, Vol. 4, 203-204.

McEwan, J. R. "Motoori's View of Phonetics and Linguistics in his *Mojigoe no kanazukai* and *Kanji san onkô*." *Asia Major*, New Series, Vol. 1. 1949, 109-118.

Miller, Roy Andrew. *The Japanese Language*. Chicago: University of Chicago Press. 1967.

___. "The 'Spirit' of the Japanese Language." *Journal of Japanese Studies* 3:2 (Summer 1977), 251-298.

Miyake Kiyoshi. *Kada no Azumamaro no koten-gaku*, Vol. 1. Urawa-shi: Miyake Kiyoshi. 1980.

Motoori Norinaga. *Motoori Norinaga zenshû*. Compiled by Ôno Susumu and Ôkubo Tadashi. Chikuma shobô. 1968-1975, 20 Vols.

Motoori Norinaga Ki'nenkan, eds. *Meihin zuroku*. Matsusaka: Motoori Norinaga Ki'nenkan. 1991.

Motoyama Yukihiko. *Motoori Norinaga*. Shimizu shoin. 1978.

Muraoka Tsunetsugu. *Motoori Norinaga*. Iwanami shoten. 1928.

Nagayama Isamu. "Zokugo." In Kokugogakkai, eds. *Kokugogaku jiten*, 604.

Nakada Norio. "Katakana." In Kokugogakkai, eds. *Kokugogaku daijiten*, 152-154.

____. "*Wajishô ranshô*." In Kokugogakkai, eds. *Kokugogaku daijiten*, 941-942.

____ and Tsukishima Hiroshi. "Kokugo-shi." In Kokugogakkai, eds. *Kokugogaku daijiten*, 399-404.

____, Wada Toshimasa, and Kitahara Yasukazu. *Kogo daijiten*. Shôgakkan. 1983.

Nakai, Kate Wildman. *Shogunal Politics: Arai Hakuseki and the Premises of Tokugawa Rule*. Cambridge, MA: Council on East Asian Studies, Harvard University/Harvard University Press. 1988.

Nippon Gakujitsu shinkôkai, trans. *Man'yôshû*. New York: Columbia University Press. 1965.

Nishimiya Kazutami, ed. *Kojiki*. Ôfûsha. 1979.

Nishimura Sey. "The Way of the Gods: Motoori Norinaga's *Naobi no Mitama*." *Monumenta Nipponica* 46:1 (1991), 21-41.

Norman, Jerry. *Chinese*. Cambridge: Cambridge University Press. 1988.

Nosco, Peter. "Masuho Zenkô (1655-1742): A Shinto Popularizer Between Nativism and National Learning." In Nosco, Peter, ed. *Confucianism and Tokugawa Culture*. Princeton: Princeton University Press. 1984, 166-187.

____. *Remembering Paradise: Nativism and Nostalgia in Eighteenth Century Japan*. Cambridge: Council on East Asian Studies, Harvard University Press. 1990.

Ôno Susumu. "Kaidai." In Ôno Susumu, ed. *Kojiki-den*. In *Motoori Norinaga zenshû*, Vol. 9, 7-29.

____. "Kanazukai no rekishi." In Ôno Susumu and Shibata Takeshi, eds. *Monji*. Iwanami kôza: Nihongo, Vol. 8. Iwanami shoten. 1977, 301-339.

____, ed. *Kojiki-den*. In *Motoori Norinaga zenshû*, Vols. 9-12. Chikuma shobô. 1968-1974.

____, Satake Akihiro, and Maeda Kingorô, eds. *Iwanami kogo jiten*. Iwanami shoten. 1974.

Philippi, Donald L., trans. *Kojiki*. Tokyo: University of Tokyo Press. 1968.

Pollack, David. *The Fracture of Meaning: Japan's Synthesis of China from the Eighth through the Eighteenth Centuries*. Princeton: Princeton University Press. 1986.

Pulleyblank, E. G. "The Nature of the Middle Chinese Tones and Their Development to Early Mandarin." *Journal of Chinese Linguistics* 6 (1978), 173-203.

Reischauer, Robert Karl. *Early Japanese History (c. 40 B.C. - A.D. 1167)*, Part A. Gloucester, Mass.: Peter Smith. 1937, 1967 reprinting.

Sakai Naoki. *Voices of the Past: The Status of Language in Eighteeth-Century Japanese Discourse*. Ithaca: Cornell University Press. 1991.

Sakamoto Tarô. *The Six National Histories of Japan*. Translated by John S. Brownlee. Vancouver: University of British Columbia Press. 1991.

____, Ienaga Saburô, Inoue Mitsusada, and Ôno Susumu, eds. *Nihonshoki*, 2 Vols. Nihon koten bungaku taikei, 67; 68. Iwanami shoten. 1967; 1965.

Sansom, George. *A History of Japan to 1334*. Stanford: Stanford University Press. 1958.

Sasazuki Kiyomi. *Motoori Norinaga no kenkyû*. Iwanami shoten. 1944.

Satô Kiyoji. *Kokugogaku kenkyû jiten*. Meiji shoin. 1977.

Shibatani Masayoshi. *The Languages of Japan*. Cambridge: Cambridge University Press. 1990.

Seeley, Christopher. *A History of Writing in Japan*. Leiden: E. J. Brill. 1991.

Stolte, Hans, trans. "Motoori Norinaga: *Naobi no mitama*." *Monumenta Nipponica* 2:1 (1939), 193-211.

Takagi Ichinosuke and Tomiyama Tamizô, comps. *Kojiki sôsakuin*, 3 Vols. Vol. 1: *Honbun hen*, Vol. 2: *Sakuin hen*, Vol. 3: *Hoi hen*. Heibonsha. 1974.

____, Gomi Tomohide, and Ôno Susumu, eds. *Man'yôshû*, 4 Vols. Nihon koten bungaku taikei, Vols. 4-7. Iwanami shoten. 1957-1962.

Thomsen, Rudi. *Ambition and Confucianism: A Biography of Wang Mang*. Aarhus: Aarhus University Press. 1988.

Tôdô Akiyasu. "Kanji gaisetsu." In Ôno Susumu and Shibata Takeshi, eds. *Monji*. Iwanami kôza: Nihongo, Vol. 8. Iwanami shoten. 1977, 61-157.

Tsuda Sôkichi. *Nihon koten no kenkyû*, 2 Vols. Iwanami shoten. 1948-1950.

Tsukishima Hiroshi. "*Kôganshô* ni tsuite." In *Keichû zenshû*, edited by Hisamatsu Sen'ichi. Iwanami shoten. 1974. 623-651.

____. "Senmyô-gaki." In Kokugogakkai, eds. *Kokugogaku daijiten*, 561-562.

Tsunoda Ryusaku, trans. and L. Carrington Goodrich, ed. *Japan in the Chinese Dynastic Histories*. South Pasadena: P. D. and Ione Perkins. 1951.

Tsuru Hisashi. "Man'yôgana." In Ôno Susumu and Shibata Takeshi, eds. *Monji*. Iwanami kôza: Nihongo, Vol. 8. Iwanami shoten. 1977, 209-248.

Ueda Masaaki. "Kuji taisei-kyô." In Kawade Takeo, ed. *Nihon rekishi daijiten*, Vol. 6. Kawade shobô shinsha. 1964, 230-231.

Utsuho monogatari kenkyû-kai and Sasabuchi Tomoichi, rep., eds. *Utsuho monogatari: honbun to sakuin*. Kasama shoin. 1943.

Vance, Timothy J. *An Introduction to Japanese Phonology*. Albany: State University of New York Press. 1987.

Varley, H. Paul, trans. *A Chronicle of Gods and Sovereigns: Jinnô Shôtôki of Kitabatake Chikafusa*. New York: Columbia University Press. 1980.

Wenck, Günther. *Japanische Phonetik*, 2 Vols. (Band I, Band II). Wiesbaden: Otto Harrassowitz, 1954.

Wilkinson, Endymion. *The History of Imperial China: A Research Guide*. Cambridge: Harvard University Press. 1973.

Yoshida Kanehiko. *Jôdaigo jodôshi no shiteki kenkyû*. Meiji shoin. 1973.

Yoshikawa Kôjirô. *Jinsai, Sorai, Norinaga: Three Classical Philologists of Mid-Tokugawa Japan*. Trans. by Kikuchi Yûji. Tokyo: The Tôhô Gakkai. 1983.

____, Satake Akihiro, and Hino Tatsuo. *Motoori Norinanga*. Nihon shisô taikei 40. Iwanami shoten. 1978.

Character Index of Postpositions, Suffixes, Adverbials, and Connectives

Listed according to radical.

Index

Cornell East Asia Series

No. 4 *Provincial Leadership in China: The Cultural Revolution and Its Aftermath*, by Fredrick Teiwes

No. 8 *Vocabulary and Notes to Ba Jin's* Jia: *An Aid for Reading the Novel*, by Cornelius C. Kubler

No. 15 *Song, Dance, Storytelling: Aspects of the Performing Arts in Japan*, by Frank Hoff

No. 16 *Nō as Performance: An Analysis of the Kuse Scene of* Yamamba, by Monica Bethe & Karen Brazell

No. 17 *Pining Wind: A Cycle of Nō Plays*, translated by Royall Tyler

No. 18 *Granny Mountains: A Second Cycle of Nō Plays*, translated by Royall Tyler

No. 28 *The Griffis Collection of Japanese Books: An Annotated Bibliography*, edited by Diane E. Perushek

No. 29 *Dance in the Nō Theater*, by Monica Bethe & Karen Brazell Volume 1: Dance Analysis, Volume 2: Plays and Scores, Volume 3: Dance Patterns

No. 32 *Tone, Segment, and Syllable in Chinese: A Polydimensional Approach to Surface Phonetic Structure*, by A. Ronald Walton

No. 35 *From Politics to Lifestyles: Japan in Print*, edited by Frank Baldwin

No. 36 *The Diary of a Japanese Innkeeper's Daughter*, translated by Miwa Kai, edited & annotated by Robert J. Smith & Kazuko Smith

No. 37 *International Perspectives on Yanagita Kunio and Japanese Folklore Studies*, edited by J. Victor Koschmann, Ōiwa Keibō & Yamashita Shinji

No. 38 *Murō Saisei: Three Works*, translated by James O'Brien

No. 40 *Land of Volcanic Ash: A Play in Two Parts* by Kubo Sakae, revised edition, translated by David G. Goodman

No. 41 *The Dreams of Our Generation and Selections from Beijing's People*, by Zhang Xinxin, edited & translated by Edward Gunn, Donna Jung & Patricia Farr

No. 44 *Family Change and the Life Course in Japan*, by Susan Orpett Long
No. 46 *Planning and Finance in China's Economic Reforms*, by Thomas P. Lyons & WANG Yan
No. 48 *Bungo Manual: Selected Reference Materials for Students of Classical Japanese*, by Helen Craig McCullough
No. 49 *Ankoku Butō: The Premodern and Postmodern Influences on the Dance of Utter Darkness*, by Susan Blakeley Klein
No. 50 *Twelve Plays of the Noh and Kyōgen Theaters*, edited by Karen Brazell
No. 51 *Five Plays by Kishida Kunio*, edited by David G. Goodman
No. 52 *Ode to Stone*, by Shirō Hara, translated by James Morita
No. 53 *Defending the Japanese State: Structures, Norms and the Political Responses to Terrorism and Violent Social Protest in the 1970s and 1980s*, by Peter J. Katzenstein & Yutaka Tsujinaka
No. 54 *Deathsong of the River: A Reader's Guide to the Chinese TV Series* Heshang, by Su Xiaokang & Wang Luxiang, translated by Richard Bodman & Pin P. Wan
No. 55 *Psychoanalysis in China: Literary Transformations, 1919-1949*, by Jingyuan Zhang
No. 56 *To Achieve Security and Wealth: The Qing Imperial State and the Economy, 1644-1911*, edited by Jane Kate Leonard & John R. Watt
No. 57 *Like a Knife: Ideology and Genre in Contemporary Chinese Popular Music*, by Andrew F. Jones
No. 58 *Japan's National Security: Structures, Norms and Policy Responses in a Changing World*, by Peter J. Katzenstein & Nobuo Okawara
No. 59 *The Role of Central Banking in China's Economic Reforms*, by Carsten Holz
No. 60 *Warrior Ghost Plays from the Japanese Noh Theater: Parallel Translations with Running Commentary*, by Chifumi Shimazaki
No. 61 *Women and Millenarian Protest in Meiji Japan: Deguchi Nao and Ōmotokyō*, by Emily Groszos Ooms
No. 62 *Transformation, Miracles, and Mischief: The Mountain Priest Plays of Kyōgen*, by Carolyn Anne Morley
No. 63 *Selected Poems of Kim Namjo*, translated by David R. McCann & Hyunjae Yee Sallee, with an afterword by Kim Yunsik
No. 64 *From Yalta to Panmunjom: Truman's Diplomacy and the Four Powers, 1945-1953*, by HUA Qingzhao
No. 65 *Kitahara Hakushū: His Life and Poetry*, by Margaret Benton Fukasawa
No. 66 *Strange Tales from Strange Lands: Stories by Zheng Wanlong*, edited & with an introduction by Kam Louie

No. 67 *Backed Against the Sea*, by Wang Wen-hsing, translated by Edward Gunn

No. 68 *The Sound of My Waves: Selected Poems by Ko Un*, translated by Brother Anthony of Taizé & Young-Moo Kim

No. 69 *Han Sŏrya and North Korean Literature: The Failure of Socialist Realism in the DPRK*, by Brian Myers

No. 70 *The Economic Transformation of South China: Reform and Development in the Post-Mao Era*, edited by Thomas P. Lyons & Victor Nee

No. 71 *After Apocalypse: Four Japanese Plays of Hiroshima and Nagasaki*, translated & introduced by David G. Goodman

No. 72 *Poverty and Growth in a South China County: Anxi, Fujian, 1949-1992*, by Thomas P. Lyons

No. 73 *The Shadow of Arms*, by Hwang Suk-Young, translated by Chun Kyung-Ja, with a foreword by Paik Nak-chung

No. 74 *Informal Empire in Crisis: British Diplomacy and the Chinese Customs Succession, 1927-1929*, by Martyn Atkins

No. 75 *Barbed Wire and Rice: Poems and Songs from Japanese Prisoner-of-War Camps,* collected by Bishop D. McKendree

No. 76 *Restless Spirits from Japanese Noh Plays of the Fourth Group: Parallel Translations with Running Commentary,* by Chifumi Shimazaki

No. 77 *Back to Heaven: Selected Poems of Ch'ŏn Sang Pyŏng,* translated by Brother Anthony of Taizé & Young-Moo Kim

No. 78 *Singing Like a Cricket, Hooting Like an Owl: Selected Poems by Yi Kyu-bo,* translated by Kevin O'Rourke

No. 79 *The Gods Come Dancing: A Study of the Japanese Ritual Dance of Yamabushi Kagura,* by Irit Averbuch

No. 80 *Korean Adoption and Inheritance: Case Studies in the Creation of a Classic Confucian Society*, by Mark Peterson

No. 81 *The Lioness Roars: Shrew Stories from Late Imperial China,* translated by Yenna Wu

No. 82 *The Economic Geography of Fujian: A Sourcebook*, Volume 1, by Thomas Lyons

No. 83 *The Naked Tree*, by Pak Wan-so, translated by Yu Young-nan

No. 84 *The Classic Chinese Novel: A Critical Introduction,* by C.T. Hsia

No. 85 *Playing With Fire,* by Cho Chong-Rae, translated by Chun Kyung-Ja

No. 86 *I Saw a Pale Horse and Selections from Diary of a Vagabond,* by Hayashi Fumiko, translated by Janice Brown

No. 87 *Kojiki-den, Book 1,* by Motoori Norinaga, translated by Ann Wehmeyer

No. 88 *Sending the Ship Out to the Stars: Poems of Park Je-chun,* translated by Chang Soo Ko

No. 89 *The Economic Geography of Fujian: A Sourcebook*, Volume 2, by Thomas Lyons

No. 90 *Midang: Early Lyrics of So Chong-Ju*, translated by Brother Anthony of Taizé

No. 91 *Battle Noh: Parallel Translations with Running Commentary,* by Chifumi Shimazaki

FORTHCOMING

Principles of Poetry (Shi no genri), by Hagiwara Sakutarō, translated by Chester Wang

Dramatic Representations of Filial Piety: Five Noh in Translation, by Mae Smethurst

Troubled Souls from Realistic Noh Dramas, by Chifumi Shimazaki

Description and Explanation in Korean Linguistics, by Ross King

More Than a Momentary Nightmare: The Yokohama Incident and Wartime Japan, by Janice Matsumura

The Snow Falling on Chagall's Village: Selected Poems of Kim Ch'un-Su, translated by Kim Jong-Gil

So Little Time to Love: Poetry by Hyonjong Chong, translated by Wolhee Choe and Peter Fusco

Ben no Naishi Nikki: A Poetic Record of Female Courtiers' Sacred Duties at the Kamakura-Period Court, by S. Yumiko Hulvey

Inventing Nanjing Road: Commercial Culture in Shanghai, 1900-1945, edited by Sherman Cochran

To order, please contact the Cornell East Asia Series, East Asia Program, Cornell University, 140 Uris Hall, Ithaca, NY 14853-7601, USA; phone (607) 255-6222, fax (607) 255-1388, internet: er26@cornell.edu.

7-97/.8M pb/.2M hc/BB

Lightning Source UK Ltd.
Milton Keynes UK
UKHW010358080622
404079UK00002B/128